Colombia

Colombia

A Concise Contemporary History

Michael J. LaRosa
and
Germán R. Mejía

ROWMAN & LITTLEFIELD PUBLISHERS, INC.
Lanham • Boulder • New York • Toronto • Plymouth, UK

Published by Rowman & Littlefield Publishers, Inc.
A wholly owned subsidiary of The Rowman & Littlefield Publishing Group, Inc.
4501 Forbes Boulevard, Suite 200, Lanham, Maryland 20706
www.rowman.com

10 Thornbury Road, Plymouth PL6 7PP, United Kingdom

British Library Cataloguing in Publication Information Available

Library of Congress Cataloging-in-Publication Data

LaRosa, Michael (Michael J.)
  Colombia : a concise contemporary history / Michael J. LaRosa and Germán R. Mejía.
    p. cm.
  Includes bibliographical references and index.
  ISBN 978-1-4422-0935-0 (cloth : alk. paper) — ISBN 978-1-4422-0937-4 (electronic)
  1. Colombia—History—1810– 2. Colombia—Civilization. I. Mejía P., Germán.
II. Title.
  F2273.L37 2012
  986.1—dc23

                                                                    2011049334

♾™ The paper used in this publication meets the minimum requirements of American
National Standard for Information Sciences—Permanence of Paper for Printed Library
Materials, ANSI/NISO Z39.48-1992.

Printed in the United States of America

To our mentors and friends,
Steve and Pilar Stein of Coral Gables, Florida

Contents

Acknowledgments

We would like to thank the many people who have assisted us with the research and writing of this book. First, Susan McEachern at Rowman & Littlefield has offered professional, thoughtful insight from the earliest days of this project's development, and we thank her for her unwavering support. Grace Baumgartner, at Rowman, has been a helpful editor and adviser. June Erlick at Harvard University and Lance Ingwersen, a doctoral student in history at Vanderbilt University, each reviewed early drafts of the prospectus; Mr. Ingwersen also assisted with editing chapters of the manuscript, as did journalist Casey M. Conley from Portland, Maine.

Professor Pamela Murray graciously offered to write a foreword to this work, for which we are extremely grateful. She also provided editorial advice. Lt. Paul J. Angelo carefully and patiently edited the entire manuscript.

Writer and editor Juan Pablo Lombana assisted with research, as did historian Lina Del Castillo. Ms. Del Castillo translated segments of the book from Spanish to English. Curator Marina Pacini and historian Guiomar Dueñas-Vargas, in Memphis, facilitated research, as did Martha Senn from Medellín.

At Rhodes College, we benefited from the support of students Andrew Howie, who helped with fact-checking and editing, and Cameron Goodman, who provided research and editing assistance; he also helped with the selection of photographs and compiled sections of the bibliography.

Dean Michael R. Drompp provided start-up funds from Rhodes College, and Professor Ann Viano supported our project with additional research funding from the college. Nannette Gills assisted with many administrative details.

In Medellín, Luis Ospina facilitated research at the Biblioteca Pública Piloto, and the director of that library, Gloria Inés Palomino Londoño, warmly welcomed us, as did Sergio Carvajal of the same institution.

Daniela López and Rubén Carvajal, history students in Bogotá, provided the copious research that went into our chronology. Pablo Silva, an architecture student at the National University in Bogotá, drew our maps, based on designs developed by Germán R. Mejía. In Memphis, graphic designers Lynn Conlee and Robert Shatzer edited and assisted with final design of the maps, and Joseph Morris, with little more than an iPhone 4 in hand, helped with statistical interpretation. Jeffrey A. Knowles compiled our index. Matt LaFevor helped review page proofs. We're extremely grateful for the patience, perseverance, and in many cases, warm friendship of the many people who assisted us with this project.

Foreword

Like the two authors of this book, my connection to Colombia is personal as well as professional. It started in the mid- to late-1960s with childhood visits to my mother's native Medellín. Compared with places like Buenos Aires, Rio de Janeiro, Havana, Mexico City, or even Colombia's own capital of Bogotá, Medellín back then was a rather obscure Latin American city. Few here in the United States had heard of it. Although humming with modern entrepreneurial energy, it still had a sedate, small-town feel—not yet that of today's hurried, more sophisticated metropolis with its sleek light rail and high-rises commanding the slopes of the Aburra Valley. It was a city of neighborhoods, churchgoing and family oriented; a place where everyone seemed to know everyone; and where guests, including the relatively rare foreigner, could expect a place of honor along with invitations to long visits (their eager-to-please hosts feeling offended if they left too soon). Children were at the center of things, the youngest and whiniest invariably spoiled and catered to. Exotic relatives such as my sisters, "gringas" all three, and I always found a warm reception, our broken Spanish tolerated with good humor. It was through this family that I first came to know Colombia and a people that were kindly, confident, and can-do, possessed of a certain flair. Life, while serious, was to be enjoyed, lived with zest. I became an admirer. Authors Michael LaRosa and Germán Mejía no doubt would find this entirely reasonable.

Which brings me to the point of this foreword. LaRosa and Mejía have performed a rare service for the broad U.S. reading public: that of offering a comprehensive, up-to-date, deeply informed, and highly readable primer on Colombia—a country that, despite its size, wealth, and geopolitical importance, remains one of the least known and most misunderstood countries in Latin America. Although both authors are professional historians, their book is no traditional academic history. It is unabashedly "presentist," as historians sometimes, rather sniffily, say. Its ten chapters aim less to dissect the mysteries of the past, an exercise dear to scholars, than to explain, as concisely as possible, how Colombia became what it is today. Overall, they stress Colombia's emergence as a viable, indeed successful, modern nation.

This claim may surprise some readers. Since the 1980s, most knowledgeable observers have portrayed Colombia as something of a failure or, at least, a huge disappointment—a country racked by chronic sociopolitical violence rooted in, among other things, inherited partisan hatreds; severe social inequities; a weak, corrupt state; and, not least, the influence of a vast, insidious, and illegal drug industry. The grim accounting of this violence and its diverse manifestations—from in-depth studies of the notorious mid-twentieth-century partisan conflict–cum–national killing spree known as La Violencia through contemporary reports on the culture of youthful assassins—has dominated writing on the country here and abroad. Then there are the traditionally lurid portrayals of Colombia in the mass media. In addition to a mainstream press addicted to coverage of murder and mayhem, *Miami Vice*, the popular 1980s television series (recently the basis of a movie with the same name), along with Hollywood films like *Blow*, have ensured that, in the United States at least, the country's image remains closely linked to drugs and violence.

LaRosa and Mejía don't deny the truth that lies behind this image. They fully acknowledge the harsh realities that have been documented by scholars and researchers both in and outside the country. Yet they do ask a question seldom asked by Colombia observers. What factors have allowed Colombia, as a nation, to endure and, despite its endemic problems, to thrive? Instead of inquiring into a presumed state of illness or dysfunction, the authors inquire into the basis of relative good health: what is working, and what has worked in this bustling country of some forty-five million? Their book, thus, highlights those aspects of Colombian history and culture that have contributed most visibly to national unity as well as sustained peace and prosperity.

The book's fourth chapter, for example, explains how institutions like the Catholic Church, the army, and a historic, multiclass, two-party political system (along with factors like the Spanish language and a public education system that taught national history and geography) each laid a foundation for unity by building bonds among Colombians of different races, classes, and regions. Its brief summary of the role of the two-party system, in particular, reflects Colombian historians' own recent reassessment of their country's nineteenth-century experience. Myriad bloody civil wars, death, and destruction weren't the only (or most important) result of the rise of the Liberal and Conservative Parties. Another was individuals' enhanced sense of belonging to a larger Colombian nation. This sense of belonging or identity came through affiliation with one or another party. In claiming the loyalty of people from across a vast territory while, with each election, mobilizing them around a great cause, idea, or moral principle, the parties connected isolated communities, lifting Colombians above the limited horizons of the local and familial. Partisan affiliation also gave ordinary people a certain protection from enemies as well as access to state services such as roads, schools, and justice, and to jobs, scholarships, and career opportunities. It helped build nationhood, however bifurcated.

Throughout their book, LaRosa and Mejía identify other constructive forces or factors that, over time, have contributed to the making of a modern, viable, and increasingly inclusive Colombia. One factor is a long tradition of bipartisan cooperation, or *convivencia*, that has served historically to curb the excesses of partisan competition and, in the twentieth century, limit damage caused by bloody conflicts like La Violencia. An important contemporary version of this tradition appeared in 1991, when Colombians from various parties, groups, and factions met to draft a new constitution—one that gives voice to previously marginalized constituencies and that, for the first time, recognizes the sociocultural rights of long-persecuted ethnic minorities, the country's indigenous and Afro-Colombian populations in particular.

Another factor has been the steady development of modern systems of transportation and mass communication that have allowed Colombians to transcend the limits of time and space, above all, the formidable barriers of the Andes. The result has been, as chapter 7 details, a true Colombian "common space" that is at once physical and virtual as well as spiritual. Nowhere is this more obvious, perhaps, than in Bogotá. As journalist June Erlick confirms in her 2005 memoir, Bogotá's recent physical transformation—its network of new parks and libraries, along with the TransMilenio transit system—has not only given the city zip and buoyancy but nurtured the rise of a new civic spirit, a renewed will to life in common. This, despite the pressures exerted by the arrival of refugees or *desplazados* (displaced persons) from at least a decade's worth of rural violence.

Readers less interested in the details of Colombia's political, economic, and institutional evolution will enjoy the chapter on Colombian achievements in literature and the arts, the latter building on the legacy of indigenous (especially Muisca) forebears. The chapter reveals that while the country has writers and artists of world renown, such as Nobel Prize winner Gabriel García Márquez and the distinguished painter and sculptor Fernando Botero, it also brims with lesser-known talent. More everyday forms of creativity are explored in chapter 9's survey of Colombian daily life and popular culture—including beauty pageants, soap operas, foodways, and the like. The chapter includes a short, fascinating account of how, sometime in the 1990s, leaders and urban planners in Medellín and Bogotá began to "take back" their cities. One of Bogotá's mayors at the time was Antanus Mockus. Mockus is a striking figure in this story, emblematic of Colombian pluck and imagination. It is these qualities that, combined with steely determination, have helped Colombians to endure and ultimately triumph over the dark forces that have besieged their nation in recent times. Their example is enviable. Colombia, I'd say, is doing all right.

Pamela Murray

Introduction

Colombia continues to be, for the United States, somewhat of an anachronism and an enigma. The country remains on the United States Department of State's "warning list," yet Colombia receives more military and defense funding from the United States than any other Latin American country. Colombia's government, under President Juan Manuel Santos, is decidedly pro–United States, yet it took the U.S. Congress five years to pass a free trade agreement (FTA) with Colombia. The FTA, signed into law by President Barack Obama in October 2011, has been strongly criticized by U.S. labor unions and human rights organizations. At the same time, the global media have shifted significantly in the way they cover Colombia. Stories focusing on tourism, restaurants, Colombian tennis stars, and positive reviews of literary works and music performances by Colombians suggest that the U.S. media's perception of the Andean nation is evolving away from the myopic, one-dimensional view that marked earlier portrayals of the country. Terrorism, kidnapping, and violence have faded into the media background while other facets of Colombia's rich, complex culture and history flourish in the conscious of readers of the international press.

Our book offers a fresh interpretation of Colombian history based on the multitude of facts, historic events, and circumstances that have come together to form that history. We focus on the modern period, that is, from around 1800 to the present. Colonialists will, no doubt, bemoan our modernist sensibilities, but our narrative does not entirely neglect the significant three-hundred-year period of Spanish colonialism.

Peruvian historian Alberto Flores Galindo reminds us in one of his most prescient books, *In Search of an Inca*, how "History should liberate us from the past, not seal us off . . . within *longue durée* prisons of ideas."[1] Our goal in writing this new history of Colombia follows Galindo's logic as applied to Colombia's recent history. We have been influenced by the excellent historiography on Colombia written by scholars both in and outside the country. But, in reviewing recent books, we noticed that a concise, contemporary interpretation of the Colombian past has not yet been published in English. The central idea in developing this project is to offer a new history based on the existent scholarship, but departing from that body of work in significant ways. New works of history should be bold, energetic, and innovative—connected to the past but not trapped by it. "If people are controlled by ghosts," writes Galindo, "it is impossible to confront the future."[2] Confronting the future would seem to invoke the methodologies of astrologers; yet the two authors of this book are both academically trained historians who understand how one's reading of the past shapes its interpretation. One of the major contributions of our 211-year (c. 1800–2011) history of Colombia is that it foregrounds themes rather than chronology. The colonial patterns, logic, institutions, economy, government, and culture form the foundation of our text—a foundation that is always present but not necessarily at the forefront of our presentation.

This book builds on the work of the late David Bushnell, who in 1993 published his groundbreaking *The Making of Modern Colombia: A Nation in Spite of Itself*. His work, the first comprehensive treatment of Colombian history published by a U.S. historian in English, is considered the standard reference text for students, scholars, and others, both in North and South America. Bushnell's clearly written text emphasizes nineteenth-century politics and society as "foundational" in explaining patterns of twentieth-century Colombia. In 2001, Marco Palacios, a Colombian historian working now in Mexico, and the American historian Frank Safford published *Colombia: Fragmented Land, Divided Society*. Their book emphasizes economic and social trends and developments and, thus, nicely complements Bushnell's more political focus.

Recently, authors from a variety of disciplines and backgrounds have published books about Colombia in English. Many of these publications focus on topics taken from media headlines during the days when those headlines focused mostly on the gloomy segment of the Colombian narrative. While some of the books are thoughtful, serious works, overall their titles suggest the limited scope of most writing, scholarship, and publication on Colombia in the past ten years. For example, in 2003, human rights activist Robin Kirk published a book titled *More Terrible Than Death: Violence, Drugs and America's War in Colombia*, which recounted the recent human rights tragedy in Colombia, ascribing drugs and U.S. military action as leading causes of contemporary mayhem. Colombian American journalist and writer Silvana Paternostro published *My Colombian War* in 2007, and in 2009, Gary Leech published *Beyond Bogotá: Diary of a Drug War Journalist in Colombia*. Canadian social scientist Jasmin Hristov's *Blood and Capital: The Paramilitarizaton of Colombia* (2009) is passionate but largely impressionistic. Collectively, these works paint an uneven, sensationalist picture of Colombian history.

Unlike many of the works mentioned above, we have not written our book from the perspective of Colombia as a country on the brink of failure. Likewise, we avoid drawing explicit comparisons to a completely distinct North Atlantic political and socioeconomic model of development. Bushnell, Palacios, and Safford study Colombia by comparing it to North Atlantic nations: naturally, "fragmentation and divided" are conclusions they draw in communicating a state of near-perpetual flux. In the chapters that follow, we depart from the relied-upon schema that scholars have employed repeatedly to write the history of Colombia. In other words, we do not use the standard comparisons, nor do we rely upon a somewhat artificial division between centuries to mark significant periods in Colombian history.

Generally, most historical texts written about Colombia focus on a strife-filled nineteenth century, with countless civil wars, conflict between the Roman Catholic Church and the state, regional rivalry and a period of détente toward the late 1880s, with a new constitution of 1886 (that endured for ninety-five years), and the signing of a treaty with the Holy See, the Concordat of 1887. Economic development during the 1880s is based on the exportation of coffee, while a major civil war at the end of the nineteenth century ushers in the twentieth century—the so-called War of a Thousand Days. Historians use this war and the subsequent separation of Panama that was orchestrated with active encouragement by the United States to distinguish between the nineteenth and the twentieth centuries. The major themes of the twentieth century are political development, the resurgence of liberal rule (after 1930), economic development, urbanization and modernization, and destructive political and social violence that dissipates for a twenty-five-year period (from about 1903 to the late 1920s) but never fully abates.

Our book adopts a new, thematic organization through which we have been careful not to foreground political and social violence, economic crises, and fragmentation. Rather than focus on this catastrophic vision of Colombian history, based on the constructs of underdevelopment, or definitions of progress or dependency that originate in more modern, wealthy, and progressive

North Atlantic societies, we have written about a Colombia that endures. We pose a few central questions throughout the text, linking those questions to our thematic structure: despite all the known problems—misrule, mayhem, and crises—how is it that the nation stays together? What are the factors that have helped unify Colombia throughout the decades? What are the cultural, economic, and social programs that have held Colombia together as a viable political and economic entity? What has been built in Colombia? What has endured? What has been rebuilt, and how? These are important questions that have been largely overlooked by authors who embrace the idea of Colombia as a chaotic failure. While we have no intention of whitewashing Colombia's contentious contemporary history, we stress those enduring institutions, cultural mechanisms, and economic patterns that have sustained the nation over the decades. The reader will notice some intentional repetition, from chapter to chapter, as key events in Colombia's history are analyzed from distinct perspectives. For example, the "taking of Panama" in 1903, an event that significantly shaped Colombia's twentieth century, is analyzed in chapter 5, on conflict, and in chapter 10, which focuses on contemporary Colombian international relations.

Colombia's history can and will be compared to the histories of its neighbors and to the projects and priorities of the more advanced industrial nations of the North Atlantic. But Nobel laureate Gabriel García Márquez warned against hasty comparisons in his 1982 Nobel lecture when he said, "The interpretation of our reality through patterns not our own, serves only to make us ever more unknown, ever less free, ever more solitary."[3] We cannot make a nation's history less solitary, but we can try to present history from a fresh perspective—thus bringing dynamism to a national narrative based largely on assumptions, established patterns, and traditions. The study of history is liberating, and new interpretations offer us the opportunity to reconsider our reading, our understanding, our sense of a nation's history.

NOTES

1. Alberto Flores Galindo, *In Search of an Inca: Identity and Utopia in the Andes* (New York: Cambridge University Press, 2010), 248.

2. Ibid.

3. Gabriel García Márquez, "The Solitude of Latin America" (Nobel lecture, Stockholm, Sweden, December 8, 1982).

Colombia in the Americas

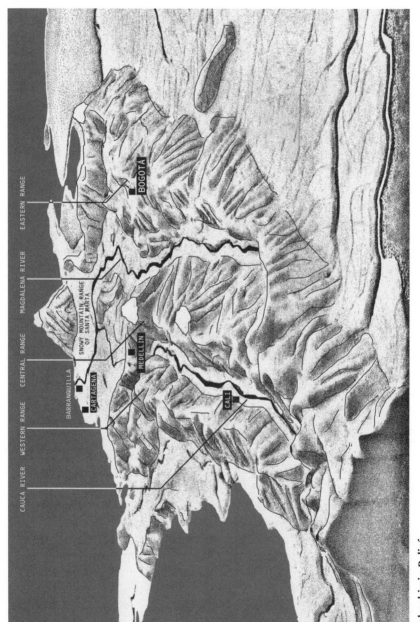

CAJUCA RIVER WESTERN RANGE CENTRAL RANGE MAGDALENA RIVER EASTERN RANGE

BARRANQUILLA

CARTAGENA

SNOWY MOUNTAIN RANGE
OF SANTA MARTA

MEDELLIN

CALI

BOGOTÁ

Colombia in Relief

Chapter One

Origins

Present-day Latin America begins some two hundred years ago. The Spanish American independence movements that flared up in 1810 opened the way for the birth of the republics and, with them, the nation-states that today make up the majority of the American continent. This transformation did not happen overnight; it took almost a century for the process to unfold fully. Yet the origins can be traced to 1808, the year that Napoleon Bonaparte's troops invaded the Iberian Peninsula (today's Spain and Portugal), imprisoning the Spanish king in French lands. This surprising turn of events wrought a vexing problem: who would govern the Spanish provinces?

Due to this early-nineteenth-century problem, Latin America's present has a clearly identifiable beginning. This is not to say that nothing has changed in the two hundred years since. The places that won independence from the Spanish Crown have had to identify the type of government that would best respect their needs; overwhelmingly, these nation-states adopted the form of a liberal republic. Colombia is one of them. The birth of Colombia can therefore be traced back to those first years of the nineteenth century, but Colombia's consolidation as a liberal republic took over one hundred years to materialize.

This chapter outlines the events that occurred from 1808 to 1830. This was a period of "firsts": several models and ideas about the future of the state and society were debated, yet, at the same time, several civil wars were fought. In short, these were the years during which the world had changed for millions of people who inhabited Spanish America. In this chapter, we consider these transformations—ideological, political, economic, and territorial—for Colombia,[1] which were inextricably linked to simultaneous changes occurring throughout the Atlantic world.

THE CRISIS OF EMPIRE

A tidal wave of transcendental transformations crashed over America two hundred years ago. The Spanish Empire had crumbled to its foundations, and although it did not completely dissolve, it nevertheless suffered a serious crisis at the hands of Napoleon and his subsequent imprisonment of the Spanish monarchs in France. People throughout all of Spain's territories argued that this crisis signified that sovereignty reverted to the people. They claimed their right to pass their own laws and elect their own leaders. Napoleon's occupation of the Iberian Peninsula and his decision to appoint his brother, Joseph, as king of all Spanish territories was the catalyst for the process of change in America whereby Spanish provinces became democratic republics. The cycle of bourgeois revolutions and the convulsions that shook the Atlantic world beginning in the middle of the eighteenth century, including the independence of the English colonies in North America, the French Revolution, the Haitian Revolution, and the almost chronic war between the emerging British Empire and the veteran Spanish Empire, all influenced the direction politics would take with the collapse of the Spanish monarchy.

The crisis of the monarchy in 1808 therefore generated protests against *mal gobierno*, or "bad government." Protesters began calling for autonomy first, and full independence later. The monarchy's authority began dividing against itself when King Charles IV left governance of the entire kingdom to his favored minister, Manuel Godoy. Godoy's excesses sparked a conspiracy against both the minister and the king, led by the king's own son, Ferdinand. In March 1808, Charles IV was forced to abdicate the throne to his son, who assumed it as Ferdinand VII. In the meantime, French troops invaded the Iberian Peninsula. Their intentions to take control of the Crown soon became obvious, so Charles and Ferdinand traveled to Bayonne, France, to settle their differences in the presence of the French emperor, Napoleon. All the while, the Spanish people, in response to the French invasion, staged an uprising in Madrid on May 2, 1808, which was supported by the provinces as well as by Spain's territories in the Americas. In this sense, Spaniards and the Spanish Americans maintained their loyalty to Ferdinand VII, but when he was arrested by Napoleon, he was no longer available to govern. A crisis of leadership ensued. The response was immediate: the Spanish provinces (in Spain) formed *juntas*, or governing bodies, that swore loyalty to Ferdinand VII at the same time that they, in his absence, provisionally took control of government until his return. One of them, the Junta of Seville, proclaimed itself as the Supreme Junta and, as such, ordered all of the provinces of the kingdom to swear loyalty to Ferdinand VII. To this end, it sent commissioners to all of the territories. To the Viceroyalty of New Granada (today's Ecuador, Colombia, Venezuela, and Panama), the junta sent Juan José Pando y Sanllorente. Solemn oaths were taken in all of the principal cities of the viceroyalty, and the viceroyalty capital city, Santafé (today's Bogotá), swore loyalty to Ferdinand on September 11, 1808. Meanwhile, the Spanish triumphed over the French at the Battle of Bailén, which forced Joseph Bonaparte, or Joseph I, to leave Madrid. The peninsular provinces subsequently sent representatives to Madrid in order to form a central junta.

On September 25, 1808, in Aranjuez, Spain, the Supreme Central and Governing Junta of the Kingdom was established. Thus, the government was again centralized and managed to stop these autonomist movements that were occurring in the Spanish provinces. But the triumphs of the Spanish armies did not last long as the French successfully retook Madrid, forcing the Supreme Central Junta to retreat to Seville. From there, and over the course of the following year, this was the junta that ruled in the name of Ferdinand VII over all of the territories that he considered his personal patrimony.

The Supreme Central Junta considered any attempt at autonomy either in the peninsula or in the Americas an act of treason. The first men to make up the junta were delegates from the peninsular provinces, but the junta quickly accepted representatives arriving from the Americas. On January 22, 1809, it decreed that all the territories of the monarchy in the Americas were not colonies but rather essential and integral parts of the monarchy itself and therefore eligible to send delegates elected by the respective populations. As a result, each one of the four viceroyalties (New Spain or Mexico, Peru, the New Kingdom of Granada, and Buenos Aires) and the six captaincy generals (Cuba, Puerto Rico, Guatemala, Chile, Venezuela, and the Philippines) were given the opportunity to elect a representative, ten in total.

Ironically, this political calculation was ultimately the reason so many populations in Spanish America called first for autonomy and later for complete independence from Spain. Why? The decree of January 22, 1809, although it recognized the rights of all Spanish kingdoms to be represented in the Central Junta, nevertheless made it clear that the territories in the Americas and the Philippines would not receive fair and equal representation. The eighteen provinces in Spain, all of which were much smaller than the overseas territories in terms of both population and geographic territory, were each represented by two delegates, that is, thirty-six total. In other words, American creoles (American, born of Spanish heritage) wished to be recognized equally as legitimate descendants of Spaniards with the same rights as a Spaniard from Spain. The skewed representation that favored peninsular interests in the junta left no doubt in anyone's mind: the Americans were clearly not equal to Spaniards.

Despite protests, Spanish America nevertheless continued an electoral process in line with the instructions that arrived from the Supreme Central Junta.

According to these instructions, each one of the viceroyalties and captaincies were to hold elections in the principal cities. The winner of each election would go on to compete for a final selection that would determine the representative for the respective territory. For New Granada, Antonio de Narváez y Latorre won the final elections on September 16, 1809. He did not travel to Spain, however. By the time he was ready to travel there, the Supreme Central Junta had dissolved.

The electoral process, together with the principle of representation that this process generated, were, no doubt, two political innovations of great importance for the coming days in the Americas. Equally important were the instructions given by the different *cabildos*, or "town councils," in New Granada to those individuals who would represent their interests to the Seville junta. The town councils did much more than merely complain of Americans' unequal representation in the junta or offer the familiar protests concerning the abuses of royal authorities. They went on to formulate enlightened ideas and true programs for governance. Narváez y Latorre received instructions from the *cabildos* of Santafé (known as the "Memorial de Agravios," or "Memorandum of Grievances"), Popayán, Socorro, Tunja, and Loja, among others. Similarly, he received a document written by Ignacio de Herrera y Vergara dated September 1, 1809, in Santafé with the title *Reflections of an impartial American for the delegate from this Kingdom of New Granada so that he may have them in mind during his delicate mission.*[2] Herrera wrote in this document that "the people are the fountainhead of absolute authority. They placed authority in the hands of a leader who could make them happy. The King is charged with this duty for his dominions."[3] Another document to be read in Spain, written by the town council of Socorro, signed October 20, 1809, called for "unproductive classes [to] be suppressed, reduction of redundant royal employment, lands and labor [should] be freed from excessive taxation and regulation, and that the imposition of taxes, their collection and distribution [should] follow the laws of justice within which the social contract has been determined."[4] They also asked that the delegate petition for the abolition of slavery and of the *resguardos*, or lands held for the exclusive use of Indians. They called for the freeing up of markets, reduction in the number of feast days and ecclesiastical tariffs, improvement of roads and education, and simplification of the civil and criminal law codes. In sum, the *cabildos* were proposing an actual program of government.

Meanwhile, back in Spain, at the beginning of 1810, the Supreme Central Junta's function collapsed and was replaced by the Regency Council, which was made up of five members. The council did not change any of the policies that the Central Junta had developed since 1808 concerning the American provinces. This meant that most Americans did not accept the legitimacy of the Regency Council to govern in the name of Ferdinand VII. This hesitation was reinforced by fear that Napoleon was about to achieve a definitive victory in Spain and Europe. The Americans, faced with the likely and total absence of their king, realized that they had to made quick and radical decisions about their future, which is exactly what they did.

1810: THE DEVELOPMENT OF THE JUNTAS

For New Granada, 1810 was a long year, which, for our purposes, lasted from September 1809 to February 1811. These eighteen months can be divided into four phases. The first, lasting from September 1809 until May 1810, saw the outbreak of violent rebellions and counter-repression and the need for urgent decision making. The second lasted from May to July 1810, when the first juntas were organized. The third witnessed the flourishing of the juntas, which lasted from the final days of July through September 1810. And, finally, the fourth phase, from August 1810 to February 1811, represented a period when the juntas consolidated their new administrations, took military actions against dissident provinces and populations, and attempted to give shape to one government for all of the provinces that were part of the former Audiencia of Santafé.

During the first phase, beginning in September 1809, creoles from Santafé thought they should seriously consider the town council of Quito's formal offer to join that city's autonomous junta, which had been organized a month before, on August 10. As explained above, the creoles in Quito and Santafé, like those in other parts of Spanish America, believed French troops would triumph over the Spanish in Spain and increasingly considered the Supreme Central Governing Junta (in Spain) illegitimate. The Spanish viceroy in Bogotá, José Amar y Borbón, however, decided to respond to the invitation by completely blocking the organization of a junta in Santafé and violently repressing any attempts to organize. For the Spanish authorities in America, there was only one option: remain loyal to only one junta, the Supreme Central Governing Junta. The creoles believed that there were other possibilities.

These creoles continued requesting that the viceroy accept the formation of a governing junta for the Audiencia of Santafé. Under pressure, Amar y Borbón accepted. He then convoked a meeting on September 6, 1809, to discuss the events in Quito of August 10, 1809, while debating the possibility of organizing a junta for their own provinces in Santafé. Not much was accomplished at this meeting, but a few days later, on September 11, another meeting took place, which accomplished little more than the establishment of two

Map 1.1.   Provinces, 1810

opposing parties: one in favor of remaining subject to the Supreme Central Governing Junta and another that backed the idea of forming a separate junta for Santafé. With respect to rebellious Quito, the viceroy decided to send individuals, reinforced by armed forces, who would "negotiate" with the junta.

The failure of these meetings and the decision to force Quito to submit under armed pressure led to the second option: conspiracy. Several printed pamphlets circulated that explicitly favored the Quito junta. The viceroy subsequently issued an edict on September 28, 1809, making it an offense to carry "seditious" documents, threatening harsh punishments and prison for anyone caught with such documents. The first of several plots to overthrow Spanish rule, now remembered as the "Revolution of the Rocket," occurred two days later but failed: an anonymous tip to the viceroy gave him time to preempt the planned revolt and imprison those he thought responsible for leading it. In a subsequent plot, a group of Santafé's residents figured out a way to take control of the armaments held by the royalist troops who marched toward Quito. The plan consisted of assaulting the soldiers, taking the arms by force, and sending the weapons to Socorro, a nearby town from where a more general insurrection could be launched. The plan failed due to poor planning by its leaders. Shortly thereafter, a rebellion broke out in Casanare, a plains region on the eastern side of Santafé's major mountain range. The purpose of this rebellion was to take the town of Pore on February 15, 1810, but the rebellion leaders were quickly captured. They were brought to trial, found guilty of treason, hanged, and decapitated, and their heads were sent to Santafé for public display. The heads (literally) arrived in the capital on May 13, 1810, but were not displayed for fear they would spark another round of protests among the inhabitants of the city.

Due to the failure of the conspiracies, the Americans in New Granada opted for a third option: to organize—on their own—governing juntas in New Granada. This kicked off the second moment of the long year of 1810: the first round of autonomous governing juntas, which began on the Caribbean coast in the city of Cartagena on May 22. After this, a series of additional juntas emerged throughout New Granada: in Cali on July 3, in Pamplona the next day, and in Socorro on July 11. The viceroy, despite this clear trend, continued to repudiate any attempts at forming a junta in the capital. By July 20, 1810, there was little more he could do; creoles in Santafé organized a junta and proclaimed it the Supreme Junta of the Kingdom. These events, occurring during the months of May to July of 1810, signified that an important threshold, brought about by the agitated situation of the previous two years, had been crossed.

On Friday, July 20, a market day in Santafé, an altercation on the city square, planned by a group of creoles against a Spaniard, sparked a major rebellion. "Don José (González) Llorente, Spaniard and friend of the ministers who suppress our liberty, lashed out with less-than decorous words against the Americans; this news spread quickly and exalted the spirits that already were disposed towards revenge. . . . All began meeting at the door of Llorente's store; the commotion brought more people, and in a moment numerous people could be seen, united and indignant against this Spaniard and against his friends."[5] From that moment, the events quickly snowballed. González Llorente was imprisoned due to the crowd's displeasure. That afternoon, three commissions arrived at the viceroy's house, demanding he convoke a *cabildo abierto*, or "open town council meeting." He refused to meet with the first two commissions, but agreed with the third commission that an extraordinary (i.e., unusual) *cabildo* could meet. Nevertheless, several creoles took it upon themselves to bring together vast numbers of people to the central plaza and stoked the crowd with haranguing speeches and complaints. Thanks to these demonstrations, by nighttime the extraordinary *cabildo* transformed into an open *cabildo*. By then it was clear—and the viceroy knew it—that the army would not act against the demonstrators. The plan worked: a junta was organized. At dawn on July 21, 1810, a document was signed that Colombians now refer to as their act of independence. Written by José Acevedo y Gómez, the act made clear the purposes and direction of the recently constituted junta:

> All authority will be placed provisionally in the Supreme Governing Body of this Kingdom, until this same Junta forms the Constitution that assures public happiness. The noble provinces will be counted on to send their representatives, and the resulting body will determine the regulations that will organize elections in said provinces. These regulations and the constitution of government should be based on liberty, the respective independence of the provinces, united only by a federal system, whose representation should reside in this capital so that it may oversee the security of New Granada. New Granada protests any attempts to abdicate essential rights belonging to the sovereignty of the people to any other individual than the august and disgraced monarch of Ferdinand VII, who will return to rule among us. For now, this new government is subject to the Supreme Regency Junta, as long as it exists in Spain, and on the Constitution that the people give it and in the terms stated.[6]

From this act, it becomes clear that "autonomy" was formally established on July 21, 1810. This autonomy was based on the right of the people to govern themselves through a constitution, to gather in a federal system, and to establish that the king was still king but only if he were to come to New Granada and follow the norms of the written constitution. A turning point had been reached, and clear separation from both Spain and the concept of absolute monarchy had been established.

July 21 and the immediate days thereafter were the focus of much agitation. The more radical element among the Americans, known as *chisperos*, or "spark makers" (or, less literally, fire starters), made it difficult for the Supreme Junta (in Santafé) to moderate their initial decisions about governance. Thus, by July 26, the junta finally declared that it no longer recognized the Supreme Regency Council, marking a decisive moment: no corporation or person located in or hailing from the peninsula would have authority over these lands, except for Ferdinand VII. Furthermore, the Santafé junta, which had declared that Ferdinand had to reside in Santafé, now established that he could not entrust any other person or institution with the authority that the people had invested in him. The next day, July 27, the junta was divided into sections so that it could more efficiently handle day-to-day governance, as had been planned only a few days earlier. The sections included: Ecclesiastical Business; Grace, Justice, and Government; War; Treasury; Police; and Commerce. On July 29, the junta sent to all provinces of New Granada an invitation to elect representatives to the General Congress of the Kingdom, which would meet in December 1810. On August 13, under pressure from the radicals, the former viceroy Amar y Borbón was placed under arrest, and on August 15, he was secretly sent to Cartagena. The following day the junta silenced the radical *chisperos* by imprisoning their leaders.

The effects of the Santafé junta's decision to organize and refuse to recognize any authority emanating from the Regency Council were quickly felt throughout the former jurisdiction of Santafé's Audiencia, or "court." On the one hand, Cartagena's junta declared its opposition to the pretensions of the Santafé junta to be "Supreme"; the Pamplona junta declared itself as a provincial junta apart from Santafé; the Cali *cabildo* began to act as a junta, however provisionally; and the junta of Socorro confidently drew up its own constitution on August 15. Simultaneously, several smaller cities and towns mobilized politically. Moreover, Santafé's July 29 invitation for the provinces to attend a Congress in December created the conditions for a new crop of juntas to sprout up throughout the former Audiencia over the course of the next two months. All communities that had served as heads of provinces, as well as many others who resented their relationship to their former governing rulers, proceeded to form their own governing entities and then elect a representative who would be sent to Santafé.

Next, the third period of this dramatic year of 1810 began taking form. In Tunja, on July 26, the residents organized an open town meeting, at which they refused to recognize the Regency Council and appointed the junta that would run the province's governance with the title "Patriotic Junta." That same day, the *cabildo* of Mariquita formed a government junta of its own, also the product of a *cabildo abierto*—an open town council meeting. Neiva did the same on July 27, taking care to heed the attorney general's request to organize a governing junta, one which, on August 13, proclaimed itself the Superior Provincial Junta. On July 30, the population of Girón gathered in the main plaza and requested that Father Eloy Valenzuela, a local priest, take charge of the town's destiny. Mompox went furthest fastest by declaring absolute independence not only from Spain, but also from Ferdinand VII and any attempt at foreign domination. Santa Marta, on the Caribbean coast, established its junta during an evening *cabildo* meeting on August 10. Popayán's junta constituted itself on August 11 and named itself the Provisional Junta of Health and Public Security. On September 6, the town of Garzón's leaders met to create an autonomous junta; their founding document included provisions that were less a junta's plan for governance policies and more akin to a constitution. On August 30, in Santafé de Antioquia, the Congress established a Superior Provincial Junta, which was attended by representatives from that city as well as Rionegro, Marinilla, and Medellín. Quibdó, in the region of Citará near the Pacific coast, declared its junta on September 1; Nóvita, in the same region, on August 27 (although other sources date its constitution from September 27). Finally, Pore created its Governing Autonomous Junta on September 13, 1810.

Elections characterized the fourth and final period of 1810, which were conducted and registered in several townships of New Granada. These were the elections that selected the representatives to the General Congress that would meet in December. Those who were elected from the different juntas took on the challenge of shaping the newly formed governments; to do this, they followed the principles of separation of powers, the crafting of laws by specialized bodies, the abolition of monopolies and other obligations detested by the people, together with other principles that likely were inspired by the United States Constitution and that of France of 1791. Finally, the juntas prepared for war. They initially worried about a possible invasion by French troops and then shifted to a consideration of the reprisals the king might act upon if he were to return to the throne. These fears justified either subduing of the dissident populations within provinces or invading the provinces that remained loyal to the Supreme Regency Council in Spain.

On December 22, 1810, the General Congress of the Kingdom met in Santafé. Cartagena boycotted the meeting from the very beginning, and signs that the Congress would fail were clear early on. Only those representatives from Socorro, Neiva, Pamplona, Mariquita, Nóvita, and Santafé attended; those from Sogamoso and Mompox were finally accepted, although the representatives present at the initial meeting did not unanimously approve these two representatives. Disagreements quickly developed over sovereignty and regional representational power, which resulted in the closure of the Congress during the first months of February 1811. In this way, with disunity and uncertainty looming, the long year of 1810 came to an end.

THE FIRST REPUBLIC (1811–1816)

The failure of the General Congress of the Kingdom led the former provinces of the Audiencia of Santafé to organize according to what each thought most convenient for their own interests. Three major political projects emerged: one sought a liberal republican order that adhered to a centralist, judicial political organization; another similarly considered republicanism but did not accept delegating sovereignty to another province and so embraced a federal program; and finally, the political order that remained loyal to the Regency Council in Spain and, as such, did not accept any change in the political order that existed prior to 1810. How a particular province adhered to a specific political project largely depended on which social groups held influence in a given region. Still, within each province, inhabitants were divided. The First Republic was, at its very inception, divided against itself. This meant that as different constitutional and government forms were considered and put into effect, civil war increasingly became inevitable. From 1811 to 1815, two major republics emerged: Cundinamarca and the United Provinces. Each was pitted against the other, and both attacked surrounding provinces that remained loyal to Spain to force them into their particular sphere of influence. Conflict diminished in 1815 when the United Provinces emerged victorious over Cundinamarca, resulting in the unification of the republic. This unification did not change the tense relations between pro-republic provinces and those that remained loyal to Spain. On the contrary, years of violent skirmishes and political upheaval facilitated the easy triumph of the occupying forces sent from Spain after Ferdinand VII reassumed the throne in 1814.

First, the Republic of Cundinamarca was born on February 19, 1811, when the people decided to convoke an electoral college that would draw up a constitution for the province. The deliberations were quick; the constitution was promulgated on April 4, bringing a definitive end to the Supreme Junta that had been created on July 20, 1810. The constitution, organized into fourteen titles and several articles, declared that the province would be called Cundinamarca and would be run as a constitutional monarchy, reiterating Ferdinand VII as king with powers that were limited according to constitutional law. Cundinamarca's constitutional monarchy established a clear division of powers among the executive, legislative, and judicial branches; determined that Catholicism would continue to be the official religion of its inhabitants; set electoral procedures, the organization of the army, and a tax code; and stated in Title XII that "the rights of man in society are: equality and liberty under the law; security and property," and that "sovereignty essentially resides in the universality of citizens."[7] This first constitution of what we now call Colombia thereby established a limited monarchy and included principles such as the separation of powers and the rights of man and citizen, and ultimately it served as a text that set the precedent for subsequent liberal constitutions.

The other provinces that had opted to separate themselves from the Regency Council, given the step Cundinamarca had taken, jealously guarded their own right to maintain sovereignty. They believed they had no other option but to organize their own forms of government founded on their own constitutions. But before even Cundinamarca's constitutional governments could form, one key issue needed urgent resolution: how to structure a state within which all provinces could participate while not requiring any one province to renounce sovereignty and, at the same time, allow all provinces to acquire the necessary power to defend themselves and be recognized as independent powers. Federalism, styled after the design of government in the United States of America, became the answer. But this step was not an easy one to take, nor did all the provinces accept it.

The president of Cundinamarca, Jorge Tadeo Lozano, presented a project to create a federal system. Simultaneously, independence leader Antonio Nariño, who was staunchly opposed to a federalist system, led a military movement against all manifestations of federalism. This polarization culminated in the violent overthrow of President Lozano in July 1811, and Nariño assumed the post of president. Worried about these developments, several delegates from different provinces organized the Congress of Delegates, which would determine the best form of governance. The result was the Federation Pact.

This pact, signed on November 27, 1811, created the United Provinces of New Granada. Signed by the delegates from the provinces of Antioquia, Cartagena, Neiva, Pamplona, and Tunja, this agreement was not accepted by Cundinamarca or Chocó. Divided into seventy-eight articles, the pact's text established that governance would be in the hands of the Congress of Delegates, which could be called into session whenever necessary; that only those provinces that existed on July 20, 1810, were eligible to join the United Provinces, in addition to those that had already voluntarily joined. Finally, the pact stated that "the United Provinces of New Granada recognize each other mutually as equals, independent, and sovereign, guaranteeing for each other the integrity of their territories, their internal administration, and a republican form of government."[8] This form of governance promised equality for all so that peaceful relations could be maintained among the United Provinces.

The key political events that occurred between 1812 and 1815 were therefore all related to the ways in which each individual province wrestled with the type of government that would order its internal affairs and how each should relate to the surrounding provinces. Those that decided to remain loyal to Spain turned to the viceregal authority, located in Panama, and enjoyed a certain level of continuity in governance. The state of Cundinamarca defended centralism as its key constitutive form of governance and raised an army that attempted to force surrounding provinces, both royalist and federalist, into submission. In April 1812, Cundinamarca reformed its constitution even further, definitively abolishing all monarchical power in the state. It declared its absolute independence from Spain on July 13, 1813. The United Provinces, for their part, each developed their own constitutions: Tunja in 1811; Antioquia, Cartagena, Mompox, and Neiva in 1812; Popayán in 1814; and Mariquita and Pamplona in 1815. They too declared their absolute independence from Spain in those years. All these constitutions share similar, basic characteristics: division of powers; one president in charge of the executive power; recognition of the rights of citizens; the adoption of Roman Catholicism as the official state religion; and the establishment of an electoral system, a fiscal system, and a military and police force to maintain public order.

The civil war that ensued among these three major political groups—Cundinamarca, the United Provinces, and the provinces loyal to the king—was long lasting and bloody. Instead of putting human and economic potential to work for the emerging republics, such potential was enlisted for war. Neither Cundinamarca nor the United Provinces was able to completely subdue the royalists, although efforts to do so were constant. Cundinamarca and the United Provinces in turn fought several important battles against each other. In December 1814, the United Provinces triumphed over Cundinamarca's army, thanks to the military leadership of Simón Bolívar. This victory brought an end to the Republic of Cundinamarca, but it could not establish a solid federal order, just as Spanish reconquest armies set sail from Cádiz to New Granada in February 1815.

THE FINAL BATTLE AGAINST ABSOLUTISM

Napoleon Bonaparte's demise allowed Ferdinand VII to return to Spain on March 22, 1814. While in the city of Valencia, he abolished (on May 4) the liberal Spanish constitution of 1812 and reestablished a reign of absolutism in all of his inherited territories in Europe, America, and Asia. To put his order into effect, especially in the American territories, he raised a powerful army of more than ten thousand soldiers headed by the renowned and successful military general Pablo Morillo. The army was sent to Venezuela and New Granada; after arriving at Margarita Island in July 1815, the Spanish forces headed to the Caribbean coastal city of Santa Marta. Morillo planned his attack on the United Provinces of New Granada from Santa Marta and decided first to lay siege to neighboring Cartagena on August 6, 1815. Cartagena fell on December 5, after suffering a disastrous six-month Spanish siege. This victory opened a clear path for Morillo and his troops, who quickly marched toward the interior of the country, arriving on May 26, 1816, in Santafé. The capital surrendered, and Morillo initiated a series of persecutions now remembered as the Régimen del Terror, or "Reign of Terror."

Prior to all of this, during a particularly harrowing military campaign against the royalists in 1813, Simón Bolívar declared *guerra a muerte*, or "war to the death." This tactic showed no mercy toward any *Peninsulares* (Spaniards from the Iberian Peninsula) who fought against the patriots but pardoned all Americans, no matter their professed allegiance. Morillo arrived to find this decree still in effect and responded to it with even further cruelty against the Americans. Once in Santafé he established the three pillars of the Reign of Terror: the Sequestering Junta was in charge of confiscating all properties belonging to the patriots; the Pacification Tribunal banished those who supported the patriot cause from the city, either by imprisoning them or exiling them; and the Permanent War Council, which was charged with the more extreme task of trying and executing those found guilty of treason. The few military men who remained in the Republic of the United Provinces just barely escaped; some took refuge in the eastern plains of Casanare, from where they organized a weak but valiant resistance.

Such violent persecutions and abuses of Americans by Morillo ultimately played into Bolívar's hands. The inhabitants of New Granada believed they were suffering at the hands of Morillo for committing the "crime" of simply being born Americans. At this point, loyalty to the king was definitively severed. Guerrilla groups emerged in surrounding mountain regions and found support through a network of urban spies who supplied information to the guerrillas about the movement of royalist troops. Slowly, these groups managed to chip away at Morillo's military dominance. Increasing numbers of inhabitants came to view Morillo's army as an occupation force, and thus, recovering independence became the primary goal. To this end, the patriots sought to reestablish a state by inaugurating the Congress at the town of Angostura (in Venezuela—currently called Ciudad Bolívar) and raising an army that would be capable of defeating the Spanish. Simón Bolívar was at the forefront of both processes.

Bolívar left New Granada for Jamaica in May 1815. The fall of the Second Venezuelan Republic and the insurmountable challenge of politically uniting New Granada and leading military actions against the royalist provinces forced him to seek refuge in the Antilles. Once there, on September 6, 1815, he wrote his famous Jamaica letter, or "Answer from a South American to a Gentleman of This Island," where he carefully examined the situation of the Spanish provinces in America; ventured predictions about their future; and following what Francisco Miranda had proposed years earlier, recovered the name Colombia for the political entity that would take shape if New Granada (Colombia and Ecuador) and Venezuela could unite into one nation. Shortly thereafter, he left Jamaica for Haiti and, with the help of President Petión, organized the Cayos expedition on March 20, 1816, a renewed effort to liberate Venezuela, which failed. By July 17, 1817, Bolívar successfully asserted control over the territory of Angostura, and a few days later, on July 24, he declared himself Supreme Chief of the Armies. Once Bolívar considered Angostura firmly under his control, he opened the Orinoco River to the British Legion, which entered Venezuelan territory through this route in order to strengthen the precarious military position of the patriot armies and provide valuable supplies and aid.

A few months later, on February 15, 1819, Bolívar inaugurated the Angostura Congress, and accordingly reestablished the republic both in the eyes of local audiences and internationally. During the inaugural address at Angostura, Bolívar stated, "I have had the honor of bringing together the representatives of the people of Venezuela for this august Congress, fountain of legitimate authority, holder of sovereign will, and referee of the destiny of the Nation."[9] He made it clear to the Congress that "the union of New Granada and Venezuela in a grand State has been the uniform vote of the people and governments of these Republics. Our luck in war has verified this link that is so very much desired by all Colombians; in effect, we are incorporated. These fraternal *pueblos* have trusted us with their interests, their rights, and their destinies."[10] Thus, the die was cast: the republic was reestablished, the army was strengthened, and Bolívar emerged as the clear military leader. The union between Venezuela and New Granada, under the new name of Colombia, was seen as an attainable goal.

One of the key military generals, who escaped from Pablo Morillo in Santafé and sought refuge in the eastern plains of Casanare, was Francisco de Paula Santander. The patriot army that held this eastern position in 1816–1817 was weak. Santander, with the help of Bolívar, rose among the military ranks, gaining the title of brigadier general. He was charged with organizing the patriot military groups dispersed throughout the vast plains region. His military prowess proved, Santander suggested to Bolívar that in order to liberate the entire northern region of South America from the Spanish armies, Santafé should be the primary target of liberation. Bolívar agreed. He inaugurated this new strategy on May 23, 1819, and on July 5, he began climbing the Andes from the east at an almost impassable point. On July 25, Bolívar led his troops to victory at the battle of Pantano de Vargas, and the following August 7, he scored a resounding military victory at the Battle of Boyacá, opening a clear path for his entry into Santafé three days later. With this victory, Bolívar did not, however, manage to completely liberate the New Granada territory from the Spanish. The harrowing path toward independence was a long one and lasted several more years. But this victory did manage to install in Santafé a government that could direct necessary military and political actions. Never again did Santafé fall to Spanish imperial dominion.

COLOMBIA: THE SECOND REPUBLIC (1819–1830)

A triumphant Bolívar returned to Angostura to announce to the Congress his military successes. With victory in hand, the Congress issued the Fundamental Law of the Republic of Colombia on December 17, 1819. The first article of the law established that "the republics of Venezuela and of New Granada are, from this day forward, united as one under the glorious title of the Republic of Colombia." The second article determined that the territory encompassed by the republic "will be that that made up the former Captaincy General of Venezuela and the Viceroyalty of New Granada." The fifth article divided the territory into "three large Departments: Venezuela, Quito, and Cundinamarca, this last Department is the one that had previously comprised the United Provinces of New Granada, a name that from this day forward will not be used. The capitals of these Departments (or Administrative Territories) will be the cities of Caracas, Quito, and Bogotá, striking the word Santafé." The eighth article ordered the Congress of Colombia to meet again on January 1, 1821, at the township of Villa del Rosario de Cúcuta.[11]

This scheduled meeting occurred, but not until May 6, 1821. The following August 30, the attending representatives signed the Constitution of Colombia, known now as the Cúcuta Constitution or the Constitution of 1821, for the place and date of its signing. This constitution set up a centralist government but one that, as indicated in its second article, was a popular representative government. The population was to exercise sovereignty through elections, and the state's administrative powers were to be divided into legislative, executive, and judiciary branches. The Congress determined that Simón Bolívar would be president and Francisco de Paula Santander, vice president. Bogotá was to serve as the capital city. From that moment on, Santander, in effect, governed as Bolívar continued to lead the liberation armies, which were actively involved in military campaigns until 1826.

From 1821 to 1826, warfare continued, as did efforts to establish a stable form of state government. Maintaining the armies in military campaigns required enormous sacrifices for a population that struggled to build and maintain civil order. Colombians nevertheless created the conditions that allowed for the founding of universities, and they constructed institutions of government and administration. Later, they established steamship navigation up the Magdalena River and built railroads, schools, and roads. Colombians also initiated trade and industry, hired foreign experts and advisers, and built their own printing presses. In short, these and other activities symbolized the intense activity Santander engaged in during these first years of the republic despite limits imposed by the need to continue fighting against the Spanish armies.

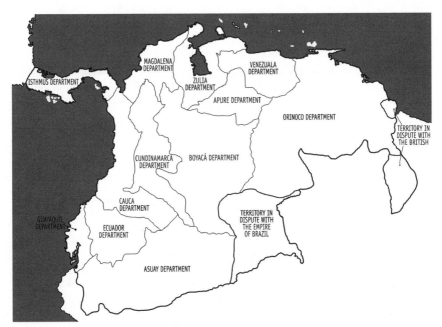

Map 1.2. "Gran" Colombia

Soon, difficult tensions emerged between the leadership of the military and that of civil society. Bolívar and Santander could not come to an agreement over priorities, and these problems were aggravated by the resentment that leaders in Quito and Caracas soon developed against the predominance Cundinamarca had acquired. The political situation grew worse as Bolívar and Santander became bitter enemies. By 1826, the Venezuelan city of Valencia held a boycott against the Santander administration. Bolívar rushed back to Bogotá from Peru en route to Caracas. He took the side of the Venezuelans against Santander and, in doing so, won the enmity of the people of Cundinamarca. The Cúcuta Constitution began to deflate, and with it the Republic of Colombia.

The two major factions in the conflict tried to negotiate their differences through a convention that took place in Ocaña from March to June 1828, but no agreement could be reached, and the pro-Bolívar delegation walked out. The convention collapsed and, essentially, the Cúcuta Constitution ceased to exist. At this point, Bolívar decided to take power for himself—as a dictator—and in essence declared his dictatorship by decree on August 23, 1828. He assumed dictatorial powers on the condition that he convoke open elections in 1830. Those opposed to Bolívar became radicalized, and on September 25, 1828, they attempted to assassinate him. Bolívar survived the attempt on his life, but politically, he could no longer establish order in the territory. To make matters worse, in March 1829, Peru declared war against Colombia, forcing Bolívar to revisit the battlefield. Upon Bolívar's return to the capital city in January 1830, Congress had already met once more to approve a new constitution, and the Venezuelans had voted in favor of separation from Cundinamarca; the Ecuadorians were similarly inclined. Colombia had simply ceased to exist. This is how Bolívar understood the succession of events; he subsequently resigned the presidency, bade farewell to his few remaining friends in Bogotá, including his lover, Manuela Sáenz, and went into exile. He died in the coastal city of Santa Marta on December 17, 1830, a bitter and broken man.

THE END OF AN ERA OF CHANGE

Many factors, not the least of which included Bolívar's death, came together to create the conditions for the civil war that brought to a close the Second Republic in 1830. Bolívar's dictatorship, the conspiracies against him, the war with Peru, the numerous rebellions against the Colombia regime, the open rebellion of Venezuela against the national government in Bogotá, the efforts by the council of ministers to establish a constitutional monarchy, the overwhelming disagreement with which so many greeted the recently issued constitution, and in particular the presence of Venezuelan troops in Bogotá were all contributing circumstances.

The so-called rebellion of the Callao Battalion marked the beginning of the end. The battalion, comprising primarily Venezuelans, was under the command of an ardent Bolivarian, Rafael Urdaneta. He dominated Bogotá politics, yet the new president of the republic, Joaquín Mosquera, refused to increase the number of soldiers as requested by Urdaneta. Similarly, he refused to name Urdaneta as minister of war. At "El Santuario," a place near Bogotá, troops from the opposing parties clashed in a violent battle. The Venezuelans emerged triumphant. The Constitution of 1830 became null and void, as did the positions of the government officials elected under its mandate. These men resigned, and the Municipal Council of Bogotá, on September 5, 1830, ratified a petition that named General Urdaneta as leader.

The death of Bolívar three months later changed the course of events. Urdaneta's legitimacy rested on the requests that Bolívar return to Bogotá to assume control of Colombia. The Venezuelans in Bogotá no longer had Bolívar as an excuse to impose their will. Although initially the actions taken by the Venezuelan Urdaneta were to pursue mercilessly any man suspected of conspiracy, the reality of events forced him to negotiate peace. The two factions met in the Juntas of Apulo at the end of April 1831. There, all parties agreed to settle their differences, accept the separation of Venezuela and Quito, and foment the union of the provinces deemed to belong to Cundinamarca under one government until a new convention could create a satisfactory political arrangement. And so it was: Urdaneta resigned his post and returned to Venezuela. On October 20, 1831, the constitutional assembly met, and on February 29, 1832, the new constitution was approved. This constitution gave birth to the Republic of New Granada.

NOTES

1. In this chapter, we use the name *Colombia* generically to refer to the Republic of Colombia with the understanding that the country had different names from 1810 through 1886.
2. In Spanish, the title is *Reflexiones que hace un Americano imparcial al diputado de este Nuevo Reino de Granada para que les tenga presente en su delicada misión.*
3. Ignacio de Herrera y Vergara, "Refleciones que hace un americano imparcial al diputado de este reino de Granada para que tenga presentes en su delicada misión," in Ángel Rafael Almarza and Armando Martínez, eds., *Instrucciones para los diputados del Nuevo Reino de Granada y Venezuela ante la junta central gubernativa de España y las Indias* (Bucaramanga: Universidad Industrial de Santander, 2010).
4. Cabildo de la Villa del Socorro, "Instrucción que da al diputado del Nuevo Reino de Granada a la Junta Suprema y Central Gubernativa de España e Indias," in Almarza and Martínez, *Instrucciones.*
5. Francisco José de Caldas and Joaquín Camacho, "Diario Político de Santafé de Bogotá," Instituto Colombiano de Cultura, *Revolución de 20 de julio de 1810. Sucesos y documentos* (Bogotá, 1996), 118.
6. "Acta de la Independencia," in Instituto Colombiano de Cultura, *Revolución del 20 de julio*, 75–76.
7. "Constitución de Cundinamarca, 1811," in Manuel Antonio Pombo and José Joaquín Guerra, *Constituciones de Colombia*, vol. 1 (Bogotá: Ministerio de Educación Nacional, 1951), 188–90.
8. "Acta de Federación de las Provincias Unidas de la Nueva Granada," in Pombo and Guerra, *Constituciones de Colombia*, vol. I, 210.
9. Simón Bolívar, "Discurso pronunciado por el Libertador Simón Bolívar ante el Congreso de Angostura el 15 de febrero de 1819, día de su instalación," *Wikisource*, www.wikisource.org. Accessed June 3, 2011.
10. Ibid.
11. "Ley fundamental de la República de La Gran Colombia," *Wikisource*, www.wikisource.org. Accessed June 3, 2011.

Chapter Two

The Colombian Nations

We think of nation-states as unified sociopolitical entities; however, Colombia contains a large number of ethnic groups, including indigenous, Afro-Colombians, gypsies (Rom), and a large *mestizo* population resulting from the mixing that began in the sixteenth century among Europeans, people indigenous to the Americas, and African slaves. Thanks to these particular historical population dynamics, Colombia became a country of nations, that is, a country that is composed of communities with profoundly different traditions in terms of their language, customs, practices, and beliefs. After centuries of subjugation, epic struggles, and contentious debates, Colombian ethnic diversity was finally recognized at the national level through the 1991 constitution; Title I, Article 7 legally recognizes and protects the ethnic and cultural diversity of the nation. Nevertheless, such institutional acceptance of diversity has not always been the case.

Considering patterns of population distribution over the course of the past two centuries, we begin with the provinces of the Audiencia of New Granada on the eve of independence. By the start of the nineteenth century, the majority of the population lived in towns and cities or relatively close to population centers. People tended to settle in temperate regions, somewhere between one thousand and two thousand meters above sea level in plateaus and valleys formed by three branches of the Andes Mountains that crisscross the country, or along the Caribbean coast. Since independence, however, populations and population centers have moved considerably, expanding the agricultural frontiers to include and occupy all possible ecological niches of an ecologically diverse country. In general, migratory trends have been driven by population expulsions in different regions and by a concentration of land ownership in the hands of few people. People have pushed (and have been pushed) into areas that over the course of the nineteenth century were considered *baldías*,

21

or "unoccupied state lands." During the twentieth century, populations began occupying rainforest areas, which until then were inhabited only by indigenous groups that had never fallen under Spanish colonial dominion.

Today's map of Colombia was initially and laboriously constructed during the nineteenth century. Modern surveying techniques show a country with several large cities that hold more than 70 percent of Colombia's total population, but almost all of these cities are concentrated in the Andean region and along the Caribbean coast. This overwhelmingly urban population obscures the country's rural past that was reconstituted after independence and that emerged out of the nineteenth-century colonizing movements and survival strategies employed by indigenous groups, Afro-Colombians, *mestizos*, and Europeans. Population movements created rural societies which, beginning in the twentieth century, shifted toward cities.

This chapter explains the emergence of contemporary Colombia by taking into consideration Colombia's multiethnic composition and urban dominance over rural areas. Demographic dynamics and population movements over the past two centuries best illustrate this aspect of Colombian history.

COLOMBIAN INDIGENOUS POPULATION

Today, Colombia—about five hundred years after European conquest— is a country with an important indigenous and African presence. Of the 41,468,384 inhabitants that occupied the country in 2005, 1,392,623 identified themselves as indigenous—that is, 3.4 percent of the total population. Meanwhile, 4,311,757 people, or 10.4 percent of the population, identified as Afro-Colombian. These statistics show how individuals who answered the census self-identified, not what a government official perceived while taking down information. We therefore have close to 14 percent of Colombians who consider themselves ethnically different from the *mestizo* population (mixed-race persons) majority or the whites who descended from Europeans. Without taking into account the 2.1 percent (860,976 individuals) of the population who did not respond to the question concerning ethnicity on the 2005 census, there are 34,898,171 Colombians who self-identify as either *mestizo* or white. It is difficult to establish absolute clarity concerning these categories because in Colombia, after five centuries of population mixing, ethnic/racial categorization is largely subjective.

The indigenous communities are characterized by their diversity: eighty-seven different ethnicities exist, speaking sixty-seven non-Spanish languages. They are present throughout the country, although the greatest number—forty-eight groups—live in the Amazonian region. This also means that the Amazon has the smallest percentage of *mestizos* and whites, although their numbers currently are growing rapidly through colonization and displacement of indigenous peoples. In the Andean region of Colombia, where *mestizos* and whites predominate, thirteen indigenous groups claim a presence, and they also hold a similar proportion in the eastern Orinoco region. The Orinoco region, nevertheless, is less densely populated in absolute terms. The Caribbean coast is home to ten indigenous groups, and the Pacific coast claims six groups.

These indigenous ethnic groups are the survivors of five centuries of domination by white, *mestizo*, and even Afro-Colombian populations. It is impossible to know precisely how many people lived in the territory today called Colombia prior to the arrival of the Spaniards in 1535; however, four million is a generally accepted figure. By some estimates, sixty years after contact only 1.5 million indigenous people remained in Colombia—paradoxically, in the areas where most of the Spaniards lived. They also lived in the dense jungles, where no contact with Europeans had occurred. By the middle of the seventeenth century, only about five hundred thousand indigenous remained in the territory that is today Colombia, representing a dramatic decline from a century earlier.

With the passage of time, the surviving populations tended to stabilize and even show signs of demographic growth. There were two major reasons for this: the first is related to the kinds of measures the Spanish Crown took to protect Amerindian populations. These included the *Leyes Nuevas*, or "New Laws" of 1542, which offered judiciary and ecclesiastic protection to Native Americans, combined with the implementation of the *resguardo* regimen (reserved lands to be used only by indigenous peoples). The *resguardo* began at the end of the sixteenth century and lasted well into the nineteenth century in some areas. The second, perhaps more significant reason for the survival of indigenous groups is found in the kind of cultural resilience and resistance that indigenous communities developed—that is, their agility at using the Spanish colonial system to their advantage. For example, by 1810 many indigenous groups disagreed with the independence movements, believing that the king of Spain provided the best form of protection against those *mestizos* and creoles (American-born whites) who seemed hungry for their land. To remain loyal to a distant king suggested that their interests would be protected via the laws and stipulations noted above. They understood that by becoming independent "citizens," they would lose their lands and would be forced to work as wage laborers. The powerful civilizing project of the emerging nineteenth-century nation-state sought to consolidate the

Map 2.1.   Regions

nation into an ideal republic of citizens. As such, it could not accept groups of people in the country who were deemed "different" from all citizens raised according to the dominant Western model. Indigenous populations would have to adapt to a growing market economy. Some of these communities became peasant societies that grew economically dependent on absurdly inadequate parcels of land, or through tenant farming—both of which held thousands of people hostage in rural poverty. Therefore, the history of rural communities during the twentieth century has been, on the one hand, a story of people's struggles against rural poverty and, on the other, the political mobilization of indigenous peoples in defense of their lands, their languages, their practices, and their beliefs.

During the twentieth century, thousands of poor, rural residents were expelled from their lands in the Andean and Caribbean regions. At about the same time, large-scale farming, forestry, and mining projects had devastating effects on indigenous communities that historically had little contact with white or *mestizo* people. These factors culminated in the mass migration, voluntary and forced, of thousands of people into particularly sensitive ecological regions such as the Orinoco and Amazon River basins, the rainforest areas of the Pacific, and the *llanos* (eastern plains) near Venezuela. Former rural peasants of the Andes and Caribbean became the new colonizers of regions that had been occupied by indigenous groups, and these *colonos* (tenant farmers/rural poor) colonized remote border regions. Recently, the magnitude of the demographic and ecological tragedy has grown incalculably, devastating indigenous groups as they become overwhelmed by colonizing rural peasants, large landowners, and agro-industrialists—not to mention drug traffickers, guerrilla groups, and paramilitaries. The mostly forgotten stories of conquest that occurred during the colonial period have been, in essence, reborn in recent times.

Therefore, although Colombia is not a country whose population is primarily indigenous as is the case in Bolivia, Ecuador, Guatemala, and Peru, it does have a significant percentage of Amerindians protected by the constitution of 1991 who are proud of their traditions. Nevertheless, they confront social and economic pressures that threaten both their continuity as ethnic groups and their right to exist as communities in the future. Independence for these populations was not about freedom from Spanish domination, a struggle that began in 1810. This was the independence that whites and *mestizos* believed in and mobilized for. Rather, the rest of the nineteenth and much of the twentieth century signified, for Colombian indigenous groups, a series of struggles for recognition of their rights that culminated in passage of the Colombian constitution of 1991.

THE AFRO-COLOMBIAN POPULATION

Colombia ranks third in the Americas for the largest population of peoples of African ancestry, after the United States and Brazil. According to the 2005 census, 4,311,757 people self-identified as Afro-Colombian. Other estimates not based on self-identification indicators use additional categories to identify racially mixed populations, such as "zambos" (mixed indigenous and African ancestry) and "mulattoes," a slightly derisive but commonly used term referring to people of mixed white and African ancestry. According to these statistics, the percentage of people with Afro-Colombian ancestry could be as high as 29 percent, or roughly thirteen million people, distributed throughout the country, including areas as remote as the Orinoco and the Amazon River basins. For socioeconomic and historical reasons, the majority of Afro-Colombians are concentrated in the Chocó Department (along the Pacific coast), where they make up 83 percent of the total regional population; the Island Department of San Andrés and Providencia, where they make up 57 percent; and in the Departments of Bolívar (28 percent), Valle (27 percent), and Cauca (22 percent). However, increasing poverty and violence during the twentieth century have caused mass displacement of individuals and family groups from their homes to large cities. Thus, Cartagena, Cali, Barranquilla, Medellín, and Bogotá currently are home to more than 29 percent of the total Afro-Colombian population.

The majority of Afro-Colombians, unlike indigenous populations, do not differentiate among themselves according to ethnic distinctions with different languages or cultures. The vast majority of people who claim African ancestry in Colombia descended from those who arrived as a result of the colonial-era slave trade. This trade began in the sixteenth century, and one of the most dynamic—that is, profitable—centers of the European slave trade took place at the port city of Cartagena de Indias in what is today the north coast area of Colombia. There, slave traders and owners attempted to impede the emergence of solidarity among slaves by deliberately intermixing individuals from different ethnic tribes. These strategies were not always successful. And while common places of origin and the hardships of the slave ship may have had initial bonding effects on some slaves in the Americas, the day-to-day experiences people lived and shared, the family and kinship bonds they developed over time, and the strategies they used to create meaning for their lives all influenced the ways in which people from Africa adapted to and adopted the specific places where they resided in the Americas as their own.

The community of San Basilio de Palenque, in the Bolívar Department of Colombia, is a significant example of Afro-Colombian adaptation. This *palenque*, or "runaway slave community," developed toward the beginning of the seventeenth century and grew rapidly as a result of ever increasing numbers of arriving fugitive slaves. The *palenque* eventually developed its own identifiable language and culture, the result of the long-term shared experiences among individuals whose origins hailed from different regions of Africa. In addition to these Colombian *palenqueros*, another group of people of African ancestry lays claim to a distinct culture and language: the *raizal* community that populates the Colombian Caribbean islands of San Andrés, Providencia, and Santa Catalina. The people on these islands arrived from Jamaica and other English colonies in the Antilles. As a result, these *raizal* communities speak a kind of mixed creole language closer to English than Spanish, and the majority of them are, religiously, Baptist, not Roman Catholic like the majority of Colombians.

Other Afro-Colombians also claim a distinct ethnic status and are recognized as such: those who inhabit the Pacific corridor that runs through the Departments of Chocó, Valle, Cauca, and Nariño. Similarly, there is a dense population of Afro-Colombians and other mixed-race populations in the Caribbean region and the Magdalena River basin, but some deny African heritage for a variety of reasons, not the least of which is the long-standing undercurrent of discrimination and exclusion of people with African ancestry in Colombia. Furthermore, the people who have been displaced from the Pacific region and the Caribbean to major cities as a result of systematic acts of racially charged violence claim an "*afrodes*" ancestry, a name that carries the double meaning of African "descendants" (*descendiente*) and "displaced" (*desplazado*), as in forced to leave their homes in Colombia. Some individuals who make up these new urban Afro-Colombian populations have found ways of coping with—and adapting to—their new surroundings by employing familiar strategies, such as creating community around common origins or around common experiences focused on the devastating reality of displacement and dislocation.

Independence from Spain did not result in an immediate and significant change for slaves or free blacks. Although *Peninsulares* (people from Spain) and patriots offered freedom to the slaves who fought among their ranks, this meant that manumission (freeing of slaves) simply became a recruiting tool for both sides during the early nineteenth century wars of independence. The constitution passed in Cúcuta in 1821 offered freedom only to those slaves born after the inauguration of the constitution. Called *libertad de vientres*, or "free womb" law, slaves who met the 1821 requirement would be free after their twenty-first birthday. At this time, freed slaves did not obtain recognition of their citizenship, nor was there any semblance of equality for ex-slaves when compared with whites or *mestizo* men, who were the only ones with citizenship rights in the new republic, provided they met the constitutional requirements of property and salary. Finally, in 1851, freedom for all slaves who inhabited the country was decreed. From that moment on, any and all forms of slavery were outlawed.

Many of the freed slaves settled in the mining areas of the Pacific and lived along the major rivers of the Andes that emptied into the Caribbean Sea and along the Caribbean cities on the north coast. The majority of freedmen remained in these areas, which explains the dense concentration of Afro-Colombians in these regions today. Descendants of the freed slaves from the nineteenth century are now peasant farmers and poor miners living in rural areas or artisans and merchants living in urban areas. Some have been able to integrate more fully into a society that predominantly self-identifies as *mestizo* and white. These are the people who best adapted and took advantage of the opportunities offered by living in larger cities. For this reason, their historical relationship with discrimination is analogous to the plight of indigenous populations—that is, independence did not bring immediate emancipation to African slaves—or political and economic equality for descendants of Africans in Colombia. Political struggles during the twentieth century ultimately brought about greater recognition for Afro-Colombians; such recognition was finally codified as "rights" in the constitution of 1991.

OTHER COLOMBIANS

In addition to the aforementioned groups, a small community of gypsy origin, also known as the Roma, lives in Colombia. According to the census of 2005, the Roma number only about five thousand individuals, organized into families that live primarily in the cities of Bogotá, Girón, and Cúcuta. They arrived in the country after independence, taking advantage of the loosening restrictions that had kept them out of Spanish America during the colonial era. Often they were fleeing the difficult discriminatory situations they faced in nineteenth-century Europe and, later in history, during the two world wars. Although the Colombian constitution of 1991 guarantees their right as a "nation" and not just as individuals, there has been historic discrimination against the Colombian Roma, and recently, many have been accused of participating in illegal narcotics trafficking.

Another significant number of Colombians descend from those who migrated during the late nineteenth century from Palestine, Syria, and Lebanon. Most were escaping violence dating from the Crimean War through the Arab-Israeli conflict of the middle of the twentieth century. Barranquilla was the major Caribbean port through which these populations arrived, and the highest density of people from the Arab world initially settled in the cities on the Caribbean coast, where today their cultural influence is palpable. Slowly, these immigrants and their children moved toward the interior of the country via the Magdalena River. The majority of these individuals self-identify as Colombian, yet in some ways they avail themselves of the constitutional principle that affords autonomy to ethnicities in order to gain special rights. By far, these citizens of Middle Eastern origin are the most numerous population of foreign origin in the country.

Generally speaking, however, Colombia is not a country made up of foreign immigrants. Except for the initial dynamics that brought Spaniards and Africans to Colombia, after independence, colonies of foreigners are notable precisely for their relative absence in Colombian society. This is quite different from Argentina and Brazil—to mention two other South American cases. Although some people from Germany, England, France, and Italy arrived in Colombia during the nineteenth century, they did not migrate in such significant numbers as to vary the demographic makeup of the country, but just enough to influence—to some degree—elite customs, tastes, and sensibilities. The twentieth century witnessed a greater variety in terms of the sending countries, but not a significant increase in the total number of immigrants. The majority of people who arrived assimilated into the urban society of Colombia, intermarrying with national families.

Notably, the Jewish presence in Colombia "emerged" in the early nineteenth century with the onset of formal separation from a restrictive, Inquisition-oriented Spain; Jews "hid" in Colombia (and throughout Spanish America) during the colonial period, but early-nineteenth-century independence from Spain allowed for more openness, fewer restrictions, and greater tolerance for Colombian Jews. In the twentieth century, a significant group of European Jews immigrated to Colombia as a result of the European persecution that occurred before and during the Second World War.

DEMOGRAPHY AND ITS NUMBERS

Colombia is a nation of *mestizos*. Today, this 58 percent of the population, in addition to the 20 percent that self-identifies as white, is the result of a significant population boom that occurred during the twentieth century. The first census taken of the population of the independent republic was in 1825, but it was never officially accepted due to deficiencies in the procedure by which it was conducted. The 1825 census nevertheless identified a total of 1,129,200 people for what is today considered Colombia, at that time referred to as the Department of Cundinamarca. Considering the entire population of what was then considered the Colombian republic (Gran Colombia), that is, the union with Venezuela, Ecuador, and Panama, the total population reaches 2,583,799. This means, therefore, that Cundinamarca was the most populated department that made up the fledgling independent nation-state, since it held close to 50 percent of the total population.

Table 2.1 shows how during the two hundred years of the Colombian republic, the population multiplied roughly thirty-seven-fold. This growth, that in absolute terms is constant, does not hold to a steady rhythm over the years: during the nineteenth century the total population multiplied threefold (from 1,129,200 in 1825 to 4,122,000 in 1905), whereas during the hundred years from 1905 to 2005 the total population multiplied more than ten times (from 4,122,000 to 41,468,384). This suggests that quality of life improved, to some extent, for most Colombians over the course of the twentieth century.

In demographic terms, the average rate of growth was about 1.6 percent during the first seventy-five years of the nineteenth century. From 1875 to 1900 that percentage grew to an average of 1.8 percent, reflecting some improvement in public health conditions in cities, the development of hospitals and medical care in urban and rural areas, and a more focused approach to tackling epidemic diseases. However, modern public health campaigns did not really begin until the early twentieth century, reflected in an average life expectancy of twenty-nine years at the end of the nineteenth century; this reality profoundly affected social customs in the nation. For example, large families were the norm at this time, people married at an early age, and very young women—teenagers in today's parlance—bore children and often died in childbirth. Colombia, unlike Argentina, Brazil, or Chile, did not grow its population via immigration, given the low number of European immigrants arriving in the republic at the end of the nineteenth and early twentieth century.

Table 2.1.   Population, 1825–2005

Census Date	Total	Census Date	Total
1825	1,129,200	1918	5,855,077
1835	1,570,900	1928	7,851,110
1843	1,812,600	1938	8,697,041
1851	2,105,600	1951	11,548,172
1864	2,441,300	1964	17,484,508
1870	2,713,000	1973	20,785,235
1887	3,666,000	1985	27,837,932
1898	4,183,000	1993	33,109,840
1905	4,122,000	2005	41,468,384
1912	5,972,604		

Source: Colombia, "Departamento Administrativo Nacional de estadística"—DANE. The statistics for the nineteenth century are approximate since no census from that century has been officially accepted; the same applies for the census of 1905.

The twentieth century witnessed a substantial change in this situation. Favorable transformations in terms of quality of life occurred first in cities, followed by similar changes in many surrounding Andean towns. The rest of the country slowly moved along this continuum, which allowed for life expectancy to surpass seventy years at the turn of the twenty-first century. The lowering of mortality rates, a greater coverage of health care for urban and rural populations, improved hygiene—in short, the progressive growth in the number of physicians and health care institutions compared with the growth of the rest of the population—caused the average annual rate of population growth during the first half of the twentieth century to reach 2.2 percent. These positive demographic shifts, together with difficulties of implementing family planning given the conservative Catholic beliefs that dominated society, resulted in a demographic explosion in the 1960s and 1970s. During these decades, the average rate of population growth was almost 3 percent. At the same time, mass migration from rural areas to cities proliferated, thanks in part to state policies. These changes are clearly reflected in the urban nature of today's Colombia.

Although the turn of the twenty-first century has seen a marked reduction in the rate of population growth, the trend in recent years has favored urban growth. Now, Colombians who were born during the population boom of the 1960s and 1970s are in the midst of their most productive stage of life, a phenomenon that does not intersect with the number of available jobs. The resulting poverty has led to the rapid growth of guerrilla or insurgency groups, drug trafficking gangs, and other criminal enterprises. Taken together, this "social crisis" is one of the most daunting challenges faced by all of the Colombian people today.

Three additional characteristics of the Colombian population during the two centuries of the republic are worth noting. First, according to the 2005 census, 51.4 percent of the Colombian population is female, a percentage that has remained largely unchanged since the end of the colonial period. Second, what has changed, and dramatically so, is the relationship between urban and rural areas in demographic terms. In 1938, 31 percent of the population lived in municipal capitals, which meant that 2,700,000 people lived closer to urban life than rural life. The rest of the six million Colombians lived either in the countryside and populated small villages, or they lived dispersed among the mountains and valleys of the country. This style of life, which we examine below, had been inherited from the nineteenth century and contrasts sharply with the census of 2005, which estimates that 86 percent of the population, that is, 35.6 million Colombians, reside in municipal capitals with clear urban lifestyles and social practices. Third, the way in which the population is spatially distributed in Colombia has remained constant. There have been some variations due to recent trends in colonization, but where people have chosen (or in many cases, been forced) to live has remained largely constant over the course of the past two hundred years. According to the 2005 census, 70 percent of Colombians live in the Andean region, preferably in areas between one thousand to two thousand meters above sea level; 20 percent live in the valleys of the Caribbean, and only 5 percent populate the immense territories of Colombia's Amazon and Orinoco River basins; 3 percent of Colombians are distributed in the jungles and rainforests of the Colombian Pacific corridor, and about 2 percent have left the country for economic or political reasons.

COLONIZERS AND SETTLERS: THE NINETEENTH CENTURY

Given the trends studied in the previous section, the preference of Colombia's inhabitants has been, since at least the colonial era, to inhabit the temperate and colder regions of the Andes and, to a lesser extent, the plains along the Caribbean basin. Table 2.2, which presents the census information taken in 1789 by the Spanish rulers, emphasizes this point.

The Andean provinces of Tunja, Santafé, Popayán, Antioquia, Mariquita, and Neiva held the majority of the population at the end of the eighteenth century: 70 percent. That population was distributed among thirty-nine cities and villas and 331 Indian towns (*Pueblos de Indios*). The Caribbean provinces of Cartagena and Santa Marta held 25 percent of the population in twelve cities, fifty-six Indian towns, and fifty *sitios* (places identified as populated by free people of color). The remaining 5 percent of the population lived in only one city and twenty-nine Indian towns in the extensive regions of Orinoquia, Amazonia, and the Pacific region of New Granada. With independence and the growing population of the nineteenth century, the primacy of key cities in different regions did not change, but significant movements of population

Table 2.2. Population by Provinces, 1789

Province	Population	Province	Population
Tunja	270,813	Mariquita	47,138
Santafé	119,779	Llanos	21,931
Cartagena	119,647	Chocó	15,286
Santa Marta	83,908	Neiva	13,000
Popayán	70,463		
Antioquia	48,604	Total	810,569

Source: Martha Herrera, "Las divisiones político-administrativas del Virreinato de la Nueva Granada a finales del período colonial." *Historia Crítica* (Bogotá, Universidad de Los Andes: 22, Diciembre 2001), 76–104.

did occur, which ultimately changed the face of the country. Colonial trends in urbanism gave way to the first republican century, and Colombia remained largely a rural/peasant nation. But many people began populating new lands that depended on recently founded hamlets or those towns and villages that the republic inherited from the colonial era. These new towns proved essential to providing a modicum of "national" unification. The towns offered newly arriving inhabitants the opportunity to link up with a market economy and receive the public services of the state, however weak the state may have been. Table 2.3 and map 2.3 offer a study of the direction and magnitude of population movements as they occurred during the nineteenth century. The table reflects population distribution in 1825, 1870, and 1912, organized by states, according to the federal ordinance of 1870.

The population growth of 1.5 million people that occurred from 1825 to 1870 was primarily centered in the states of Antioquia, Boyacá, Cauca, Cundinamarca, and Santander; a less significant increase is seen in the states of Bolívar and Tolima; and barely any change occurred in the State of Magdalena. It is worth pointing out that while the demographic changes in Cundinamarca and Boyacá were primarily due to natural increase, demographic growth in Antioquia, as well as in Bolívar, Cauca, Santander, and Tolima resulted from internal migration. These movements accelerated during the final decades of the nineteenth century.

The major migratory paths took people from the Andean region of the Eastern mountain range in the center of the country toward the Western mountain range or toward the Eastern mountain range's extreme north to what is today Norte de Santander. Similarly, people moved from the Central and Eastern mountain ranges toward the savannahs in the interior of the Caribbean coast, what is today the Departments of Córdoba and Sucre.

Table 2.3. Population in the Nineteenth Century

State	1825	1870	1912	Increase 1825–1870	Increase 1870–1912
Antioquia	104,017	365,974	1,082,135	261,721	716,161
Bolívar	121,663	241,704	535,617	120,041	293,913
Boyacá	208,762	498,541	620,730	289,779	122,189
Cauca	149,778	435,078	865,728	285,300	430,650
Cundinamarca	188,695	413,658	717,714	224,963	304,056
Magdalena	56,320	88,928	202,560	32,608	113,632
Santander	201,207	433,178	604,465	231,971	171,287
Tolima	98,496	230,891	440,617	132,395	209,726
Total	1,129,174	2,707,952	5,069,566	1,578,778	2,361,614

Source: Hermes Tovar Pinzón, *Que nos tengan en cuenta. Colonos, empresarios y aldeas: Colombia 1800–1900* (Bogotá: Tercer Mundo Editores, 1995), 28.

Department	Capital
Atlantico	Barranquilla
Amazonas	Leticia
Antioquia	Medellin
Arauca	Arauca
Bolivar	Cartagena
Boyaca	Tunja
Caldas	Manizales
Caqueta	Florencia
Casanare	Yopal
Cauca	Popayan
Cesar	Valledupar
Choco	Quibdo
Cordoba	Monteria
Cundinamarca	Bogota
Guainia	Inirida
Guaviare	San Jose de Guaviare
Huila	Neiva
La Guajira	Rioacha
Magdalena	Santa Marta
Meta	Villavicencio
Narino	Pasto
Norte de Santander	Cucuta
Putumayo	Mocoa
Quindio	Aremenia
Risaralda	Pereira
San Andres y Providencia	San Andres
Santander	Bucaramanga
Sucre	Sincelejo
Tolima	Ibaque
Valle del Cauca	Cali
Vaupes	Mitu
Vichada	Puerto Carreño

Map 2.2.   Political/Departmental Capitals

In this way, an increase of more than two million people over the course of forty-two years from 1870 to 1912 distributed people between the Antioquia area on the Central and Western mountain ranges, the Caribbean states, and the state of Cauca. By contrast, Cundinamarca and Tolima had a relative decrease in population growth, and Boyacá and Santander had an absolute loss in population. In other words, the source of populations for the colonizing movements of the late nineteenth century primarily sprang from Boyacá and Santander, where people—pushed from their lands or seeking more space—came to inhabit what is commonly called Greater Antioquia. This region was opened by machete-wielding colonizers who tamed the land and built the thriving city of Medellín, today's capital of Antioquia. These same migrants also came to populate the more temperate regions of Cundinamarca and Norte de Santander, which ultimately produced the first coffee-centered economy in the country through the hacienda system.

The expansion of the agricultural frontier in Colombia during the nineteenth century moved toward more temperate climates, down the mountain ranges. Interestingly, Colombia's western expansion lines up with a similar narrative of U.S. westward expansion in the nineteenth century. In general terms, Colombia's westward movement was undertaken by *colonos* (agricultural peasant colonizers). With their families or in small groups, they moved and cleared lands that they considered national state lands, territory not held privately. The national state supported these endeavors because it was in Colombia's economic interest to economically integrate large swaths of fertile land into the emerging national project. It was also part and parcel of the political-economic ideals held by the Radical Liberal Party in power during the late nineteenth century. That is, democracy (or so it was assumed) would be favored by connecting democratic development to citizens who held small and medium parcels of land, a sort of "Jeffersonian democracy" in western Colombia, modeled after the North American example.

This ideal, however, was never met. Quickly *colonos* began competing with large landowners, speculators, and jurists who had managed through a variety of strategies to appropriate the newly cleared lands worked by the *colonos*. Their tactics pushed *colonos* to settle newer lands or to become day laborers and tenant farmers on the large haciendas that wealthier, politically influential individuals constructed. Ultimately, then, although the new agricultural frontiers were developed as a result of the movements of thousands of *colonos*, many of these individuals and their families saw opportunities curtailed by the abuses of wealthier groups that managed to gain ownership over large swaths of land, often the very same land cleared and worked by *colonos*. The tensions generated from this process blossomed into a new form of land-based violence in Colombia. The civil wars of the nineteenth century

had largely been a series of ideological and strongman (*caudillo*)-led conflicts. By the end of the nineteenth century, landownership and the conditions
of work on the land became the two major causes of violent clashes among
the Colombian people.

The dynamic of opening the internal agricultural frontier of the country
during the nineteenth century was accompanied by an important phenomenon: colonization did not result in the dispersion of the population throughout
the territory, but to the contrary, brought people together around towns and
cities. These processes of increasing populations around town centers worked
as an important organizing principle over territory, which in turn benefited
the process of building capacity for the national state. Thus, a great paradox
of the nineteenth century emerged: while the country was becoming ever
more agricultural, the number of towns that existed in the country increased
significantly. These towns brought together a large number of people, and
most importantly, it was in these towns where institutions for the emerging
republic were situated: the mayor's office, the market, the church, the store,
the school, the court, the notary public, the doctor's office, the jail, the café,
the inn, the transport terminal, and the telegraph station. These new towns
became the new centers of a kind of institution that was inherited from the
colonial period and that survived independence: the municipality. In the modern United States, the municipality translates to "county."

The national state made a concerted effort to develop the level of institu-
tionality required for maintaining a clear presence throughout the country's
territory. As a result, *cabeceras municipales*, or "heads of municipalities"—
towns that were considered the most important in a particular area—became
the critical centers for political organization and socioeconomic integration. It
was here where all of the institutions of the emerging state were found. In this
sense, the colonizing movements of the nineteenth century, which gave rise
to our modern rural peasantry, were accompanied by the systematic foundation of towns, which became the nucleus of municipalities. Therefore, instead
of people dispersing haphazardly, towns allowed the agricultural frontiers
of Colombia, on the sides of mountains, to be slowly integrated with the
national state and connected in various ways to the manners and practices of
urban sites. In short, the majority of the population became increasingly rural
during the nineteenth century as the agricultural frontiers expanded into the
valleys and mountains where *colonos* worked their own lands or lands owned
by others, but they never lived so far from a town that they could not travel
to it with relative frequency and benefit from, or at least approach, the basic
services offered in the town.

AN URBAN COUNTRY: THE TWENTIETH CENTURY

In 1912, a few more than five million Colombians lived in about eight hundred municipalities; still, within them, the majority of the population lived
outside of heads of the municipalities, that is, 75 percent of those people, or
3,750,000 individuals—rendering Colombia's population as predominantly
rural. But, as noted, the remaining 25 percent (or about 1.25 million people)
ultimately held real control over the territory because they dominated market
relations, the institutions of the state, and the other sociocultural dynamics
of the nation. For this reason, the municipal leaders became the force that
marked the direction, pace of growth, and population settlement during the
decades that followed. By the end of the twentieth century, Colombia had
transformed into a largely urban country: according to the 2005 census,
more than 74 percent of the population lived in heads of municipalities, while
the rest lived in the rural regions of municipalities.

The demographic dynamics of the twentieth century allowed for a tenfold
increase of Colombia's population over the course of the century. Two trends
emerged, which were not entirely new, given the dynamics of the nineteenth
century. On the one hand, at the same time the population was growing in
size, it was increasingly being pushed from one region to another, expanding
the agricultural frontier and generating the foundation of more municipalities.
Today, a total of 1,102 municipalities exist. On the other hand, a significant
proportion of the expelled or migrating population no longer sought out new
lands. Instead, people preferred to migrate to large cities, a movement that
gained further momentum due to governmental policies and the unique development of Colombian capitalism. From this perspective, to say that Colombia
increasingly became an urbanized country means that there was considerable
growth in the number of urban poor.

Concerning the expansion of the agricultural frontier, expulsion of populations favored the growth of agribusiness in rural areas while at the same time
poor people were expelled from their homes and forced to find new lands
in the limited fertile areas remaining, which were concentrated in the hotter
regions of the inter-Andean valleys and especially the rainforests and jungles
of the Colombian Amazon and Orinoco basin. In cities, the consolidation of
the state and of capitalism, at the same time that it overwhelmingly enriched
a few people and dramatically impoverished others, nevertheless permitted a
significant increase among the ranks of the middle class, in part because of
the development of the service sector and wage labor, which was accompanied by the professionalization of wide segments of these populations.

Today, the principal component of the Colombian nations—the *mestizo* and white population—is primarily urban (in a social and cultural sense), although many members of this population may have ties to rural areas through their parents or grandparents. This fact creates even greater distances between the majority and the indigenous and Afro-Colombian populations, which primarily inhabit rural areas of municipal regions that have been most recently colonized. The general preference for the Andean regions and the Caribbean basin by Colombia's population has not changed much over the years, and the cultural differences found in each geographic region continue to mark the most profound characteristic of the Colombian population.

The last table of the chapter, table 2.4, brings together the general statistics of the 2005 census related to the distribution of the population according to departments. It specifies the population that resides in each departmental capital and the number of municipalities that comprise each one. This information offers a quick overview of a Colombia that has emerged during a two-hundred-year period of history.

Table 2.4. Population, 2005

Department	Total Population[a]	Population in the Capital[b]	Number of Municipalities
Bogotá D.C.[c]	6,824,510		1
Antioquia	5,601,507	2,175,681	125
Valle del Cauca	4,052,535	2,083,171	42
Cundinamarca	2,228,682	—[c]	116
Atlántico	2,112,001	1,142,312	23
Santander	1,913,444	509,216	87
Bolívar	1,836,640	842,228	46
Nariño	1,498,234	312,377	64
Córdoba	1,462,909	286,575	30
Tolima	1,312,304	468,647	47
Boyacá	1,210,982	146,621	123
Cauca	1,182,022	226,978	42
Norte de Santander	1,208,336	567,664	40
Magdalena	1,136,819	385,122	30
Huila	1,001,476	295,961	37
Caldas	898,490	353,312	27
Cesar	878,437	299,065	25
Risaralda	859,666	371,239	14
Meta	713,772	356,464	29
Sucre	762,263	219,639	26
La Guajira	655,943	136,183	15
Quindío	518,691	273,114	12
Chocó	388,476	101,134	30
Caquetá	337,932	121,898	16
Putumayo	237,197	25,751	13
Casanare	281,295	90,218	19
Arauca	153,028	62,634	7
Guaviare	56,758	34,863	4
San Andrés y Providencia	59,573	48,421	2
Amazonas	46,950	23,811	2
Vichada	44,592	10,032	4
Vaupés	19,943	13,066	3
Guainía	18,797	10,793	1
TOTAL	41,468,384	31,890,892	1,102

Source: Colombia: Departamento Administrativo Nacional de estadística—DANE. Censo 2005.

[a]Population count, no adjustment
[b]Population adjusted on June 30, 2005
[c]Nation's capital

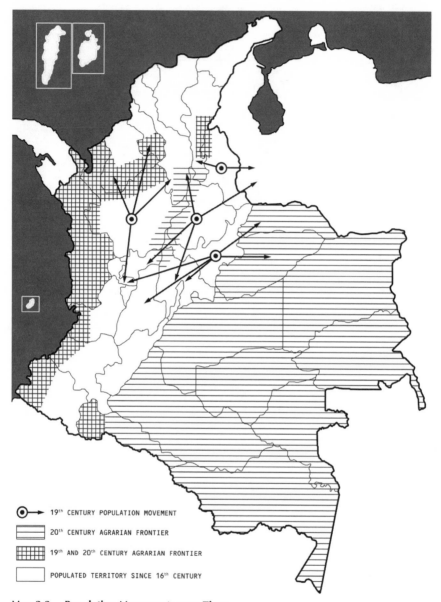

Map 2.3.   Population Movements over Time

Chapter Three

The Dynamics of a
Political Community

In 1830, the Republic of Colombia dissolved. Historians remember this republic as Gran Colombia because it brought together under one government the current South American republics of Colombia, Ecuador, and Venezuela. New republics were born out of the ashes of the civil war fought between 1830 and 1831. The territory that Gran Colombia called Cundinamarca became the Republic of New Granada. Following Simón Bolívar's resignation of the presidency in May 1830 and his death in December of that year, Rafael Urdaneta assumed leadership of New Granada's national military and controlled the government in Bogotá, acting as dictator. Regional *caudillos* opposed not only Urdaneta's dictatorship but also any other attempt to establish a monarchy or to concentrate all political power in one person.

The project to unite northwestern South America into one single republic called Colombia was originally imagined by Francisco Miranda, but it was Simón Bolívar who made the union of New Granada, Quito, and Venezuela a political reality by proposing this measure to the Congress of Angostura in 1819. The Congress approved, but soon thereafter, this extensive and expansive political entity ran into problems. In 1826, the Districts of Venezuela and Quito made it unequivocally clear that the Cúcuta Constitution—and especially the centralist project it proposed for the national state—displeased them. They had a point. All power would be concentrated in Bogotá, and since Bogotá was located in New Granada, both Venezuela and Quito would be beholden to New Granada. Furthermore, they vehemently opposed what seemed to be pro-monarchical ideas in the constitution, especially Bolívar's decision to enact the constitution he created for the recently liberated Bolivia. Federalists squared off against centralists, arguing that necessary and rigorous control over the people and institutions of government was possible only in a federalized system. The centralists, in turn, countered that only a

centralized system that applied laws equally throughout the nation could protect individual liberties. This quickly led to the formation of irreconcilable
political factions in Gran Colombia. The situation reached a critical juncture
in 1828 when the Ocaña Convention failed to enact the Cúcuta Constitution.
It instead paved the way for the secession of Venezuela and Ecuador, both of
which separated from the union of Colombia during the first months of 1830,
precisely when the convention was supposed to be in session, shaping what is
now called the Admirable Constitution. The absence of Venezuela and Quito
from this convention, their ability to transform themselves into individual republics, and the resignation of Simón Bolívar from the Colombian presidency
meant that the Admirable Constitution was born as a dead letter.

Secession and the civil war it created allowed a new *caudillo* leadership to form in the New Granada provinces. The *caudillos*, powerful men
with loyal soldiers by their sides, opened political space for themselves by
participating in a new legislative convention. From October 20, 1831, to
February 29, 1832, a new constitution was discussed in Bogotá. Presidential
elections were held, and Francisco de Paula Santander won, despite the fact
that he was living in exile at the time due to his alleged participation in the
failed conspiracy to assassinate Bolívar on September 25, 1828. Santander
happily sent in his notice of acceptance from exile in New York and was
inaugurated into office on October 7, 1832, three days after having returned
to Bogotá, the city that had been selected as the new capital for the new
Republic of New Granada.

This change opened a new historical era for Colombia. Independence had
been fought for and won. The Gran Colombian Republic, no longer facing a
threat from the royalist forces, dissolved. February 1832 marks the beginning
of 180 years of history lived by the juridical-political entity that is now the
Republic of Colombia. After two decades of political agitation and negotiation of new liberties and the laws that would guarantee them, institutions,
potential administrative models, and solid principles had been formulated
and a new horizon expanded the limits of what was possible. But these were
the initial years, the years during which the state was in the process of being
born. The task of making the state function began in 1832. The idealized state
had a republican form that not only was difficult to enact but transformed and
expanded with the march of time.

This chapter covers the beginning of the collective construction of what
we now know as Colombia. Building a state was an arduous and sometimes
bloody task. Those who maintained principles of democracy and modern
republicanism nevertheless engaged in entrenched and bitter conflicts. The
chapter begins with the history of the Colombian state and its transformation from a liberal state (in the nineteenth-century definition of liberal, that

is, guided by European Enlightenment philosophies and precepts) to a state guided by an expanding sense of society and law.

CITIZENSHIP

During the last years of the eighteenth century, news about revolution in the United States and France circulated among inhabitants of New Granada's cities. Creoles (Americans, descendants of Spaniards), *mestizos*, and *Peninsulares* all commented on the events, the rights of man and citizens, the right to elect and be elected, and the sovereignty that would allow a society to make its own laws. Some of these individuals began to think it legitimate to live within a democratic republic—founded through the recognition of civil and political rights of a new kind of political entity: the citizen.

Independence from Spain quickly demonstrated that the organization of new political entities would have to deal with the rights of citizens; this is why the first constitutions, such as that of Tunja in December 1811, or the Constitution of Antioquia from May 1812, included passages such as this: "God has conceded equally to men certain essential, inalienable, natural rights, such as to defend and conserve his life, acquire, enjoy and protect his properties, find and obtain his security and happiness. These rights are reduced to four principal rights: Liberty, legal equality, security, and property."[1] In other words, the essential principles of the French charter of the rights of man, considered the basis for Western civil rights, were already included in the first constitutions of the republics that were forming in the former Audiencia of New Granada. Something similar was happening with political rights, or the right to participate in government. In its twenty-first and twenty-third articles, the same Tunja Constitution of December 1811 stipulated that sovereignty meant the ability to make laws; that no part of the nation could dominate another; that no person without legitimate delegation could exercise authority over others or realize public functions; that all elections should be free; and that each citizen has the right to assemble, in the short or long term, for the purpose of forming laws and the naming of representatives or public functionaries. Thus, confronting the separation from Spain meant creating civil and political liberty through the transformation of subjects into citizens. But what constituted a citizen?

The constitutional developments that created the contemporary Colombian state, which began with the constitution of 1832, provide an answer. First, to be a citizen of the republic, one must necessarily belong to the territory through birth or naturalization. This principle was included in the charters of 1811 and has not varied since. Second, an individual must, in addition to forming part of a political community that exists within a territory, meet the provisional or permanent requirements to exercise that citizenship. These requirements have changed in important ways over the course of the past two centuries. At first, citizenship was exclusive and formalist and was based on the ideal of homogenizing all the inhabitants according to a single definition of the individual. Now, citizenship is inclusive and accepts diversity as part of belonging to the community—that is, the "Estado Social de Derecho."[2]

The constitution issued in 1832 established rules for citizenship. Citizens were men who were over twenty-one years of age, married, who possessed properties with a minimum value of three hundred pesos or an annual income of at least 150 pesos that did not come from domestic service or day labor, and who knew how to read and write (although this requirement was deferred to 1840). The constitution of 1843 qualified and simplified these requirements, stating that citizenship was for males over twenty-one years of age who paid taxes on properties or income as required in the constitution of 1832 (again, the literacy requirement was deferred, this time until 1850). The constitution of 1853, however, significantly lowered the requirements for citizenship by dropping property and income requirements; thus, in 1853, an individual male had to be at least twenty-one years of age and married (or married at one point) in order to be considered a citizen.

The provincial legislature of the town of Vélez, north of the capital city, went further still and voted to extend suffrage to women, adding that women be duly represented along with men in local electoral boards to ensure that their participation was truly effective. The Supreme Court nullified this law, arguing that the states did not have the right to grant more political rights than the rest of the nation. The federal constitution of 1858 maintained universal male suffrage for those over twenty-one years and married, as did the federal constitution of 1863. But the latter ensured that the constitutions of the states within the union should all guarantee the principles of popular elective, representative government that alternates and that is responsible, leaving it up to each state to decide the requirements for citizenship. Finally, in 1886, the last of the constitutions of the nineteenth century established that "citizens are those Colombian males older than twenty-one years who have a profession, art or office, or hold legal employment or another form of legitimate and known source of subsistence."[3]

Fifty years later, in 1936, the Colombian Congress reformed the constitution of 1886. Beginning in that year, citizenship belonged to men who were twenty-one years or older. All other requirements were stricken. This reform also opened a viable space for political participation by women in public office: it determined, after reiterating that the condition of valid citizenship was required to elect, or to be elected, that "the Colombian woman who was of age may execute public office, even if [such work] connotes authority or jurisdiction."[4] In other words, women could be appointed to positions of public authority—even to positions that required executive decision making. Women, with this reform, began attending university and, to some degree, modernity began to emerge for women in Colombia. A few years later, in 1945, another reform of the constitution eliminated the reference to males in the definition of citizenship, leaving citizenship open for any Colombian over twenty-one years of age. However, the following article of the same reform document expressly limited its exercise to men with respect to the right to elect or to be elected. A fundamental change finally occurred in 1957: women were granted the right to vote by the national state, and women now held the same political rights as men. In 1975, the constitution was reformed yet again in order to reduce the voting age to eighteen. Last, the constitution of 1991, which is the governing constitution of Colombia today, considers questions of citizenship but only in terms of when it may be lost or suspended, and maintains legal age at eighteen years of age. In this sense, the formal characteristics of citizenship have been universalized to the maximum degree. The one unchanging characteristic is that citizenship is still considered the single most important requirement needed in order to vote, to be elected, and to hold public offices.

There is a new aspect to the 1991 charter, however. This constitution gives an exhaustive list of the rights and responsibilities of the Colombian citizen. Formal citizenship, which had implied that all people, men or women, indigenous or Afro-Colombian, had to be homogeneous in terms of citizenship, now allows for citizenship based on cultural or ethnic distinction and heterogeneity. The 1886 constitution—which guided the nation for 106 years—conferred citizenship based on cultural connection to Spain in addition to being white, male, and Catholic.

RIGHTS

Although the Colombian state's capacity is still limited in its ability to guarantee all citizens the benefits of the rights that the current social contract recognizes and grants, the situation today, after almost two centuries of republican life, has obviously evolved since 1832. Civil and political rights have expanded over time, which is important, but they are not as definitive as those of today's charter in establishing social, economic, cultural, and environmental rights together with the institutional infrastructure to guarantee them. This was the fruit of political rebellions, cultural resistance, ideological and partisan battles—in short, clear social conflicts and fratricidal wars that are part of the contemporary history of Colombia. The formal democracy that was inaugurated during the first decades of the nineteenth century now consists of a political system that understands the individual as a social and cultural being with the inalienable right to be distinctive—culturally, ethnically, racially, religiously, sexually, and so on.

From the basic list of civil rights, taken from the French charter of 1789, and consigned in the first constitutions, independence allowed for the contentious battling for the inclusion of a system of political rights. In this sense, the history of democracy in Colombia forms part of an initial moment, one whereby it was understood that in order for an individual to claim rights, such rights had to be guaranteed via political sovereignty. For this reason, it is not surprising that as early as April 1811, the Constitution of Cundinamarca, while maintaining the monarchy as the formal system of government, limited the monarchy's exercise of power to a charter of laws and the sovereignty of the people. Similarly, the sixteen articles of the 1811 constitution's Title XII gave legitimacy to the following rights of man and citizen: equality, legal liberty, security, and property. It also made the right to free expression explicit and prohibited taxation without representation or without an explanation of how such taxes would benefit public use. Furthermore, men and citizens could not be called to trial, stand accused, or imprisoned except through formal processes prescribed by law. Finally, citizens would participate in the formulation of laws and in the naming of representatives. This last right, that is, the right to participate directly by being elected or indirectly through the right to elect, supports popular sovereignty.

Subsequent constitutions allowed for little change in the conception of rights. Expanding these rights was limited by two factors that were not easily transformed. The first factor was related to the restrictions on citizenship explained above. These restrictions limited political rights to a small portion of society. The second factor was the de facto distance that existed between the enjoyment of political rights and the enjoyment of civil rights. Take, for instance, private property. Private property was equally guaranteed for whites, indigenous people, and blacks once the abolition of slavery occurred in 1851. This right to property grew through a rapid dismantling of *mayorazgos*,[5] the confiscation of properties held in mortmain, the commissioning of property surveys, and other inheritances from the colonial regime, including the largely successful attempts at abolishing indigenous *resguardos*. During most of the nineteenth century, the right to be elected, to elect, and to carry out public office was the exclusive domain of wealthy property-owning men twenty-one years old or older. This situation helps explain the meaning and importance of the social struggles that occurred in the nineteenth and twentieth centuries. The main struggle centered on the extent to which political rights could be expanded, given the economic advantages the wealthier classes enjoyed by restricting suffrage. Guilds, ethnic organizations, women's groups, unions, leftist democratic organizations, revolutionary groups—in short, individuals and collectivities with progressive agendas—have at different times pushed, through different forms of struggle, to expand the democratic nature of civil and political rights of Colombians. These struggles have meant the transformation from equality and liberty under the law, proclaimed and defended in 1811, to social equity as enunciated in the new constitution of 1991.

A new category of rights took shape in the world during the second half of the twentieth century: social rights. These were introduced into Colombia through the above-mentioned social groups and people. Thus, the debate over the need to expand the participative base of the Colombian state occurred when ethnic, women's, and political opposition and armed groups led a strong resistance against a bipartisan structure that had held power since the middle of the nineteenth century. This push for greater sociopolitical inclusion in Colombia gained momentum when the student movement of the Seventh Ballot, organized in the last days of 1989 and beginning of 1990 as a result of the murder of three opposition candidates to the presidency, reinforced the need for a change to the constitution. The constitution of 1991 was born out of that movement, opening space for a renewed social pact that would establish new bases for rights of all Colombian citizens.

The 1991 constitution established Colombia as a social state of rights. Title II of the document organizes the fundamental rights of Colombians, which begin with the defense of life and the prohibition of the death penalty. The second chapter brings together social, economic, and cultural rights. The third brings together rights associated with the environment and collective rights to use of the environment. The fourth establishes how all these rights will be protected and applied. And, finally, the fifth chapter determines the duties and obligations of Colombians. Debates about the applicability of these rights have generated actions such as the right to "*tutela*,"[6] the right to petition, and the right to sue; judges and public functionaries must oversee these rights under penalty of prevarication. In short, this new system established a seemingly infinite horizon of possibilities for Colombians and set social equity as the primary objective of the national state.

THE DEMOCRATIC MODEL AND POLITICS

Since 1810, the possibility of setting up a monarchy in Colombia has never been seriously contemplated, although on some occasions the idea was proposed. In 1811, the Constitution of Cundinamarca did so, and then, in the late

1820s, a faction that opposed the Cúcuta Constitution proposed a monarchy as an alternate form of government. Nonetheless, the breakup of Gran Colombia indicated that Colombia would emerge as a democratic representative republic. With some regularity, however, the national landscape saw the appearance of proposals to transform the government into a parliamentary system, which quickly were abandoned because they did not fit with the presidential tradition that had taken root in the nation. What was argued over, and several times with force of arms, was the centralist versus federalist character of the nation's organization and the relative balance of power between branches of government. In general terms, the country had seen centralism as the predominating form of organization, which consequently produced an imbalance in favor of the executive power.

Debates over the strength of centralism in the nation began very early in the republic's history. After the dissolution of Colombia, the Republic of New Granada that took its place in 1832 was centralist, favoring a strong executive power. This tendency continued well into 1853, when the constitution of that year opened the way for the autonomous organization of the provinces, which in turn allowed for a short yet monumental epoch in nineteenth-century history. From 1854 to 1857, the corporative and baroque traditions of the colonial period were well on their way to being systematically dismantled, and during these years, the centralized state was also disassembled. New norms were adopted at this time, including legalization of divorce, a secular state separate from the Catholic Church, direct taxation, and other measures that highlighted the importance of the individual before the state. Some of these changes were short lived. The constitution of 1858 tried to rein in the extremes that resulted, with some success. It was a federalist constitution that sought to recover political space for centralism and the executive power. However, the competing forces of the 1853 and 1858 constitutions provoked a visceral civil war that, in turn, generated a new constitution in 1863, which was equally federalist and followed the North American model of 1787; the constitution took cues from positions elaborated by George Washington, John Adams, and the Federalist Party—all favoring more control over the associated states by a central national power.

The centralist, presidentialist system returned more quickly than expected. The brief civil war of 1885 ushered in the new constitution of 1886, which returned Colombia to a centralist state with a strong executive power. Additional civil wars broke out in 1895 and from 1899 to 1902, as the centralist system was still contested by a significant portion of the population. This second conflict was the most destructive of the nineteenth century and is remembered as the War of a Thousand Days. No clear winners emerged, but the war did set the stage for the first major reform of the constitution in 1910.

This reform moderated the centralist excesses of the 1886 charter and allowed for a relatively long period of political peace that lasted until the 1930s. Nevertheless, the reform of 1910 did not manage to successfully resolve the deepening party conflicts that had channeled not only political interests but also political violence. Both liberals and conservatives battled to control the executive branch, as well as related institutions of the state, to the exclusion of the other. Instead of opening a space for debate, where decisions could be made through congressional discussions of ideas and programs, or allowing state bureaucracy to be managed by technocrats and specialists, both parties sought a monopoly over all public offices. This assured that key decisions that had significant consequences for the future were made in ways that favored political party clientelism and guaranteed party loyalty. Battles moved from the field to the ballot box and, through this channel, to public administration at the precise moment when the governmental bureaucracy was expanding in size and complexity, given the increasing modernization of the country.

The lesson of Colombia's nineteenth century was clear: presidentialism/centralism created fertile ground whereby party-led management of the state became the factor that contributed most directly to chronic violence. A monopoly of state offices by one or the other political party was viewed as the most efficacious manner of operating government, and such monopoly was typically enforced through violence. Triumphs at the ballot box granted political power to one party to the exclusion of the other. The party out of power often determined that violence was the only way to overturn such a situation of exclusion. Although formal civil wars disappeared in the twentieth century, political party violence remained one of the basic characteristics of the Colombian political model; violence was the manner through which control over the Colombian state was ensured.

In this sense, the twentieth century witnessed the continuity of centralism and presidentialism as the consequence of political party struggles over control. This, in turn, led to a crisis of violence at midcentury and eventually to what is remembered as the National Front. The National Front was an elite-led agreement among leaders of the Liberal and Conservative Parties to alternate their hold on the presidency with calculated parity in each and every possible public office. This regime lasted from 1958 until 1974, and in some ways it lasted into 1986, when the Liberal president, Virgilio Barco, decided to return to the government of one-party rule, which represented the apex of presidentialism for the country. The bipartisan agreement, by obliging each party to alternate its hold on the presidency, managed to solve one problem: it dramatically slowed political violence that not only bloodied the country from 1930 to 1958 but also had subjected the nation's institutions to a profound crisis. For example, Colombia's only military dictatorship

(1953–1957) occurred during this period. Similarly, the parity in public offices solved part of the bipartisan dispute but significantly debilitated the party base ideologically. Thus, clientelism became the principal mechanism through which party loyalty was rewarded. Although there were some earlier attempts to build a state around modern technocratic principles, the reform of 1958—the peace ushered in by the National Front—accelerated this trend. Nevertheless, the consequences of this transformation and of the so-called peace generated profound impacts on the society and political culture of Colombians. Politics as an exercise of citizenship was stripped of its virtue, instead favoring the technocrat and punishing the career politician. At the same time, new, dangerous actors exploded onto the national political scene: the guerrilla fighter, the drug trafficker, the paramilitary, and the corrupt public official. A society that was becoming ever more urbanized increasingly grew politically apathetic, a phenomenon that was made evident by the significant abstention that characterized all elections during the last two decades of the twentieth century.

Unfortunately, the model of state imposed upon Colombia after the National Front coalition government up until the constitution of 1991 was unable to respond to challenges posed by the radical transformations of Colombian society and culture. Nor could it expand the bases of political participation within the state. One solution was offered with the constitutional reform of 1986, which expanded political participation and democracy via direct, popular election of governors and mayors and through overall administrative decentralization. Direct elections of regional and local government officials livened up political activity and, at least in the larger cities, helped reinvigorate the rise of third parties and even civic candidacies. Nevertheless, many regions and population centers could not completely eliminate cronyism or political clientelism. And once the leadership of the major parties lost control over the electoral process, the path was clear for other actors to enter the state apparatus, primarily drug traffickers and paramilitaries. Furthermore, decentralization has not led to more regional autonomy regarding decision making as the central state, that is, the executive branch, continues dictating what should be done at the local level.

The constitution of 1991 sought to create a new model for the state. This is what the moment demanded: a guerrilla movement had radicalized due to the failure of the peace talks at the end of the 1980s and especially due to the systematic assassination of all members of the Unión Patriótica, a leftist political party founded by the insurgent group FARC (Revolutionary Armed Forces of Colombia) and the Colombian Communist Party that had successfully won public office in many municipalities throughout the country. Moreover, paramilitary groups were on the rise at this time, and their agendas went beyond controlling local processes and affairs; they became national political actors with agendas of their own. Drug cartels also gained increasing political power, having won seats in Congress and influence among businesspeople, politicians, and government officials. The economic crisis of the 1980s and innumerable other problems made it necessary to rethink the model of the Colombian state.

Changes came swiftly; in less than a year a new constitution was created. It proposed as a formula for the state a social state of rights and a renewed relationship among the branches of government from that of the past. The excesses of presidentialism were curtailed by strengthening the legislative branch and expanding the area of action in which the high courts of the judicial branch could act. The results have been limited, but nevertheless, what it means to govern Colombia today is beginning to change significantly from what it meant in the nineteenth and twentieth centuries.

GOVERNMENT

A significant paradox exists in the history of the Colombian state: at the same time that centralism and presidentialism have generated chronic violence due to their combined exclusionary character, which still has not been solved by the current state model, they have allowed for significant achievements in the modernization of the country and improvements in the quality of life of its inhabitants. Of course, it is impossible to state that poverty, which is the result of social, economic, and even political inequalities and discrimination, has been eradicated. Nevertheless, the challenges that have defined the work of governing over the course of time, as a product of ideological and cultural changes and of pressures that have emerged out of social struggles, indicate that today the nation is moving forward with the consolidation of a social state of rights.

From early on, Colombia has defined what it means to govern: since the constitution of 1832, which evidenced clear continuities with the first charters approved in 1811, the Colombian state has dictated that supreme power would be divided among the separate legislative, executive, and judicial branches. The object of governing is to protect liberty, security, property, and equality among a nation's inhabitants. Additionally, from its beginnings in 1832 until 1991, Colombia has dictated that the government is obliged to protect its inhabitants in their practice of the Roman Catholic religion. The changes in this conception of the state have been few but significant: on the one hand, the 1991 constitution considered the need for administrative decentralization; on the other hand, the 1991 constitutional assembly had to decide on the types of issues that needed government direction and consequently made decisions concerning the adequate management and balance of modern measures of public administration. These factors, taken together, allow for a clearer understanding of the particularities of the history of the Colombian state.

The first factor that has shaped the Colombian government is the extent of administrative decentralization. The origins of the issue lie in the tension that municipal governance generates in the political lives of Colombians because of the diversity of Colombia's regions. The regions vary according to the characteristics of the national territory, the ways in which a particular region was populated, and the chronic imposition of centralized government and institutions. The constitutions of 1832 and 1843 imposed a change toward centralism, since all local authorities could be elected only through the direct intervention of the central power. For example, in the constitution of 1843, the governor of a province was named directly by the president, who could recall the governor at any time—this ensured immediate political power for the executive in the provinces. The nine states that finally gave shape to the Granadine Confederation (1858–1863) and to the United States of Colombia (1863–1886) offered an intermediate solution for governance between the municipality and the central state. Authority at this time was found in a sort of permanent tension between the central and federal levels, and this tension prevented the municipality from actually governing. The conditions of the federal conception nevertheless established that the central government would govern only in those matters that were expressly delegated by federal governments. For this reason, the tendency of states to govern themselves autonomously and the conflicts that emerged among states when regional political offices were controlled by the opposing party or faction weakened government and, in general, the federal state.

With the constitution of 1886, the state was centralized, and the government was left in the hands of only one political party. The government returned to an exclusive, centralized executive power with agents throughout the country, once again causing an unequal distribution of power among the branches of government in favor of the president, his ministers, the governors, and mayors. These were the political figures that most dominated the political scene for the following century. This situation did not change until the constitutional reform of 1986, the year in which popular election of governors and mayors was approved, and in this way, presidential power and that of the coalition that brought him to office was tempered. Notwithstanding the resultant revival of political participation at the regional and local levels, especially in urban areas, caused by this transformation, the reform did not achieve a significant expansion of the powers of these new public officials.

Centralism suffered a mere scrape to its power. After two hundred years and even taking into account changes to the social pact, in Colombia the regional and local levels of government remain limited in their capacity to make fundamental administrative decisions. These decisions are primarily made at the highest levels of central government.

Second, the matters of government have varied as society has grown in complexity over the course of centuries. In spite of the different ideas concerning who should govern during the nineteenth century, the democracy that predominated was maintained without any major changes concerning its liberal conception—that is, a state composed of individual citizens whose rights needed to be guaranteed. In this sense, the nineteenth-century state did not intervene in matters of liberty and equality before the law, nor did it intervene to limit private property. The world economic crisis that occurred in the 1930s, which forced a profound transformation in liberal democracies, equally affected the Colombian state and challenged the common conception of the purpose of government. The interventionist state took shape, and in this way it limited, through predetermined rules, the rights to property, extending the concept of equality beyond that of the law by introducing the consideration of social well-being. Regarding respect for liberty, which could be restricted as stipulated by the constitution of 1886, the capacities of government were expanded in terms of their provisional ability to place limits on liberty. The crises of the 1930s and the emergence of new social actors of the late twentieth century, which eventually led to the constitution of 1991, forced the most important governmental change that has occurred in the past two centuries. The social state of rights means governing officials must enforce both equity and society's well-being.

The executive power, during the nineteenth century, centralized or federated, understood that its circumscribed principal tasks were to control political and military order within the state and international relations (both political and commercial) and to expand and consolidate the national treasury. These matters gave shape to the "secretariats of the office," referred to as such until the constitution of 1886 renamed them "ministries." It is noteworthy that from 1843 until today the constitutions did not dictate what the secretariats/ministries should be, leaving this to the needs of the moment. In this sense, studying the creation of different ministries leads to a clearer understanding of the substantial changes the executive power underwent. For example, law 7 of 1886 inaugurated the modern state because it created the Ministry of War (now Defense), Development (now Economic Development), Public Instruction (now Education), Treasury and Public Credit, Interior, and International Relations. A few years later, it was necessary to create the Ministry of Justice in 1890, and fifteen years later, in 1905, a Ministry of Public Works (today

Transportation). This shows that in two decades, half of the ministries that currently help the president of the republic run the country were created. In 1913 the Ministry of Agriculture and Commerce (today Agriculture) was organized, and in 1923 the Ministry of Mail and Telegraphs (today Communications and Technologies of Information) was established.

An important governmental reform of 1936 created a welfare state—modeled after, to some degree, the United States under President Franklin Delano Roosevelt's government reform during the 1930s; thus, in Colombia the Ministry of Labor, Hygiene, and Social Provision (today Labor and Social Security) was created in 1936. In 1940 the Ministry of Mines and Petroleum (today Mines and Energy) was established, and in 1946 the Ministry of Labor organized all health-related issues in order to create a separate Ministry of Hygiene (today Health).

Several decades passed before any new ministries were created. Not until 1991 did the External Commerce Ministry (today Commerce, Industry, and Tourism) emerge. The Environment Ministry was formed in 1993, and finally, in 1997, the Ministry of Culture was created. These developments, since the government's beginning in 1832, have been accompanied by activities directly guided and enforced by the executive power, according to the needs of each particular historic moment. For example, these ministries guided the development of manufacturing industries; also, state lands were conceded, immigrants of European origin were courted, railroads and roads were built, normal/teaching schools were established, school textbooks were produced, and museums/libraries were opened. In short, everything from vaccinations and hospitals to agribusinesses and telecommunications, including radio and television, were aspects of the many changes managed by successive Colombian government administrations to ensure the progress of the nation.

Third, and finally, the capacity to *assure* the future of the governed via the management of modern public administration tools took on a constitutional demeanor. Thus, the introduction of planning in government was initiated with the state reform of 1936. Soviet state planning of the 1920s inspired this change, as did the need to intervene effectively in individual liberties in order to bring welfare solutions to the crises of the 1930s. This kind of intervention developed into an alternative political formula to the communist system proposed and supported by the Communist Party of Colombia, the PCC—a system never adopted in Colombia.

Planning became a key role of government and continues to be today. The constitutional reform of 1958 permanently established planning in Colombia. Colombian law requires departments and municipalities to have a planning institution. Furthermore, the interventionist state made it possible for the executive branch to develop many public entities, such as the Superintendencies of Commerce and Finance, among others; the Administrative Departments of Security (DAS—closed in 2011), Public Function (DAFP), and Statistics (DANE), among others; and Industrial and Commercial Works of the State (Ecopetrol, the state-run oil company, for example). Taken in their totality, these public entities have allowed the government to complete its tasks more efficiently but also to intervene directly in the development of the country.

THE FORMATION OF LAW

Congress, comprising the Senate and the House of Representatives, has always served as the institution charged with forming the laws of the Colombian Republic. Its function, with a few notable exceptions, has been constant in Colombian history. During the First Republic, legislative bodies were organized. During Gran Colombia, Congress was in session between 1823 and 1828 and ceased to exist when Simón Bolívar decided to close Congress so that he could create the political circumstances for a new constitution. From 1832 to 1905, Congress functioned with only occasional short closures caused by civil wars or conflicts between factions within each party. The longest of these occurred during the civil war of 1860 to 1863 and the War of a Thousand Days from 1899 to 1902. From 1904 to 1909, President Rafael Reyes dissolved Congress and imposed a national assembly. Congress was not closed again until 1949, when by decree President Mariano Ospina Pérez did so at a time when rural and urban violence grew dramatically. Congress remained closed until the fall of the dictatorship of Gustavo Rojas Pinilla in 1957 and through the end of the transition regime known as the Military Government on July 20, 1958. The most recent closure, which in effect was not caused by a government decision but by the creation of the Constitutional Assembly, which created the new constitution of 1991, occurred between 1990 and 1991.

The relatively consistent activity of this institution has been one of its defining characteristics. Nevertheless, what has in reality marked its nature within Colombia has been executive officials' preference for a *weak Congress*. This has allowed the executive power to carry out legislative initiatives in the country, either because many of the law projects discussed in Congress have been developed in the offices of the different ministries or because the constitution of 1886 allowed the president to govern by decree. Often, presidents would abuse this clause of exception and make it the rule. The constitution of 1991 prohibited these excesses and has tried to place the country under the dictates of a strong Congress, which existed only during the years of nineteenth-century federalism. The difficulty in activating a strong Congress is explained by looking to the weakness of the Colombian political parties vis-à-vis the executive power: clientelism has not completely disappeared as a mechanism of political negotiation and control by the opposition in the country. Also, unfortunately, the parties continue to approach politics in a manner that places a high value on coercive customs associated with political *caudillos*.

The formation of laws in Colombia has followed the dictates of a government led by a strong executive power. A weak Congress has been maintained. Given that Congress makes laws and is the body charged with overseeing the approval of laws based on majorities in Congress, the executive has limited the capacity of the legislative branch to solve some of its most entrenched vices by making it difficult for Congress to enact a transformation of itself. One can argue, however, that the permanence of a weak Congress gives the appearance of a kind of de facto executive dictatorship. However, Colombia has managed—with major difficulties—to avoid the emergence of actual dictatorships, except during one period in the 1950s. The exercise of resistance has been, therefore, positive for the health of the state, but the cost in terms of human lives and social instability has been enormously high for Colombian society.

NOTES

1. "Constitución de la República de Tunja, 1811," in Manuel Antonio Pombo and José Joaquín Guerra, *Constituciones de Colombia*, vol. 1 (Bogotá: Ministerio de Educación Nacional, 1951), 246.

2. This term refers to the fact that the 1991 constitution insists that the Colombian state is organized along a complex charter of human rights—in the contemporary sense and usage of the term. Roughly, the term translates as "Social State of Rights."

3. "Constitución de 1886, artículo 15," *Biblioteca virtual Miguel de Cervantes*, www.cervantesvirtual.com. Accessed June 3, 2011.

4. "Acto legislativo No. 1, agosto 5, 1936," in "Reformas de la Constitución de 1886." *Biblioteca virtual Miguel de Cervantes*.

5. This Spanish colonial system, concerned with holding large Spanish-controlled territories intact, forbade any person except the eldest male son from inheriting property.

6. *Tutela* comes from the Spanish verb *tutelar*, which gives guardianship over something or someone. The 1991 constitution forced government officials to respond to individuals who wished to use the law to protect their guaranteed rights.

Chapter Four

The Cadence of Unity

Over a period of two hundred years, the country we now call the Republic of Colombia underwent several name changes. The Republic of New Granada that emerged out of the dissolution of Gran Colombia was renamed in 1858 as the Grenadine Confederation. This name, in turn, was replaced in 1863 by the United States of Colombia. Not until 1886 did the name Republic of Colombia return, though it referred to a place significantly different from the Colombian Republic of 1819. It is therefore worth asking which forces and/ or social dynamics allowed this entity to remain united as a single territorial state given that, as these multiple name changes suggest, the nation (a unifying culture) that would give rise to the state (institutions) did not exist when the state first formed. Even today a "Colombian nation" is difficult to identify. What emerges out of the depths of Colombia's republican history is a state that had to construct the "nation." By actively producing both governmental and cultural institutions over its territory, Colombia would begin to gain stability and, over time, would consolidate into a unified nation.

The changes in name were not accidental. As we have seen in previous chapters, the nineteenth century may be characterized by the search for a state model that would accommodate itself to what elites understood as best for their interests and, by extension, those of the country. Nevertheless, powerful elite power brokers were regionalized. The particular spatial distribution of elites into regions explains in part why the name of the country changed so often; regional elites fought one another in various civil wars. The history of these conflicts reveals the kinds of political and social tensions that, once resolved, allowed the Colombian state to unify its "parts." Those parts were vastly different from one another and for centuries had developed unique modes of existence and ways of using space. They were separate nations.

This chapter studies the principal dynamics that facilitated the construction of a state that was viable in terms of its social and territorial control. It may be said that the nineteenth century inaugurated the kinds of political and cultural dynamics that began to change the centrifugal tendency of the Colombian social order. This tendency was most pronounced in the dispute among the different Colombian federalisms that were obliterated by the triumph of centralism in the late 1800s. Once this inclination toward dispersion was thus resolved, the twentieth century saw the excesses of regional autonomy solved through an extremely centralist and presidentialist system that grew more moderate with time. In this context a contradiction needed to be resolved: the problem of how to consolidate a strong state without excluding wide social sectors from representation. Mechanisms had to be developed that would help Colombians understand their place within the social and cultural body politic. The most difficult challenge would be to overcome the geographic and cultural barriers that separated the old provinces. Foremost, substantial improvements in communications were needed. Trade could then expand and allow for the colonization of the intermediate zones, those areas that still needed colonizing. Increased urbanization would then allow for the installation of ample midlevel professional sectors that could employ workers and laborers who shared common notions of citizenship and future aspirations—thereby creating authentic mechanisms of social ascent.

The primary forces that helped forge national unity are varied. The two traditional political parties, the Liberals and Conservatives, have been crucial unifying forces. Additional mechanisms of national unity include Roman Catholicism as a common religion and Spanish as the national language. Other important unifying factors include the establishment of the army and a national currency.

THE PARTIES AND THE NATION

Differences among political parties, which focused on monopolizing the state and its institutions, were the primary cause of the political violence unleashed on the country throughout its republican history. This was considered in detail in the previous chapter, and we will return to this political violence as it relates to social conflicts. The purpose of examining political parties here, however, is a bit different. Although it may seem paradoxical, understanding the political party system in Colombia during the nineteenth century is critical to understanding the permanence of the Colombian state through time.

The traditional political parties were ultimately a key unifying factor in the construction of a nation. The reason stems not from the ideological principles laid out by one or another party, which shaped each party and remained consistent for decades. Rather, it was the social composition of the parties and their distribution throughout the territory that generated a measure of unity and stability. In this sense, Liberals and Conservatives developed multiclass, regional political organizations.

Both parties were born at the same time as a means to provide ideological positions with regard to the conflicts that reigned during the mid-nineteenth century, particularly in terms of the model of state that would be most efficient for the complex society that inhabited a territory still unknown and largely uncontrolled. Toward the end of the 1840s a kind of solution and cause for violent confrontation emerged. In 1848, as tensions rose with the elections that were to be celebrated in 1849, the initial political platforms of the two parties were first published. Over the course of the next 130 years, these were the only two political parties in Colombia with the capacity to control the entire state and its institutions.

Before examining the trajectory of the two parties, a clarification is in order. This concerns the argument that the parties were founded within the context of Bolivarianism and Santanderism of the Gran Colombia epoch. For the leaders of the mid-nineteenth century, it was clear that there was no reason to ransack the pages of history to find origins for their political parties in the early republic. All debate and ideological differences were actually rooted in a basic agreement over which there was no dispute at all: the republic, no matter its formal organization, would be popular and representative and would share a balance of power among its branches of government. Mariano Ospina Rodríguez, one of the founders of the Conservative Party, stated it this way in an article published in 1850: "Today in New Granada there are no Bolivarians nor royalists. . . . Today there is no discussion on whether or not New Granada should be united or separated from Spain; whether the government should be a monarchy or a republic. Similarly, there can be no discussion over whether or not the states that form Colombia should separate. These questions have been decided, and these decisions are consummated facts, and there is no turning back."[1]

These words demonstrate the ways in which emerging party leaders confronted what had been perceived as a necessary reform of the state of New Granada. This reform was brought about as a result of the decentralizing changes the *caudillo* leader Tomás Cipriano de Mosquera put into effect during his first presidential administration (1845–1849). Ezequiel Rojas published the text that now is recognized as the first program of the Liberal Party in the newspaper *El Aviso* on July 16, 1848. In the text's final section, Rojas states that the Liberal Party wants

a government that is organized for the benefit of the governed; it wants a Republic, a truly representative system; an independent congress, an executive power that can only do what the law permits; positive responsibility, and for that, independent tribunals, good laws, an eminently national and American policy emanating from the Executive Power, impartial justice for all, that the actions of the State have no other consideration other than the public good, and it wants all this so that those who obey do not become the slaves of those who govern; this way there will be true liberty; we will liberate ourselves from a theocratic government, and assure the people that they are secure in their homes and in their property, and that these guarantees are not false promises.[2]

Less than three months later, on October 4, 1848, the newspaper *La Civilización* published an article by Mariano Ospina Rodríguez and José Eusebio Caro titled, "Conservative Program of 1849," which today is recognized as the first document of that party because it details the eight principles that guided Conservatives into the future:

First, constitutional order against a dictatorship; second, law will triumph over the power of direct action; third, the morality of Christianity and its civilizing doctrines against the immorality of corrupting doctrines of materialism and atheism; fourth, rational liberty in all of its applications against despotism, albeit monarchical, demagogic or literary; fifth, legal equality against aristocratic, university, or other privilege; sixth, the real and effective tolerance against exclusivism and persecution, whether it be a Catholic against the protestant or the deist, or the atheist against the Jesuit or friar, etc.; seventh, property [will be protected] against theft and usurpations executed by communists . . . or anyone else; eighth, security against the arbitrary actions of any kind; Civilization, in short, against barbarism.

The program ends by clarifying that "to be or to have been an enemy of Santander, of Azuero, or López does not mean one is Conservative."[3]

These parties quickly became national. This is precisely the point that must be emphasized. One reason both parties became national political parties is that both were born in Bogotá. Though it is true that native sons, or *caudillos*, led regional autonomies, it is also true that in order to triumph nationally, these regional leaders had to take Bogotá politically. Affiliating oneself with a particular party was a kind of personal guarantee, as other party members in other regions could support the cause and help block opponents from using government mechanisms against a candidate and his allies.

Additionally, political party systems offered continuity. Systems of authority based on kinship and labor, consolidated during the colonial period via patriarchal and corporative social organization, were firmly rooted in the country. From father to son and from patron to client (worker), these hierarchical relationships continued. One's choice of political party affiliation often merged with those in one's kinship and labor sphere. Transgression could have serious repercussions on family relationships and on the loyalties that emerged out of the principle of obedience to one's patron. Such inherited party loyalties adapted as a result of expanding family relationships or modernizing labor relations that followed the migrations of populations. Moreover, political parties easily transitioned into new territories and paralleled the demographic growth of the country.

The electoral system, either through secret universal ballot or through "indirect" (that is, nonuniversal) elections, facilitated the maintenance and growth of the parties in the regions. As ideological or regional interests clashed within the same party, internal fissures would occur, but rarely would a new political party emerge. Both parties managed to exert a level of control over electoral machinery and did so through their ability to name government functionaries to posts. This kind of patronage shaped the major pathway through which people accessed political office and administrative positions at all levels of the public sector. Thus the people could receive benefits from the state, but only through their ties to a recognized political party. Political party leaders managed to impose a monopoly on the bureaucracy of the public sector. This loyalty to one or another party allowed a person access to the state mechanisms that prompted development, justice, or protection from adversaries. Finally, as the state and the political parties increasingly intertwined, a dynamic of growth and consolidation occurred such that neither one could be distinguished completely from the other.

This last aspect conditioned one of the problems that helps explain, in part, the reasons for the chronic weakness of the Colombian state. The act of governing was subject to the capacity of one party to control the state's apparatus not only in the center but also in each region of the country. Regional control was never completely possible since partisan control varied from region to region and even from province to province within a region. In other words, to control the central state and to monopolize its principal institutions were no guarantee of obedience throughout the territory. If one party's ability to exert control were cut off, it would resort to armed resistance and political violence. In this way, the same mechanisms that had permitted the parties to extend their reach nationally, generating either Liberal Colombians or Conservative Colombians, no matter their place of residence or provincial culture, strengthened the state but also, paradoxically, divided it. Party rule became government rule, and minimal separation of political affiliation from the exercise of public administration persisted.

Colombian nation building is therefore tied to political partisanship. Having either a Liberal or Conservative political affiliation formed an essential part of what it meant to be Colombian, at least until the National Front years. It is important to note, however, that within these affiliations there was room for nuance, even differences, but rarely were these expressed outside of or independent from either one of the two parties. The reasons for differing opinions within either party varied, but they almost always developed as conflicts of opinion between the radical members of a party versus those who held more moderate views. The former steadfastly held onto doctrine, while the latter preferred the opportunities presented by holding a more politically pragmatic position, especially so that capitalism and bourgeois life could advance. Similarly, when conflict arose between parties and reached such extremes as to threaten the very viability of the state, the more moderate members of each party tended to negotiate, creating interparty agreements that served as escape valves for potentially explosive pressure. The first such negotiation occurred in 1854 as a result of the violent reaction by the artisan guilds against the increasing individualization imposed as part of the requirements called for by a nascent capitalism and the increased gentrification of society. Similarly, from 1880 to 1884, the National Party allowed for reconciliation between many moderate Liberals and Conservatives; in 1910, with the triumph of Republicanism in elections held that year, moderate Conservatives allied with Liberals; in 1946 and 1948, Colombia saw negotiations, however tepid, between moderate Liberals and moderate Conservatives given the sociopolitical debacle that was looming on the horizon. Most significantly, between 1958 and 1974, the National Front, the official political power-sharing pact between Liberals and Conservatives, continued into the mid-1980s to help resolve the political party crisis that emerged during the dangerous era of political exclusion in the mid-twentieth century. The collaborative National Front also helped dismantle the military political model imposed by the dictatorship of Rojas Pinilla in the mid-1950s.

The National Front, through its agreements to alternate governance between the two traditional political parties, hid the kinds of disputes that had afflicted the state up until 1958—conflicts that were no longer about ideology as much as they were about control over bureaucracy. The emergence of the National Front also coincided with a notable secularization, urbanization, and gentrification of Colombian society. Similarly, parity in public office prompted citizens to change their political party affiliation as a kind of survival strategy so as to maintain or find employment with the state bureaucracy. This led to the breakdown of traditional loyalties at the same time that young people in cities no longer found political affiliation to be an important factor, either in terms of family unity or as a force in provincial or generational identity.

The state reform of 1991 favored the creation of new political parties, organized as an electoral strategy or as a clear political alternative to the dominant traditional political parties. No less important at this time was the increasing corruption of some politicians, either through their ties to drug traffickers or guerrilla or paramilitary groups or through their use of public funds for personal benefit. The public became aware of the number of government functionaries who increasingly won political posts in return for political favors and not for their abilities, merit, or knowledge. This led to widespread skepticism by voters, if not outright abstention and depoliticization among a broad spectrum of the population. All this favored the "personalization" of politics during the twenty years since the constitution of 1991. Political parties are now electoral machines run by a single leader, who through personal charisma may acquire the characteristics of a *caudillo*. In this way, the traditional parties are no longer an essential aspect of Colombian national identity, but without them, it is impossible to maintain an adequately functioning state. Despite this, for all their faults and foibles, and for all of the violence they have unleashed, the traditional political parties have been essential for the construction of a shared political identity that unites and divides Colombians as they search for solutions to some of their most entrenched historical challenges.

COMMUNION IN BELIEFS

Catholicism emerged as a central force in building a common identity for Colombians during the formative years of the nineteenth century and well into the twentieth. Catholicism unified a state that was trying to construct a nation. The religion dominated for centuries, clearly shaping and homogenizing a system of common cultural practices for the population. This was in part underscored by a state that offered the Catholic Church a kind of protection by supporting its institutionalism and moral dictates. The protection was expressed in constitutions and through the granting of a monopoly over education to the Church over the course of several decades. Children and adolescents in every corner of the country received Catholic instruction. Furthermore, the Church, via its religious orders, engaged in active missionary work among the more far-flung regions of the country, incorporating indigenous and Afro-Colombian populations into Colombian society that had been marginalized during previous centuries. In this way, Colombian society increasingly constructed an identity as a community not through participation based on a civil code of ethics, but rather through obedience to the rules dictated by Catholic morality. Thus, the political community was indistinguishable from the community of believers. Today, this situation has changed in favor of a secular state. This has not necessarily occurred because of the social effects of secularization of the population, which is quite limited, but rather due to the loss of command and control held by the Church hierarchy over the general assembly of the nation and the state.

The Colombian nation was born in the Catholic faith and remained so until 1991, but this also does not mean that religious intolerance has uniformly prevailed in Colombian society. Except for the final years of the nineteenth century and during the mid-twentieth century, citizens respected freedom of religion. But in Colombia, no denominational church except the Catholic Church could have access to state institutions and proselytize to its own advantage. Similarly, if the nation was constructed from the state, and the state made its Catholic identity dominant, then the resultant identity was clear: to be Colombian meant to be Catholic.

To ensure that Colombia's identity remained Catholic, churches were built in each and every plaza of all Colombian towns. These were in addition to the many Catholic parishes, schools, convents, hospices, and hospitals that, without exception, counted on the exclusive support of the state and local societies. Thus, the Catholic Church maintained itself in daily life and in the festivals and celebrations of the Colombian population, granting a certain sense of community to a new nation.

Of course, Catholicism was one of the legacies inherited from centuries of Spanish rule that pro-independence republicans refused to renounce. The very statements/declarations of independence that were produced in 1810 invariably guaranteed the continuity and protection of the Catholic Church in the new autonomous province. This is expressed, for example, in the minutes of the newly formed Santafé Junta of July 20, 1810, which describes the oath that the deputies had to take: "With one hand on the Holy Gospels and with the other making the sign of the cross, in the presence of Jesus Christ crucified they said: 'we swear by the God who exists in Heaven, whose image is made present, and whose sacred and worshipful maxims are contained in this book, to religiously carry out the constitution and will of the people expressed in this act, concerning the form of provisional government that has been installed; and to defend our sacred Roman Catholic Apostolic Religion until the last drop of blood has been sacrificed.'"[4] Subsequent constitutions, including that of 1991, but with the exception of 1863, were enacted with a formula that in one way or another expressed that God was the source of all authority or at least invoked God's protection.

The mid-nineteenth-century debate over the nature of individual liberties prevented the Church from initially exerting a clear monopoly over state institutions and limited the state from assuring special protection of the Church. The situation radically changed in 1886. Since the civil war of 1876, it was clear that neither Conservatives nor increasing sectors of the Liberals were willing to accept a secular state—a formula proposed by Radical Liberals who had dominated the state from 1863 until 1880. The Constitution of 1886, although in no way banning religious freedom (Article 39), nevertheless limited these freedoms to the worship of religions that did not offend Christian morality and law (Article 40), and Article 38 clearly established that "the Roman Catholic Apostolic Church is the religion of the Nation. Public powers were to protect it and ensure that it would be respected as an essential element of social order. It is understood that the Catholic Church was not, and would not be ruled by the state, and it will maintain its independence."[5] The reform of 1936 completely suppressed Article 38 and limited the powers of the Catholic Church over the state. It did not, however, change the state's religious identity, although it ultimately upheld freedom of religion provided such "freedom" did not run contrary to Catholic morality or law. And so it remained until 1991, when the formulation of a so-called social state of rights forced the eradication from the Constitution of any consideration of origin or religious preference. A ruling by the Constitutional Court in 1994 reaffirmed this:

> The Constitution of 1991 establishes the pluralist character of the social state of Colombian law, of which religious pluralism is one of its principal components. Similarly, the Charter precludes any form of sectarianism and enshrines full rights to religious freedom and equal treatment of all religious denominations, given that the invocation of the protection of God, which is made in the Preamble, has a general character and does not specifically refer to a particular Church. This implies, therefore, that in the ordering of the Colombian constitution, there is a separation between the state and the Churches because the State is secular. In effect, that strict neutrality of the state in religious matters is the only way in which public powers may ensure pluralism, an egalitarian coexistence, and the autonomy of the different forms of religious worship.[6]

The power the Catholic Church gained with the victory of the Conservatives allied with moderate Liberals in the civil war of 1885 and the subsequent 1886 constitution was reinforced by the agreement signed between the Colombian state and the Vatican in 1887. Known more formally as the Concordat, this treaty gave the Catholic Church, among its already existing safeguards, control over the official registry of citizens, uniting the entire population through baptism, assuring control over public education of children and adolescents, and mandating the kinds of materials that could be taught in private schools with respect to morality. The Catholic Church also obtained economic aid and tribunal exemptions, especially in areas where indigenous populations lived "unincorporated" into Colombia, and where there was an extremely limited presence of the state and the Church. In 1902, the Concordat reached the pinnacle of power when, by Decree 802, the state was consecrated to the Sacred Heart of Jesus, and as a consequence, a temple was built in Bogotá, the "Church of the National Devotion" or El Voto Nacional, which served to remind everyone that the Colombian state and the nation were Catholic.

The relative autonomy sought in this arena with the reform of 1936 only served to further radicalize the partisan animosities that bathed the country in blood during the mid-twentieth century. In 1952, the decree of 1902 celebrated its fiftieth anniversary under the complete dominance of the state by the Radical Conservatives, led by Laureano Gómez. The first law of that year not only renewed the consecration made in 1902 but also ordered that this consecration be made by the president of the republic or his representative. Moreover, it made certain that this conservative ceremony be repeated yearly on the day that the Catholic Church celebrated the day of the Sacred Heart of Jesus—a Catholic "movable" feast day celebrated each year nineteen days after Pentecost Sunday. This date, thereafter, became a national holiday called Acción de Gracias—Thanksgiving. This imposition continued during the following years as the dictatorship of Rojas Pinilla honored its ties to the moderate sector of the Conservative Party and the government administrations of the National Front. Subsequent regimes (through 1991) refused to challenge this public linkage of state and church, fearing disruption in public order were they to do so.

Contrary to what many feared, the step taken in 1991 to end the profound alliance between Catholicism and the Colombian state did not cause a public disruption in Colombia. By 1991, the global Catholic Church was itself in a state of crisis. In Colombia, the additional dynamics of a society that was growing increasingly urban and welfare oriented and more open to the values and conceptions of "materialism" prepared Colombians for a more secular society. These changes gained momentum during the mid-twentieth century and finally allowed the Colombian state to declare itself openly secular by 1991. As in the case with political parties, this change occurred only after Catholicism had significantly influenced the creation and consolidation of the nation. The Church has had a profound social, cultural, and political impact and is still visible today in the holiday calendar of Colombians, through shared practices of celebration and mourning, and in the number of children and adolescents who continue their education in Catholic social and moral teachings. Today the state is not officially Catholic, but that is largely because it is no longer necessary to declare it as such. Despite the fact that most people do not acknowledge this openly, Colombian society is, in many ways, as Catholic as it was a century ago.

A COMMON MEMORY

In the midst of controversy and confrontations concerning what Colombia would become, all sides agreed on three fundamentals: first, the urgent need to educate people; second, that people should know about the wealth and possibilities offered by the territory in which they live; and finally, that people should share a common explanation concerning what it meant to be Colombian as compared to other peoples. By the twentieth century, it was clear that all Colombians shared a common memory, one that efficiently created a kind of identity that continued into the end of that century. This occurred through education and its institutionalized system for control over its content; by conveying detailed knowledge of the territory and its people, which not only facilitated governance but also allowed Colombians to know and identify one another; through the defense of Spanish as the national language; and through the construction of a collective past that adequately explained the origin of the nation.

The centrality of education is critical in any democratic system. The electoral process is based on rational decision making, which is facilitated through growing literacy rates. For this reason, as noted above, the constitutions of 1832 and 1843 required that citizens be literate. But since the majority of inhabitants were not literate, the implementation of this requirement was deferred until the state met its obligation to educate all those who could be citizens—namely, males with a certain level of economic security and income. Subsequent constitutions failed to mention the literacy requirement since it came to be understood, during the nineteenth century, that providing free, basic education for all inhabitants was an indisputable function of the state. This notion and practice continues today. The basic state obligation to educate, therefore, emerged during the earliest days of the republic.

Scarce resources during much of the nineteenth century prevented universal education, but when funding was made available, monumental disputes developed over the content of education in Colombia. In general, a consensus developed that all students should be taught according to a single, similar program that should be obligatory in every corner of the country so as to create a unity of consciousness and, at the very least, the same basic skills needed to confront the requirements of modern life. Most everyone agreed that the basic function of education was to train the populace in the basic requirements of writing, reading, and mathematics. Beyond this, however, there was no agreement among contenders who sought to control Colombian education. Like most disagreements in Colombia from the mid-nineteenth century to the late twentieth century, educational disputes merged with political party factionalism. The civil war of 1876 is an example of disagreement over education resulting in conflict. This war represented the rage of the Conservative Party, with the Catholic Church, against the education reforms introduced beginning in 1870 by Radical Liberals in power. Their reforms imposed a secular education, state intervention in education, and the hiring of a pedagogical mission of German Protestants with the purpose of creating teacher training schools in all of the states in the federation.

The resultant Conservative backlash inspired the 1886 constitution, which litigated on behalf of the Catholic Church during the next fifty years for control over education in the country. The constitution turned complete control of public education and the right to oversee private education to the Roman Catholic Church. Article 41 of the Constitution of 1886 established that public education would be organized and conducted in accordance with the Catholic faith. This resulted in dissidents turning to the private sector, supported through the principle of freedom of education, also upheld through the 1886 constitution. Nevertheless, that freedom was limited because the Church had the capacity to intervene and oversee education with respect to "moral" issues. Liberals, who held power from 1930 to 1945, limited the power of the Church, but the Church still held control over the education system. Notwithstanding this trend, the processes of urbanization and secularization during the last years of the twentieth century meant that the church eventually lost de facto power over the Colombian education system.

At the same time that controversy over education took root, the state encouraged the development of scientific expeditions that would provide greater knowledge of the territory and its inhabitants. The Chorographic Expedition, organized during the first administration of Tomás Cipriano de Mosquera (1845–1849) and led by the Italian Agustín Codazzi, explored practically every inhabited region at the time and ventured into territories that had yet to be settled in the eastern regions of the country. The purpose of the Chorographic Expedition was to develop a single cartography that would prove fundamental for the emerging state and governing officials. Thus, financing the expedition became a national priority, and disseminating its results occurred via the educational system. The state made the study of geography an obligatory subject in schools; texts were written that offered a uniform idea about what Colombia was in its regions, its peoples, its customs, and its resources. Thus, the geographer and the cartographer were indispensable to the state. The need for trained professionals in this endeavor gave rise to the Office of Longitudes and Borders in 1902 and the Geographical Society of Colombia in 1903.

The defense of the Spanish language as the only language for the nation emerged from independence as a banner for the new governing officials. The Spanish language, together with the Catholic religion, would be the two legacies of the colonial era that would be consciously preserved. All other traditions of the monarchical regime, such as control over production and commerce and an educational system that ignored sciences and mechanical trades, were to be abolished. Regarding language, it was relatively easy for independence leaders to agree that all citizens needed to speak the same language. Both Liberal and Conservative constituents supported the dissemination and purity of the Spanish language via education in all schools. For this they founded the Colombian Academy of Language, which began its work on August 6, 1872, as an institution that would ensure the health of the language, allow for control over neologisms, support philology, and publish grammar texts.

Similarly, since the mid-nineteenth century, Colombians would work to establish the origin of a repertoire of Colombian literature. This issue is important because it ultimately implied defining what was properly national—that is, what is Colombian. José María Vergara y Vergara was a major figure of this literary generation of the mid-nineteenth century. In 1867, he published *Historia de la literatura en Nueva Granada*, the first of many significant works. The value of this work, in particular, lies in the fact that it confronted the question of origins and resolved the problem through a catalog of Colombian literature written *prior* to 1810. In fact, the texts and writers historicized in the chapters dealing with the colonial era formed the basis from which the repertoire of national letters of the early republic would emerge. For example, a few years after Vergara y Vergara's work, Isidoro Laverde Amaya, in his *Ojeada histórico-crítica sobre los orígines de la literatura Colombiana*, listed Gonzalo Jiménez de Quesada, the "Spanish" founder of Bogotá, as the first "Colombian" writer. He continued with the colonial chroniclers and ended his work with the founder of Colombian journalism, Manuel de Socorro Rodríguez. The independence model in Colombia, which prevented any consideration or discussion of pre-independence literature, had matured: national literature, by the mid-nineteenth century, could now be traced back beyond the watershed of the break with Spain. Colombian literature finally had a past, and the Spanish language thereby became patrimony—a constitutive legacy of the nation.

Something similar happened with historiography. The construction of the state and its consolidation required the writing of its history from its origins, inheritances, and great patriotic deeds. This task had already been clearly realized when the celebration of the first centennial of independence took place. It was made to coincide with July 20, 1910; the celebration spilled out onto the streets of Bogotá and was celebrated in other regions of the republic. The story of Colombian independence was no longer tied only to several provinces; it became a history that was common to all, and independence

history was now a history of the state. July 20 signified the unified and collective celebration of a triumphant, democratic, centralist state born out of
the constitution of 1886. The main figures of the independence movement
were presented as founding fathers, who were accompanied by new heroes,
those who gave their lives, in multiple nineteenth-century civil wars, for the
sake of a centralist state. The judgment passed on presidents prior to Rafael
Núñez (1884) was based on the extent to which each had contributed toward
the consolidation of the Colombian state of 1886. This new vision of the past
was accompanied by a new civil liturgy, the Acts of the Twentieth of July,
which were regulated and reproduced throughout the country. To consolidate
historic memory and oversee the "truth" in such matters, the Colombian
Academy of History was established in 1902.

The twentieth century inherited this historical construction and maintained
it, keeping it alive into the present among some social classes, although it is
now evident that this idea of history no longer holds a firm grip on the historical imaginations of the youth, academics, or ethnic groups. Newer history
texts relay wider, more complex versions of history.

During the 1960s, new history books were developed for high schools that
completely revised what had been considered undisputed at the beginning
of the twentieth century. This "new history" had already been the subject of
much discussion at the university level and quickly filtered down to basic primary education. The social movements that in one way or another developed
during these years created a different historical framework, a new past, and
this led some sectors of society to a wider understanding of the parameters set
out in the constitution of 1886. New interpretations of history called for the
creation of a new state, grounded in pluralism, to include all Colombian historical and cultural heritages. The deep sociohistoric questions of the 1960s,
developed in Colombia and elsewhere in the West, forced a reconsideration
of the centralized state and politics and ideological purity while pushing for
expanded heterogeneity of the Colombian nation.

A SINGLE INSTITUTIONALISM

Other social forces and activities developed by the state strengthened the
idea that all Colombians belong to the same community. This did not mean
that local customs and practices were abandoned. In this sense, Colombians' capacity to understand themselves as Catholic, as Spanish speaking, as
members of one or another political party, as educated according to the same
foundations and contents that others had experienced, and as the inheritors
of a learned common past—did not mean that regional particularities were

erased. This was because the ideological superstructure imposed upon all Colombians generated ties among inhabitants. The Colombian nation is not based, per se, upon one common culture, but rather on the idea—imposed by the state and dominant elite—that all Colombians form part of the same community. Similarly, the actions taken by the elites who run the state, who come from different regions of the nation, ended up strengthening the idea of unity among all Colombians who have had to learn to live under the guidance and protection of the same institutions.

Several forces worked toward this end. We will begin with the armed forces, which began to take shape as a unified and hierarchically organized institution in 1886. Until that date, which represents the triumph of centralism and the beginning of presidentialism, each state organized and financed its own army. The central state counted on only a national guard, which never had more than seven hundred men, since the midcentury Radical Liberals were ideologically opposed to a strong, centralized military. Thus, social and political forces that brought forth the triumph of centralism also saw that the organization of a single army would concentrate the monopoly of force in the state. Dissolving the regional armies and militias was a primary task for the central government during the last years of the nineteenth century.

The serious political tensions that emerged among the radical factions of both parties blocked the process of unification of regional armies into a single national army. Professionalization and institutionalization of the army occurred in 1907, under the presidency of Rafael Reyes. His administration founded the Military School of Cadets, and he hired a military mission from Chile to help organize the new institution.

With the passage of time and the presence of other military missions hired from abroad, the national military took a definitive shape. Starting in 1919, the Colombian Military Aviators (renamed the Colombian Air Force in 1994) joined the national armed forces. The National Navy, after several attempts at organization during the nineteenth century and beginning of the twentieth, was finally established in 1935, the same year the Navel Cadet School was founded in Cartagena. This school was designed with national unity in mind: two cadets from each department and five from the nation's capital city would be admitted annually to this prestigious academy.

The National Police, organized in 1890, was actually born out of the police force raised for Bogotá under the influence of the French *gendarmerie*. This occurred despite a presidential decree in 1891 that ordered the elimination of departmental and municipal police forces but, at the same time, provided funding for a new police force under the Ministry of Government. The national character of the police thereby took shape, but its character as a civil or military institution was increasingly debated. Conflict over its political use by the particular political party in power overshadows this institution's history during the first five decades of the twentieth century. In 1953, the dictator Rojas Pinilla incorporated the police in the Ministry of War and, in doing so, converted it into a military force. This lasted until 1991, when the new constitution restored its civilian character.

Colombian political economy from 1886 to the present illustrates a history of national unification that is rooted in the conceptions and practices of the central state. Of course ideological differences that were often irreconcilable emerged over time, leading to deep divisions among elites who understood themselves as "national" elites. What is worth noting is that such disagreements were discussed and resolved through partisan control of the state. Thus the elimination of the federal states went hand in hand with the abolition of duties, tolls, and other obstacles to internal trade and free movement of people within a truly national territory. On the other hand, political economy and, in particular, all aspects related to the agro-export system, distribution of uncultivated state lands, and imposition of labor conditions favored entrepreneurs in cities and landowners in rural areas. These capitalist-friendly policies were defended by the moderate sectors from both parties, facilitating the implementation from early on of an economic bipartisan system at the national level.

Similarly, the creation of the National Treasury, as the only system of taxation and administration of national assets, generated the necessary resources for the state to promote policies, build institutions, and pay for a bureaucracy that was required for running the country. Equally important was the appearance of associations to generate income with offices in all regions where particular activities were important, usually in the provincial capitals. These included the Agricultural Society of Colombia (1871), the National Federation of Coffee Growers (1927), the National Association of Manufacturers (1944), and the National Association of Merchants (1945), to mention just a few of the most influential associations still active today. They served to control the links between the sectors of power in an economy that was already national in scope.

The consolidation of a national currency, the *peso*, and the creation of the Bank of the Republic as a result of the Kemmerer Mission of 1923, which created a uniform set of policies and controls over money and credit, gave stability and credibility to the economic system in all regions and municipalities of the country. This system also had a symbolic value, one of unity, in that it inspired within the Colombian citizenry trust in the *peso* as the only medium of exchange. Another example of state unification includes the implementation of unique systems of control throughout the state such as the comptroller general or the different superintendencies. These structures were designed to strengthen the central character of the state by developing uniquely Colombian institutions throughout the territory. This occurred at the same time that a central ideology increasingly gave rise to the consciousness of what it meant to be Colombian. Colombians began to travel along the same path, but perhaps not all in the same way.

NOTES

1. Mariano Ospina Rodríguez, "Los partidos políticos en la Nueva Granada," in Jaime Jaramillo Uribe, *Antología del pensamiento político Colombiano*, vol. 1 (Bogotá: Banco de la República, 1970).

2. *El Aviso*, July 16, 1848.

3. Mariano Ospina Rodríguez and José Eusebio Caro, "Programa Conservador de 1849" in *La Civilización*, October 4, 1848.

4. "Acta de la Independencia," Instituto Colombiano de Cultura, *Revolución de 20 de julio de 1810. Sucesos y documentos* (Bogotá, 1996), 77.

5. "Constitución de 1886," *Biblioteca virtual Miguel de Cervantes*, www.cervantes virtual.com. Accessed June 3, 2011.

6. Corte Constitucional de Colombia, Sentencia no. C-350/94.

Chapter Five

Conflict

Colombia's history has been defined by epic conflicts. In recent years, judging from book titles and articles published in the international press, the words *Colombia* and *conflict* are almost synonymous. This chapter explores the historical dimensions of conflict in Colombia by organizing the discussion of conflict around four key categories: politics, international relations, social structure, and (more recently) illegal narcotics. Some conflicts, of course, fall into more than one category, such as the long period of violence known simply as La Violencia during the late 1940s and 1950s. During the nineteenth century, political conflict was the norm rather than the exception, but Colombia is not unique in a Latin American context; comparing Colombia with Mexico or Argentina during the nineteenth century reveals common patterns of conflict surrounding the difficult task of constructing a nation after three hundred years of Spanish colonial rule. For the twentieth century, historian Michael F. Jiménez points out dramatic social strife in Colombia. Though quasi-social harmony (defined as the relative absence of fighting) existed for about a twenty-five-year period, from 1904 to the end of the 1920s, the Colombian twentieth century has been marred by a complex array of conflicts—conflicts that have spilled over into the twenty-first century and have affected neighboring countries such as Ecuador and Venezuela.

Despite endemic conflict, Colombia has held together as a territorial entity, with the exception of the separation of the Province of Panama, which resulted from a myriad of colliding national and international factors. Colombians have been able to resolve conflicts through creative methods and intermediaries. At least four distinct historic examples help illustrate this. First, the Comuneros rebellion began in Socorro in 1781 and gathered strength as frustrated folk marched to Bogotá to demand an end to the hated tobacco monopoly and increased taxes on tobacco, cane liquor (*aguardiente*), and other products. The folk army, some twenty thousand strong, was stopped at the town of Zipaquirá, about twenty-five miles or a day's walk from the capital. The crowd dispersed, which prevented the sacking of Bogotá, after the archbishop, the Spaniard Antonio Caballero y Góngora, negotiated a settlement with the rebel leadership. The archbishop reneged on the agreement, and the primary leaders of the movement were captured and killed; the principal leader, José Antonio Galán, is viewed as a hero and martyr in Colombia.

Next, in the early twentieth century, President Marco Fidel Suárez pushed for a diplomatic and political realignment with the United States. Diplomatic relations had been frozen with the United States since the 1903 Panama intervention, but Suárez recognized the importance of aligning his nation with the vibrant nation to the north, the "Polar Star"—the United States. Diplomatic efforts led to the final payment of a twenty-five-million-dollar indemnity to Colombia for the arbitrary, aggressive Panama intervention of 1903.

Third, during the late 1950s, the Colombian ruling elite came together to try to end a decade of unrelenting sociopolitical violence. They created the Frente Nacional (National Front), which represented a creative, functional power-sharing arrangement between the two established political parties. The Liberals and Conservatives—rather than kill each other in rural sectors of the nation—agreed to alternate in the presidency for two four-year terms. The unintended consequence of this power-sharing arrangement was that it pushed people who belonged to neither party toward the sociopolitical margins and eventually into armed guerrilla forces.

Finally, by the late twentieth century, Colombians came together to recast their society, via the rewriting of their outdated constitution. The Constitutional Assembly was designed to mediate some of the social tensions that had caused so much mayhem and havoc during the 1970s and 1980s; in 1991, a new Colombian constitution was ratified. It modernized the state by declaring Colombia a multiplural rather than "Hispanic" nation and guaranteed civil rights to all citizens, but it did little to solve the severe economic inequality that has allowed both the guerrilla forces and *narcotraficantes* to remain active.

THE SPANISH EVACUATION

The Latin American wars for independence were epic in scope, territory, and organization. There were at least four "theaters" to the independence processes, resulting in the complete evacuation of Spain from America in the early nineteenth century, leaving a European ruling presence only in the Caribbean, at Puerto Rico and Cuba. In post-independence Colombia, the central problem involved the ever-recurring, anticentralizing tendency of Colombian history, geography, and culture. Regional cliques, shaped by unique cultural standards and independent elite rule, did not immediately turn their attention to the capital city, Bogotá, for leadership or inspiration. Gran Colombia,[1] organized and maintained from 1821 to 1830, was the dream of Simón Bolívar, "the liberator," who concluded that a strong central authority was the only solution for Latin American people. Bolívar was frustrated in his attempt to rule, as dictator, over this group of nations, and one of his final pronouncements expressed his disillusionment: "America is ungovernable," he declared in 1830, shortly before his death. "Those who served the revolution have plowed the sea." Reflecting on more than twenty years of fighting against a centralized, overseas monarchy, people, particularly in Colombia, refused to return to any model that suggested absolute rule.

POLITICAL CONFLICT IN THE NINETEENTH CENTURY

Bolívar's death in December 1830—as noted earlier—at the north coast Colombian city of Santa Marta represented the literal end of the Gran Colombia experiment and the beginning of intense rivalry among factions that dominated Colombian politics and society for the next fifty-five years. An early conflict, the 1839–1842 "War of the Supremes," represented a revolt by people from the southwestern part of the nation, in and around the city of Pasto, who decried the federal government's meddling in local affairs. The uprising, which was suppressed by the central government under Jose Ignacio de Márquez, offers thematic clues to understanding future national conflicts. Regional interests would be pitted against the centralizing tendency at Bogotá; the Roman Catholic Church would fight to protect its power, special ecclesiastic privileges (or *fuero*), properties, and right to exclusive authority over the national education system. Colombia's church-state conflict was not outside the Latin American norm during the nineteenth century: Argentina and Mexico both engaged in armed conflict to determine the boundaries between secular leadership and the rights, duties, obligations, and power of the Roman Catholic Church. In Mexico, the Church essentially went to war against the state over implementation of the Mexican liberals' anticlerical constitution of 1857. The Church (and its Conservative allies) lost the war but continued to fight, going so far as to support an invasion of the country by a European monarchy—the disastrous French intervention of 1862–1866.

Though by 1825 the Spanish monarchy had ceased to rule over the Latin American people, the strong vestiges of Spanish culture and society remained, most notably in the spoken language and the European religious system imposed in the earliest days of the conquest. The Catholic Church, with the demise of the monarchy, supported colonial-style hierarchy, fought against any social and economic change that might threaten its power and prestige, and worried about lax morality and Protestant education. The Church generally adhered to a Conservative sociopolitical agenda. The Liberals who ascended to power at midcentury would make it a point to harass the Church, but the Church would fight back energetically.

General José Hilario López ascended to the presidency of Colombia in 1849 and continued the modernizing policies of General Tomás Cipriano de Mosquera, who exerted significant influence over the third quarter of the nineteenth century in Colombia. López managed to abolish slavery by 1851 but antagonized the Church by expelling the Jesuits in 1850 (the Jesuits were expelled three times from Colombia, something they have not forgotten even to this day) and ending ecclesiastic privilege. Disunity in the Liberal Party resulted in the short civil war of 1854 and ensured that the Conservatives would come to power under the leadership of Mariano Ospina Rodríguez, an elitist law professor who was "committed to the bourgeois values of orderliness, practicality, and hard work."[2] Ospina's government was racked by regional factionalism and demonstrated the difficulty of effectively ruling over the entire Colombian nation from remote Bogotá. Communication was slow, laws from the capital were ignored, and local military and economic elites held de facto power in far-off regions—particularly in the southwest Cauca Valley, where General Mosquera was the primary political and military force. Sensing Ospina's weakness to control the nation at large, Mosquera decided to rebel; civil war (1860–1862) concluded when Mosquera and the Radical Liberals finally took power and wrote a new federalist, anticlerical constitution that prohibited executive re-election after a two-year term.

Colombia should not be singled out among nineteenth-century nations of the Americas as more prone to conflict than others. Mexico went through a midcentury civil war and between 1838 and 1862 suffered at least three outside interventions. As mentioned, the 1858–1861 Mexican civil war, the "War of the Reform," left tens of thousands dead and represented a dramatic loss for the forces of tradition and conservatism. The 1857 anticlerical constitution in Mexico was the spark that led to conflict. In the United States, the Civil War started in 1861 and lasted until 1865, leaving 630,000 dead. That war had less to do with religion and was more focused on the issue of federal versus state sovereignty, the tensions surrounding the economic model for the young nation, and the role of slavery in American society.

General Tomás Cipriano de Mosquera emerged as the undisputed political and military leader during this period in Colombia. A nineteenth-century *caudillo*, Mosquera fit the pattern of the all-powerful leader, but by 1876, new political forces came to dominate Colombia that were more in line with modern party rule. By 1880, the political pendulum had begun to swing away from Liberal anticlerical excesses and toward a more Conservative governing structure for Colombia. This is the year that Rafael Núñez emerged on the national scene, elected president from the north coast city of Cartagena. His election represented an important regional shift away from Mosquera's Cauca Valley power base and an ideological shift that favored traditionalism in politics and social structure. He was re-elected in 1884, and in the following year, Radical Liberals staged a revolt against him, which he used as a pretext to dissolve the constitution of 1863. Núñez's "Regeneration" movement became the political platform that would represent a long period of hegemonic Conservative rule. A new centralizing constitution was written in 1886. This constitution returned power to the central executive and restored the prestige and power of the Roman Catholic Church. Colombia became a Hispanic, Catholic, and centralized nation. The 1886 constitution attempted to correct the decentralized, excessively federalist, anticlerical 1863 constitution, and the Conservatives' ties to the Church inspired them to sign a concordat with the Holy See in 1887. This concordat came to define Colombia's special relationship with the Roman Catholic Church and ensured that Colombia would be a Catholic nation—a reality that would impact Colombian culture, education, and politics for generations.

The political excesses and conflict of the fifty-year period from about 1830 to 1880—marked by confusion, Conservative rule, a Liberal political reaction, the emergence of Mosquera as regional ruler, civil wars, and revolts—all happened within the framework of a written, acknowledged constitution and a concern with elections—though they were hardly universal or representative competitions. This is one of the fascinating ironies that emerges when considering Colombia's nineteenth- and twentieth-century history: violent conflict has tended to occur within the strictures of constitutional procedure and process; and though the political conflict in Colombia during the nineteenth century seems almost interminable, it never reached the level of lurid madness of Mexico under Antonio López de Santa Anna (who ruled from about the mid-1820s through 1855) or the cruel, arbitrary brutality in Argentina under Juan Manuel de Rosas, who ruled from 1829 to 1852. The Colombian nineteenth-century conflict is confusing because it is regionally focused, reflecting the geographic obstacles that define the nation and defy easy unification or political collaboration. These geographic challenges during the tumultuous nineteenth century provided the impetus to resort to regional rule, yet forced Colombians to see the need for some sort of centralizing, unifying set of principles or documents.

The Conservatives' plan of government represented little more than political maneuvering designed to ensure that they would remain in power. Much like the Liberals before them, they ruled to the exclusion of their political adversaries. The extremely doctrinaire, traditional, and ultra-Catholic Miguel Antonio Caro emerged as the de facto leader of the nation after Núñez's death in 1894. Caro's arbitrary, exclusive rule, coupled with the declining price of coffee and an 1895 export tax leveled against the coffee industry, rankled Liberals, and by 1899, their frustrations boiled over in armed conflict. This conflict, the War of a Thousand Days, was a major South American civil war. For one thousand days, war was conducted throughout much of the national territory, which left approximately seventy thousand dead, slowed economic growth, and set back the fortunes of Colombia at the dawn of a new century. This partisan slaughtering, which sputtered to a halt by 1902 and represented real victory for neither Liberals nor Conservatives, established the precedent for a dangerous pattern in twentieth-century politics in Colombia: political exclusion as a catalyst of armed conflict. While other Latin American nations were forging modernity more or less in accordance with established "positivist" principles of the time (political order was equated with material progress, modern science, and technology, which were seen as elements of salvation), Colombia engaged in a costly civil war that altered the pace of modernization.

Thus, compared to other nations of Latin America, Colombia seemed an anachronism at the turn of the century: Mexico, in 1899, was swept up in the Porfirio Díaz dictatorship and modernization plan, Argentina welcomed European immigrants and pushed forward a successful agro-led export economic plan, and the young Brazilian republic was consolidating under the (literal) banner of a new positivist-inspired flag, "*ordem y progreso*" (order and progress). The devastating war in Colombia, by contrast, hurt the internal and export sectors of the economy and left the nation so weak, politically and economically, that the stage was set for some sort of outside intervention. By November 1903, Colombia was engaged in an international conflict with the United States that resulted in the separation, or independence, of the Colombian province of Panama. Though virtually no physical conflict ensued, the 1903 separation was one of the most devastating and humiliating events in Colombia's history as an independent nation and suggested the need for bipartisan compromise in the country, the so-called *convivencia*, which emerged by early 1904 with the rule of Rafael Reyes and lasted for about twenty-five years.

PANAMA SEPARATES

In the spring of 1902, the United States Senate ratified a treaty known as the Hay-Herrán Treaty, named for U.S. Secretary of State John Hay and the Colombian chargé d'affaires in Washington, Tomás Herrán. The treaty allowed for U.S. control of a seven-mile-wide interoceanic strip of territory through the Province of Panama and authorized the United States to construct a canal there; the U.S. military would control and occupy that territory via a lease agreement with the Colombian government for ninety-nine years. The treaty was the final piece of a complex international diplomatic process dating back to 1850 and involving four nations: Great Britain, France, the United States, and Colombia.

The Colombian government at Bogotá hardly represented the aspirations or ideology of the people who lived on the distant north coast, including the Province of Panama. The Bogotá ruling oligarchs were traditionalists, lifelong members of the ruling Conservative elite who looked derisively on the culture, traditions, and political affiliations of the coastal residents, who gravitated toward Liberal Party principles and priorities. Panamanians had never felt fully integrated into the Colombian national ethos. The capital city of Colombia was distant and foreign to most Panamanians; Bogotá was accessible via an arduous, monthlong journey that took the traveler out to sea, up the Magdalena River, and, from Honda, up bumpy mountain roads to the capital. Panamanians paid taxes to the government but received almost nothing from Bogotá in social services (hospitals, schools, roads, and basic infrastructure) that would improve the lives of the people. Thus, in August 1903, when the Colombian Senate unanimously rejected Hay-Herrán and the prospects for construction of a canal fell apart, some Panamanians rebelled—with encouragement from the United States. The United States, in defense of the Panama Railroad Company (in which U.S. investors owned shares) and the uninhibited movement of goods over the isthmus, declared that Colombian troops would not be allowed to land at Colón on the Caribbean coast or Panama City on the Pacific. The separation of Panama, or Panamanian independence, never escalated to actual war between the United States and Colombia, but it represented international conflict between the two nations and resulted in a diplomatic stalemate that would last for more than a decade. Of course, Colombia permanently lost a key coastal province, and politicians at Bogotá began to think of national rather than regional interests once the sobering lessons of this loss began to set in. Also, Colombia's geostrategic significance meant that competing interests would enter into conflict in the earliest days of the twentieth century, a pattern which would repeat itself later as conflict generated by production and transshipment of illegal narcotics took hold.

The separation of Panama marked a profound turning point in contemporary Colombian history. Colombians began to worry about their pattern of oversized conflicts and settled into a period of what has been called "the

New Age of Peace and Coffee."[3] The new Colombian president took office in 1904, shortly after the stinging loss of Panama; Conservative and elitist Rafael Reyes understood the meaning of the term *convivencia* ("living together as one," roughly translated) and sought to strengthen society through inclusion of alternate ideas in his government. Thus, he appointed Liberals to lower-level government positions and helped promote Liberal leadership in the officer corps of the Colombian National Army. Peace ensued for a generation or two, and higher coffee prices helped produce internal social and economic stability during the first decade of the twentieth century.

CONFLICT IN THE TWENTIETH CENTURY

If peace is defined only as the absence of formally declared war, Colombia could be considered "at peace" during the period leading up to 1932, when the nation engaged in a brief war with neighboring Peru. During the period after the First World War, Colombian elites worked to improve infrastructure through investment in costly and, given the realities of Colombian geography, untenable railroad construction. Railroad construction implied "modernity," and the network of railroad lines nearly doubled during the six-year period 1922–1927, with a total of about 2,500 kilometers constructed. Road construction, air transportation, and other signs of modernity coincided with the 1920s coffee export boom. With the conclusion of the First World War, Europeans and Americans expanded their view of coffee as a luxury reserved only for the wealthy. Coffee drinking became the norm for elite and working-class tastes and sensibilities, and a mild roast coffee—the Colombian trademark—was the product preferred by U.S. consumers.

Despite the coffee boom, however, three areas of conflict came to define this period for Colombia, and one in particular resulted in thousands of deaths. Labor, land, and foreign conflict with Peru brought the "New Age of Peace and Coffee" to an end and, domestically, returned political power to the Liberals in the election of 1930, after a forty-five-year period of rule by the Conservative Party. Labor disputes, fueled by European labor theories and the internationalization tendency of the recent Bolshevik revolution in Russia, arrived in Colombia, where labor conditions were trapped in a past that seemed, in some cases, medieval.

One place where a synergy of sorts developed between abusive labor conditions, foreign enclave ownership of land, control of a specific commodity (in this case, bananas), and the dynamics of a port city, privy to foreign ideas and forces, was Santa Marta on the north coast. There, in 1928, thousands of banana workers, fed up with abusive treatment by foreign management, payment in meaningless company scrip, and subhuman living conditions that contrasted so glaringly with the palatial luxury in which the foreign management lived, went out on strike. The ensuing massacre, at the town of Ciénaga, described in the next chapter (and in chapter 10), was frightening in its severity and set an unfortunate paradigm for the remainder of the century: disagreements would be settled through violence—massive violence in this case—rather than through negotiated settlement.

Agitation in the countryside characterized this time period as well: the Great Depression shrank demand from the agricultural sector of the economy, and land consolidation occurred since the price of land remained relatively low at this time. Thus, poor people were pushed off the land by owners of large estates, and the people pressured the government to act on their behalf. These land disputes grew intense, particularly in the early 1930s, when poor people, confined to generations of grinding poverty in the countryside, expected reform out of a new government that promised to rule on behalf of all Colombians, not just the powerful and well connected. There would be no Bolshevik-style reform in Colombia, as pragmatism, elitism, and hierarchy still defined, to some degree, the character and tone of the Liberal republic. Marco Palacios puts it best by noting how, "On the whole, the Liberal republic left the social structure of the Colombian countryside more or less intact."[4]

A major conflict involving a Latin American neighbor developed in 1932: the war with Peru, or the "Leticia Affair." In September of that year, Peruvian forces occupied the Colombian Amazon city of Leticia, resulting in a wave of national indignation and jingoistic, patriotic fervor the likes of which had not been seen even after the 1903 separation of Panama. Colombia moved armed forces to Leticia by boats and planes to take back what was rightfully its territory, according to a 1922 treaty between the two nations. The war was brief; Colombians are generally credited with having won the war, and Leticia remains, to this day, part of Colombia's national territory, its window on the Amazon. The war represented a needed boost for the armed forces and national leadership which, by 1932, had not yet recovered from the humiliation and mistrust resulting from the banana workers' strike at Ciénaga four years earlier.

Latin America responded to the political, social, and economic crises of the 1930s by turning to "populist" leaders—charismatic men and, in the case of Eva Perón of Argentina, a woman—who helped open up some space between entrenched economic elites and the poor, many of whom made their way to the major cities from the countryside looking for work and opportunity. The populists challenged elites to invest in better housing and city sanitation for the poor, to allow workers to unionize, and to offer basic financing for evening classes and other opportunities whereby the poor could improve their position in society. The populists were pragmatic operators and rhetorically gifted, intent on maintaining social control while advancing their own political agendas.

Colombia's populist leader was a young, charismatic Bogotá lawyer from the lower classes named Jorge Eliécer Gaitán. Gaitán studied law in Italy and was influenced by the rhetorical prowess of the fascist dictator Benito Mussolini. Gaitán identified with the working poor—his humble origins from a decidedly lower-middle-class, center-city neighborhood helped him connect with the people. He held a number of important political posts, including member of the Bogotá city council, minister of education and labor, and mayor of Bogotá. He ran for president in 1946 and won important cities, such as the capital and the coastal city of Barranquilla, but never enjoyed the support of the official Liberal establishment, which ran its own candidate that year, Gabriel Turbay, splitting the Liberal Party, handing the presidency to the Conservative candidate, Mariano Ospina Pérez, and breaking a sixteen-year period of Liberal political rule.

Gaitán was the favored candidate for the presidency in 1950, but he was murdered in the center of Bogotá on April 9, 1948, a day that changed the history of the nation, much as the assassination of President Kennedy in 1963 changed U.S. society. The marginalized working class, people who felt that government, laws, and society were stacked against them, were stunned when their hope for a better future—mystically tied to a Gaitán presidency—evaporated with four shots of a revolver. The ensuing riot, known in Colombia as the "nueve de abril" and outside of Colombia as "the Bogotazo," left vast segments of downtown Bogotá looted and smoldering; the trolley car system was badly damaged, churches and ecclesiastic archives were burned, and businesses—especially those that seemed to sympathize with the Conservative political agenda—were ransacked.

Of the major Latin American populist leaders of the era, including Lázaro Cárdenas of Mexico, the Peróns of Argentina, Getúlio Vargas in Brazil,[5] and Víctor Raúl Haya de la Torre in Peru, Gaitán is the only one to have died by assassination. Thus, the populist program ended abruptly, dramatically, and violently in Colombia, on April 9, 1948, and the urban chaos that followed in the capital and other cities throughout the nation reflected a sense that something monstrous had happened, engineered (allegedly) by the wealthy and Conservative establishment, to prevent the people from ever having a real voice in politics or society.

Urban political violence on April 9 intersected with rural political violence that had escalated after the 1946 election, when the return to national Conservative rule implied a return to the past—the days of Conservative hegemony of the nineteenth century. But political Liberals, having tasted power for sixteen years, were unwilling to return to a position of subordinate citizenry. The feckless, insulated Ospina regime, highly offended by the riots and looting in Bogotá, could hardly be counted on to provide national leadership at this time. And, with Gaitán gone, a creeping sense of disorder took hold and spread, growing gradually out of control. La Violencia, or "the violence," came to define the period from about 1946 to 1960 in Colombia. Some historians, including Catherine LeGrand, Michael Jiménez, Herbert "Tico" Braun, and Álvaro Tirado Mejía, argue convincingly that the violence dates back to the 1930s, originating from the onset of agrarian conflicts and pressures on the countryside. Those pressures, instituted largely by policies that favored large-scale producers in the agrarian sector, coincided with Liberal party political ascent and resulted in the consolidation of landholding patterns and dislocation of poor agricultural workers. Weak central political leadership could not prevent social and political conflicts in regions that lay largely outside of the literal domain of the ruling political class at Bogotá.

It is impossible to date the origins of "the violence," but it is safe to say that Liberal-Conservative tensions, the root cause of the violence, had been boiling over since the 1930s. The return to Conservative rule in 1946 frustrated poor people, who felt they had been tricked, and the assassination of the most charismatic, engaged, and determined political leader of the era, Gaitán, led to an undisciplined era of outsized violence throughout the nation. Finally, the violence wound down by the late 1950s, thanks in large measure to a political program—an elite power-sharing arrangement called the National Front.

LA VIOLENCIA

In a country of regions, a nation that geographically defies unification, La Violencia was a phenomenon that clearly demonstrated the weakness of the Colombian state. The Colombian government, for all intents and purposes, was confined to the Plaza de Bolívar, the main square in Bogotá, and other main plazas at regional capital cities. People in the countryside had no incentive to obey arbitrary laws, radiating out from a distant capital and written by politicians who never understood rural life in Colombia. When the Liberal Party decided not to run a candidate in the 1950 election, politics became something other than electoral contests and governance: for Liberals who held no stake in the official political apparatus, violence seemed to be the only means for political participation. Thus vengeance killings, cattle theft, and long-standing familial and territorial disputes came to define reality for vast segments of Andean, rural Colombia, and the distant Colombian government was both unwilling and unable to stop any of this. Perhaps as many as 80 percent of the victims of the violence, roughly a quarter of a million people killed during a fourteen-year period (1946–1960), were young, male, and poor. The violence demonstrated a severe disconnect between urban and rural Colombians and between the wealthy and the poor, highlighting the dangers of demonization of political adversaries. Myopic, anemic leadership at Bogotá made people in the rural areas realize that the government could not respond and would not respond, so poor people took political matters into their own hands in the manner that was most functional to them. They destroyed their enemies, their neighbors, through visceral, brutal violence, and it took years for the nation's decision makers to take note and to develop a plan of action to stop or at least diminish the violence. That plan—a creative, collaborative effort called the National Front—was organized by elites in the capital city and offered some political breathing room for both parties. The National Front was the political agreement whereby the two traditional political parties, Conservatives and Liberals, would rotate in and out of the presidency every four years through competitive elections, though the competition would be interparty. This arrangement grew out of Colombia's unique nineteenth- and twentieth-century political history—discussed earlier—whereby one party would rule to the complete exclusion of the other party, offering little more to the party out of power than a challenge to mobilize for violence. There is little doubt that the National Front succeeded in dampening down rural violence, but hostility, anger, and revenge killings in the countryside did not end overnight because of an elite political agreement at Bogotá. Gradually, as in other Colombian conflicts, the violence grew counterproductive, as a developmentalist model took hold and work began (with millions of dollars in funding from the United States) to rebuild the battered nation.

Another often-overlooked factor that contributed to a Colombian quasi-consensus against the violence was a book, published in two volumes in 1962. Three Colombians, the jurist Eduardo Umaña Luna of the National University at Bogotá, a prelate, Monsignor Germán Guzmán Campos, and a young intellectual, a sociologist who earned a doctorate at the University of Florida, Orlando Fals Borda, authored *La violencia en Colombia: Estudio de un Proceso social.*[6] The book painted a clear, unsentimental account of the years of violence, based largely on fieldwork, interviews, and graphic photographs. The published work shocked the literati in Bogotá and throughout the cities; people in Colombia knew that violence occurred in rural areas of the nation, but the wealthy and well connected—most of whom could protect themselves from such phenomena—read this dispassionate report as one that seemed to come from a distant land. The book clashed with their concept of modernity and national development. *La violencia en Colombia* was published, it should be noted, just months after U.S. president John F. Kennedy visited Colombia as a way to show solidarity with the nation's political and economic elite. Kennedy allocated millions of dollars to Colombia—a nation he viewed as a model of democracy and gradualist development—for his signature development program in Latin America, the Alliance for Progress. He also, ironically, promoted the U.S. Peace Corps while in Colombia. Colombia would serve as the first nation in the Western Hemisphere to welcome the arrival of sixty-one Peace Corps volunteers in the fall of 1961.

The first paragraph of *La violencia en Colombia* expresses the lack of clarity that certainly existed in the early 1960s and, to a certain degree, characterizes contemporary Colombia. The authors wrote, "Much has been written about the violence, but there is really no agreement as to what it means."[7] The book established "violence" as a legitimate area of academic research—the researchers were referred to as *violontologos* or (roughly translated) "those who study the violence." For many years, during the 1960s up until quite recently, political and social violence seemed to be the major concern and focus of the academic community, especially scholars living outside Colombia, including American Robert Dix, American-born Paul Oquist, and French sociologist Daniel Pécaut, to name a few.

The creative solution to "the violence"—the emergence of the National Front—led to a new and unforeseen substructure of violence in the form of leftist guerrilla insurgencies throughout the country. Colombians who wanted nothing to do with traditional Conservative or Liberal Party platforms were dismayed by the narrowness of the elite bipartisan agreement. How would the politically unaligned or disenchanted engage politically after the 1958 implementation of the National Front? Part of the answer came in the form of a revolution on the not-so-distant island of Cuba, months after implementation of the National Front. The Cuban Revolution of January 1959 provided enormous energy for the disenchanted, those who questioned traditional politics, political alignments, and economics in the Americas. The accommodating nature of the National Front represented, by January 1959, an opportunity for organization outside of the traditional party alliance in Colombia and gave birth, in effect, to the modern leftist armed insurgencies in Colombia, at least two of which—the FARC and ELN—are still operational in the country, though certainly their objectives and philosophy have mutated during their difficult, nearly half-century existence.

INSURGENCY INTERVENTION

The ELN (National Liberation Army) burst onto the scene in Colombia in the department of Santander in the early 1960s. Disaffected university students, some of whom had traveled to Fidel Castro's Cuba in 1962, were the foundation of this group, which sought to imitate in Colombia Castro's path to power. The students neglected the specific historical and cultural dissimilarities between Cuba and Colombia and chose to focus on theory, most of which had been drawn up in Europe. The most famous recruit for the ELN was a dashing, bourgeois, Bogotá-based Roman Catholic priest, Father Camilo Torres Restrepo. Father Torres joined the ELN forces in October 1965 and was—foolishly—sent to the front lines. He died in combat in February 1966, and most Colombians consider his entrance into the forces an example of youthful naiveté and a national tragedy. Father Torres had a wide following, especially among the urban sectors, university students, and those who believed that historical political and economic inertia in Colombia prevented any type of social mobility for the poor.

In 1964 the FARC (the Revolutionary Armed Forces of Colombia) formed; less cerebral or theoretical than the ELN, the FARC continues to challenge the Colombian state even today. It can be seen as a rural-based agrarian movement that came into being out of frustration with the failed agrarian struggles of the 1930s and 1940s, struggles that elicited little more than repression from the Colombian state. The FARC, which might have numbered fifteen to twenty thousand armed fighters in the early 1990s, has diminished in size and significance. Its founding director, Pedro Antonio Martín Marín (nom de guerre, Manuel Marulanda; nickname, "Tirofijo" [Sure-shot]) died of natural causes in March 2008, never having been captured by Colombian authorities. His death reminded people of an inconvenient reality: the Colombian state does not really control the entire Colombian territory. Tirofijo's death hurt the organization's morale, as evidenced by hundreds of deserters—many of whom had entered the guerrilla forces as teenagers. Leadership passed to Alfonso Cano, but a persistent campaign against the FARC by the Colombian armed forces, a campaign financed largely with U.S. dollars, has continued to disable the group, as evidenced by the September 2010 killing of the FARC's top military commander, "Mono Jojoy" (né Víctor Julio Suárez Rojas; nom de guerre, Jorge Briceño Suárez) about 120 miles outside of the capital city. Cano (né Guillermo León Sáenz Vargas) was killed by Colombian military forces in early October 2011. Today, the FARC operates with perhaps six thousand to eight thousand armed fighters, and over the past twenty years has used kidnapping, extortion, and protection of the illegal narcotics industry as a means to finance its operations. The vast majority of Colombians view the FARC negatively.

After a period of severe state-supported repression in the late 1970s, during the administration of Julio César Turbay—characterized by extrajudicial killings, illegal imprisonment, and a "state-of-siege" mentality and reality—the Betancur administration in 1982 offered a more conciliatory approach. Belisario Betancur is remembered fondly as a leader who offered a peace plan and amnesty to the various insurgencies that competed for power and attention in Colombia during this time period. The peace initiative came to a halt at the end of 1985 when the urban guerrilla group M-19 stormed the Palacio de Justicia—the Colombian Supreme Court building.

The M-19 emerged in opposition to the presidential election of 1970, when Conservative Party leader Misael Pastrana won narrowly over Gustavo Rojas Pinilla, who ran as the ANAPO—Alianza Nacional Popular—candidate, representing the interests of students and workers. Many in the country viewed this presidential election as flawed and fraudulent, and the M-19 took to the streets with dramatic folkloric flare as an "urban guerrilla" organization. Its members stole arms from a military installation and even managed to capture the sword of "the Liberator," Simón Bolívar; in 1980, they overtook the Dominican embassy in Bogotá and held diplomats hostage. Their most daring act, and the beginning of their undoing, occurred in November 1985 when they stormed the Palace of Justice and held the Colombian Supreme Court hostage. They intended to hold a "show trial" of the Betancur administration, but military hardliners, meeting in the Presidential Palace across the Plaza de Bolívar where the drama unfolded, found nothing humorous in the humiliating tactics of the M-19. The military stormed the palace, battering down the front door with a lightweight Brazilian tank, and the siege ended with the deaths of all but one of the M-19 insurgents, eleven members of the Supreme Court, and dozens of others; the siege left about one hundred dead. Some people, about a dozen, seen leaving the palace under military escort, simply "disappeared." This tragedy is a benchmark in modern Colombian history and represents the beginning of yet another tragic phase in the context of the contemporary Colombian conflict.

Betancur's optimism and hope for a peace settlement crashed in November 1985, and the same year as the Palace of Justice tragedy, the FARC—reacting to the Betancur amnesty—formed a political party made up of demobilized fighters known as the "Unión Patriótica." This party made impressive gains in local elections in 1986, but over the next four years, into the early 1990s, the leadership of the UP was systematically eliminated by a number of webs of mysterious forces that included the military, hired murderers/paramilitary forces, members of rival leftist organizations, and, increasingly, powerful drug cartels. The violence against the UP diminished the prospects of a negotiated settlement to the conflict and has spawned a general sense of distrust between the government and those who have challenged the government's political authority through the use of force.

NARCO-VIOLENCE

As the leadership of the UP was systematically eliminated—some 3,500 people killed by 1992, with an alarmingly low level of arrests or prosecution—the message from Bogotá was that extrajudicial killings of subversives, former or otherwise, would be tacitly ignored. Such an environment helps explain the dramatic growth of drug traffickers, so-called *narcotraficantes*, during the 1980s, when cocaine production, shipment, and financing became the principal domain of a group of audacious and savvy businesspeople based in three principal cities: Bogotá, Cali, and Medellín. The most notorious, Pablo Escobar, born in 1949 in Rionegro, Antioquia, began his career as a low-level thief—making money by stealing gravestones, grinding away the inscriptions, and reselling them (at a discount rate) to unsuspecting families of the more recently departed. Escobar was elected in 1982 as an "alternate" member of Congress (from Medellín) as his fortunes grew through the illegal production and shipment of narcotics, mostly cocaine, to U.S. and European markets. Colombia, for reasons both geographic and political, became the epicenter of the exportation of drugs from South America. Its status as the only nation in South America that fronts two oceans helped; its mountainous valleys provided geographic cover for clandestine laboratories and the coca leaf thrived at the midaltitude regions of Colombia (and in Peru, Bolivia, and other nations of the Andes). Politically, the decentralized, regional power structure, accompanied by a historically weak central government, allowed people like Escobar to command and control a vast network of land, labor, funds, and politicians.

By 1984, the power and wealth of Escobar's Medellín cartel had become both notorious and obnoxious—Escobar had a zoo built at one of his palatial *fincas* in the Antioquian countryside and ordered the Colombian government not to interfere with his business. When the young, ambitious Colombian minister of justice, Rodrigo Lara Bonilla, decided to prosecute money laundering and shut down some of Escobar's illicit laboratories, he was assassinated in 1984 on orders from Escobar. Lara's death sparked a ten-year war that pitted an often reluctant, sometimes outgunned Colombian government against well-financed, outlandish drug lords who took advantage of poverty and historic social inequality to form cadres of hired killers, known as *sicarios*, to do their dirty work. These teenagers, mostly from the Medellín slums, would accept the equivalent of about one hundred dollars to assassinate people, including police officers and politicians. The war intensified from 1989 to 1990, a period that historian Marco Palacios refers to as "the free fire zone."[8] In August 1989, Luis Carlos Galán, while campaigning for the presidency in Soacha, just outside of Bogotá, was gunned down on orders, most likely, from Escobar. Galán, the presumed successor to President Virgilio Barco, had promised to use the power of the state to dismantle the drug cartels, and his murder represented a gloomy descent into violence and despair; four candidates campaigning for the 1990 presidency, including Galán, were murdered. A terrible counteroffensive began.

Car bombings, kidnappings, and assassinations became part of daily life in Colombia until December 1993, when Escobar was finally captured and killed by an elite military unit in Medellín. With the death of Escobar, the Colombian police and military turned their focus to the Orejuela brothers, who controlled the Cali cartel. By the mid-1990s, the cartel system of systematic and complete control of all aspects of the narcotics business had been replaced by smaller, more dispersed, less visible, and less outwardly aggressive *cartelitos*. Drug production and shipment out of Colombia continued, protected by extralegal paramilitary and guerrilla forces, but the struggle between entrenched cartels and the state seemed to have ended, though certainly not in a peaceful or harmonious way.

At the same time the Colombian state was engaging the drug cartels and the leftist insurgencies, a relatively new actor emerged in the early 1980s. This was the AUC (the United Self-Defense Forces of Colombia), or paramilitary fighters. The stories of the AUC's formation are multiple and hazy. One account, as told by the Mexican journalist Alma Guillermoprieto, describes a feud among friends that essentially grew out of context and control. She notes that FARC fighters kidnapped "the father of a small-time drug and emerald dealer called Fidel Castaño."[9] Fidel and his brother Carlos would organize a formidable, highly disciplined fighting force to avenge the death of their father, who died while in FARC captivity. The AUC grew to as many as thirty thousand fighters at the apex of its power in the mid- to late 1990s, and its mere presence and the ghastly, gruesome massacres it orchestrated caused reasonable people to question who, in fact, was in charge in Colombia. Tens of thousands were killed in a new phase of conflict wherein the paramilitary forces moved in to take territory left behind by a retreating FARC and ELN and a shifting, lower-profile drug production process. By the late 1990s, the FARC and ELN were fighting the military, the AUC were fighting the leftist guerrillas, the military was supposedly fighting the AUC, the FARC, and the ELN, and the drug barons were fighting the government while simultaneously fighting and collaborating with the guerrilla forces. It was a confusing time in Colombia, and in the confusion and chaos, as the body count grew, the country seemed to be spiraling out of control.

PLAN COLOMBIA, 2000

Andrés Pastrana Arango, former mayor of Bogotá and son of President Misael Pastrana (who ruled from 1970 to 1974), took control of Colombia in

1998 as international attention focused on the nation and its ever more complex and seemingly impenetrable structure of conflict. Colombia was becoming somewhat of an anomaly in the region; peace accords had been signed in El Salvador in 1993 and in Guatemala in 1996. President Alberto Fujimori in Peru declared victory over the "Shining Path" insurgents with the capture of their leader, Abimael Guzmán, in October 1992. Yet in Colombia, the actors involved in the various conflicts seemed more entrenched than ever, and the state seemed no longer to hold the upper hand. This perception was reinforced by a new "peace plan" orchestrated by the Pastrana administration. Pastrana authorized a "safe zone," or *zona de despeje*, in the southeast of the country, more specifically at San Vicente del Caguán, a place where the military would no longer operate, as a sign of goodwill toward the FARC commanders. This gesture was intended to show the government's resolve to negotiate in the *campo* on terms familiar to the FARC fighters, many of whom had never seen the capital city of Bogotá. But the FARC, never particularly savvy political operators, used the 42,000 square kilometer—Switzerland-sized—*zona* to warehouse weapons and their kidnapped victims; they loaded in cases of liquor and cartons of contraband cigarettes. Widespread reports of relaxing leftist insurgents living rent free on the government's dime infuriated the urban elites and working-class citizens alike; Pastrana's popularity plummeted.

The peace process—the occupation of a Switzerland-sized territory in the middle of Colombia—alarmed the United States, and President Pastrana, while ostensibly planning for peace, successfully lobbied U.S. president Bill Clinton for an enormous aid package, worth 1.35 billion dollars of mostly military aid. This aid package, known as "Plan Colombia," was hurriedly debated in a U.S. Congress that never fully understood the complexities of Colombia but came to view it as a Western society spinning out of control. Pastrana prudently pressured and lectured Clinton and Washington power brokers on the importance of "saving" Colombia from itself. Plan Colombia was approved in the final days of the Clinton administration, and at that time, "Plan Colombia" turned Colombia into the third-leading recipient of U.S. foreign aid, after Israel and Egypt.

Toward the end of Pastrana's term of office, with no serious peace prospects in sight, the president ordered the military to move into the demilitarized zone and retake the territory. This occurred on February 20, 2002, and represented a defeat for everyone, but especially for President Pastrana, who seemed to have been outmaneuvered by the FARC commanders. This failed peace initiative paved the way for an outside candidate, the former governor of Antioquia and a vowed hard-liner against the left, to win the Colombian presidency in May 2002. Álvaro Uribe Vélez, whose campaign pledge was "mano dura, corazón grande" (a strong hand, with a big heart), an Oxford-trained technocrat with an unassuming political style and presence, became president in August 2002 and immediately went on the offensive. His decision might have been influenced by a FARC-organized rocket attack on the presidential palace in Bogotá, televised nationally on August 7, 2002, during his inaugural celebration. Neither the new president nor any of the dignitaries was injured, but wayward rockets did kill fifteen people and injured fifty, most of whom lived in a *casa de consumo*—"drug rehabilitation house"—in a seedy, notorious downtown neighborhood called "El Cartucho," which has since been bulldozed and turned into a public park.

President Uribe, utilizing the funds from Plan Colombia (which total, as of this writing, about eight billion U.S. dollars over the first decade of this century), made headway against the FARC, pushing the fighters into the country's corners, but the FARC remains operational, even after Uribe's two terms as president. Even so, President Uribe clearly won the public relations war. He presented himself as an indefatigable patriot who would stop at nothing to defeat the FARC and other insurgents. He refused to refer to the FARC or the ELN as "political" actors, instead adopting the lexicon that became most fashionable after 9/11: he called them, simply, terrorists. His redefinition campaign was facilitated by Washington, which put three Colombian organizations on its terrorist list: the FARC, the AUC paramilitary forces, and the ELN.

Uribe's determination to derail the FARC led to a Colombian armed incursion into neighboring Ecuador, where FARC forces were encamped, including the number-two commander, Raúl Reyes, who was killed in the March 2008 attack. Prior to the attack, the FARC lost (as noted above) its founding leader, Manuel Marulanda, and Iván Ríos, another member of the ruling secretariat. Though Uribe pronounced Marulanda's death as a sign of success for his policies, others noted that the guerrilla leader had never been captured and had, in fact, eluded Colombian military forces for forty-four years.

The 2008 cross-border attack nearly led to war between Ecuador, Colombia, and Venezuela. Leftist Venezuelan president Hugo Chávez ordered troops to the Colombian border in an apparent show of solidarity with leftist president Rafael Correa of Ecuador. Cooler heads prevailed, and a regional war was avoided, but tensions in the region remained heightened until a new Colombian president, Juan Manuel Santos (August 2010–), re-established normal diplomatic relations with both Andean neighbors. This is discussed in more detail in chapter 10.

The Colombian paramilitary forces continue to wreak havoc over the Colombian land. Though technically demobilized, they have since become criminal bands with de facto power in many places throughout the country. Their campaign against leftist insurgents, *campesinos*, and unionists has been truly terrifying. Union leaders, human rights activists, and those who call for just wages, better working conditions, or land reform for the poor have faced the terror of self-sufficient, unregulated, for-profit hired killers.

Searching for some sort of solution to this situation, the government initiated a discussion and approved, through Congress, "Ley 975" of 2005, which is now known as the "Law of Justice and Peace." The objective of this law was to allow all extra-official combatants—guerrilla and paramilitary forces—the opportunity to voluntarily demobilize in exchange for freedom from prosecution and sentencing. The law sought to facilitate the reinsertion of armed actors into society provided these individuals turned in their weapons, confessed to the crimes they committed, and promised never again to join an armed group outside of the official military forces of the nation.

The Justice and Peace Law put into practice alternative sentencing, based on the idea that in order to advance national peace, and in collaboration with justice and reparations to victims, it is not always necessary to apply the maximum sentence to guerrilla or paramilitary fighters. Thus, Colombians created the National Commission of Reparations and Reconciliation, an institution charged with carrying out the new law as applied to the *insertados* (guerrilla or paramilitary fighters who had, in fact, turned themselves in) while protecting the rights of the victims by determining the truth and seeking both justice and compensation for physical and material suffering and loss. Additionally, a "Commission for Historic Memory" was created and has been successful in developing detailed reports regarding some of the most terrible actions committed against the civilian population. These documents are all the more significant given that they have been diffused and discussed in Colombia during a time of open warfare. Today, in Bogotá, Colombians are building a museum and archive dedicated to preventing Colombian society from forgetting the violent decades that have marked the recent past.

Conflict has been endemic in Colombia since the earliest days of the republic's founding. It has resulted from geographic factors which, in isolating large segments of the country, created strong regional identities and culture. Political factors paired with the historical weakness of the central government and the immense power of the Church and oligarchy contributed to tension in the nineteenth century that would spill over into armed conflict at various periods in Colombia's history. Outside meddling by the United States in the early twentieth century and disagreements with neighboring countries generated conflict, but most of the conflict in Colombia has been produced internally; vacillating leadership, inadequate prosecutorial customs, a tepid press, distant, diffident political officials, and outright fear have allowed murderers to kill with impunity in contemporary Colombia. But conflict does not define the Colombian nation or its people. The resilience of the Colombian nation, a nation that has endured so much conflict, is evidenced in a difficult-to-quantify "Colombian style," which is informal, warm, accepting, and refreshingly suspicious of those who take too much for granted. Colombians have learned to live with great ambiguity and uncertainty. Conflict is part of everyday life, but so too is warmth, generosity, and a spirit of collaboration. Most Colombians try to transcend the daily political and social conflict by spending as much time as possible with family, friends, and visitors—a style of endurance influenced by Colombia's unique historical and cultural development.

NOTES

1. Gran Colombia is a nickname for the time period when Colombia comprised Ecuador, Colombia, Venezuela, and Panama, 1821–1830.

2. David Bushnell, *The Making of Modern Colombia: A Nation in Spite of Itself* (Berkeley: University of California Press, 1993), 118.

3. See chapter 7 of Bushnell, "The New Age of Peace and Coffee (1904–1930)."

4. Marco Palacios, *Between Legitimacy and Violence: A History of Colombia, 1875–2002* (Durham: Duke University Press, 2006), 107.

5. Tragedy characterized the demise of several Latin American populists; Getúlio Vargas committed suicide in his bedroom in the Presidential Palace in 1954, and the much beloved Eva Perón died of cancer at thirty-three years of age in 1952.

6. Germán Guzmán, Orlando Fals Borda, and Eduardo Umaña Luna, *La violencia en Colombia: Estudio de un Proceso Social* (Bogotá: Tercer Mundo Editores, 1962).

7. Ibid., 23.

8. Palacios, 213.

9. Alma Guillermoprieto, *Looking for History: Dispatches from Latin America* (New York: Vintage, 2001), 31.

PHOTO ESSAY

The sixteen photos in this section are from two sources: Collection Germán Mejía (CGM), all taken by Germán Mejía, and the Biblioteca Pública Piloto de Medellín/Archivo Fotográfico (BPP), taken by various persons, as noted below.

1. Palenque de San Basilio
Source: CGM, 2010
Place: Near Cartagena, Colombia

The Palenque de San Basilio is a community of about three thousand persons living on the outskirts of Cartagena, Colombia. *Palenque* is the Spanish term for "runaway slave community," and this particular community dates back to the sixteenth century. The people living in this community have created a unique culture and, though they speak Spanish, they also preserve a language that combines a variety of African languages. The Palenque of San Basilio is recognized as a unique ethnic community by the Colombian constitution of 1991. This photo demonstrates the Afro-Colombian presence on the Colombian coasts, and although the culture is strong, this group has not shared in the wealth generated by the modern Colombian economy.

2. Bogotá from La Candelaria
Source: CGM, 2010
Place: Bogotá, Colombia

The city of Bogotá as viewed from the historic segment of the city, "the Candelaria." The architecture seen in this photo is a mixture of eighteenth-, nineteenth-, and twentieth-century structures. There are no structures from the sixteenth century in Bogotá and very few from the seventeenth. The center of Bogotá is dynamic and fluid; it functions as the center of government, culture, and university life. There are several important universities in the city center, including the Universidad de los Andes and the Universidad Externado. The Candelaria has been, since the 1960s, a protected historic zone, which means the government regulates all architectural modifications and construction in the neighborhood.

3. El Carmen—plaza
Source: CGM, 2009
Place: El Carmen, Norte de Santander

This town dates from the late seventeenth century. El Carmen is a typical town in Colombia that serves as interlocutor between the people who live in the countryside and the larger cities. This town plaza is the center of power in the locale; the notary, mayor's office, bank, and—most prominently—the Catholic Church are all present in the town center. During the twentieth century, parks such as the one seen here were constructed in town centers and named "Jardines de la República" (Republic Gardens); normally a statue of a Colombian patriotic hero would be prominently featured in the square.

4. Galán
Source: CGM, 2009
Place: Charalá, Santander

José Antonio Galán, a captain and leader of the Comuneros rebellion in 1781, is heroically depicted in this statue, which occupies a central location on the main plaza of Charalá, the hometown of the hero. Galán, depicted shirtless and muscular, reminds people of the struggles of the past against foreign domination, in this case, the Spaniards. The Spaniards negotiated with the advancing Comunero army—which sought a relaxation on taxes and end to the hated tobacco monopoly—but reneged on the agreement. Galán continued the rebellion, was captured by Spanish forces, and was drawn and quartered publicly.

5. Midterm elections, 1961
Source: BPP, Horacio Gil Ochoa, 1961
Place: Medellín, Colombia

Midterm elections in Medellín while the Liberals hold onto national political power. Carlos Lleras Restrepo was the head of the Liberal Party, and his cousin, Alberto Lleras Camargo, had been elected president of the republic in 1958. This is the period when the "Frente Nacional" is in effect; the photo suggests a folkloric electoral process, complete with musicians; the National Front alleviated political and social tensions to some degree, by alternating political power every four years between the two major parties, Liberal and Conservative. The electoral workers take their task seriously, as suggested by the woman examining the *cédula*—the official government-issued identification document—of the voter.

6. Pope Paul VI arrives in Colombia
Source: BPP, Alberto Palacio Roldán, 1968
Place: Bogotá's El Dorado International Airport

Pope Paul VI arrived in Bogotá, Colombia, in August 1968—the first visit by a pontiff to Latin America. The pope's arrival coincided with the closing of the 39th International Eucharistic Congress, held in Bogotá; the congress was designed to foment spirituality and prayer on the continent as a counterforce to advancing secularism and revolutionary activity in Latin America. Rome viewed Colombia as an integral ally in the defense of the Catholic faith, dating back to the 1887 concordat, a treaty between the Holy See and the Colombian state. Pope Paul also provided encouragement to the Latin American bishops meeting in Medellín. That meeting, in late August 1968, is seen as the organizational event from which a Latin American liberation theology would emerge.

7. Gaitán with family
Source: BPP, Francisco Mejía, n.d.
Place: Colombia

   Dating from the early 1940s, this photograph shows Jorge Eliécer Gaitán as "family man"; he is photographed with his daughter Gloria and wife, Amparo Jaramillo de Gaitán. This photomontage (the photo of the family is superimposed onto a background photo) is designed to show the liberal leader as both family man and man of the people. *El pueblo*—the people—literally surround Gaitán and family. The leader's expression of humility and calm contrasts with the way he is generally depicted: as a fiery populist politician, delivering speeches in crowded city plazas.

8. Missing bust at El Carmen
Source: CGM, 2009
Place: El Carmen, Norte de Santander

   The bust of Jorge Eliécer Gaitán in El Carmen was destroyed in 1949, and this monument reminds visitors of the violence in the region during the 1940s. El Carmen, a Liberal town, was attacked on November 16, 1949, by a Conservative armed police force, resulting in about fifty deaths. One of the casualties of this day was the bust of the Liberal leader Gaitán, whose murder one year earlier in 1948 set off urban and rural violence. The inscription reads, "Here, the bust of the Colombian leader Jorge Eliécer Gaitán Ayala was destroyed by a violent horde."

ACUI
SE LEVANTÓ EL BUSTO
DEL CAUDILLO COLOMBIANO
JORGE ELIECER GAITAN AYALA
DESTRUIDO
POR HORDAS DE VIOLENCIA

COMITE TRICENTENARIO EN CUCUTA

JUAN A. CACERES A.   SANTANDER PINZON C.
JESUS GUTIERREZ F.   HUGO CASTRO LOBO

JULIO 16 1986

9. Quibdó, Chocó
Source: CGM, 2010
Place: Quibdó, Chocó

   This photo, shot from the Atrato River toward the city of Quibdó, reflects the precarious condition in which many people live in this region of Colombia. Quibdó is the capital city of the west coast department, Chocó; this region is rich in mineral resources and straddles a region of indigenous and Afro-Colombian peoples. Quibdó is a city mired in poverty, and little progress has been made at bringing social development to this region of Colombia. The housing on stilts is designed to resist the fickle waters of the Atrato.

10. Chapolera
Source: BPP, Gabriel Pérez Carvajal, n.d.
Place: Coffee region of Colombia

   Chapoleras (from the Spanish verb *chapolear*—"to flit from flower to flower")—are Colombian migrant workers who move from place to place cultivating agricultural products. They were mostly associated with the coffee harvest, as seen here. Chapoleras were hired during harvest time in the coffee region, and they travelled in family units; landowners generally preferred women coffee pickers—women were viewed, in general, as a less troublesome labor force and as more able than men to carry out the delicate work of picking coffee beans. This photo is probably from the 1950s and was most likely taken in the Colombian coffee-growing region.

11. Fishermen
Source: CGM, 2005
Place: Cartagena, Colombia

This photograph, shot at Cartagena's popular beach known as "La Boquilla," shows fishermen in a human-powered *lancha* (raft or canoe) leaving to fish using traditional equipment. This photo captures the struggles of hard-working fishermen and conveys an active determination and willingness to work and venture against seemingly insurmountable odds.

12. Camino Real
Source: CGM, 2009
Place: Guaduas, Cundinamarca

This photograph of a segment of a Colombian *camino real*, or "royal road," is a beautiful example of the road system envisioned and constructed by the Spaniards throughout the Americas. This road, probably dating from the seventeenth century, was designed to facilitate communications between towns in the far-flung empire. Royal roads where built wherever there was a Spanish presence; thus they can be found in Argentina and even in what is today California in the United States. Spanish road builders were likely influenced by the legacy of Roman road builders given Rome's extension into the Iberian Peninsula and their rule there for about six hundred years.

13. Magdalena River and Girardot
Source: CGM, 2004
Place: Flandes, Tolima

This view of the Magdalena River and the town of Girardot is taken from Flandes, on the other side of the river. The Magdalena is the central artery of Colombia, and in the period prior to aviation, it was the only viable link between the capital city and the north coast. Many towns and cities developed along the Magdalena, surviving off of commerce generated through river traffic. Steamship service during the nineteenth century seemed to offer a modern manner of conquering the mighty Magdalena, but funding flowed toward more fashionable railroad technology after midcentury, and the steamships, with the advent of the automobile in the twentieth century, disappeared altogether. The towns along the river, however, remain.

14. Mule at Charalá
Source: CGM, 2009
Place: Charalá, Santander

   This lonely mule in the middle of the plaza at Charalá reminds viewers of a period in time when pack animals moved a wide array of products over long distances in Colombia. Colombian muleteers, called *arrieros*, drove hundreds of mules and burros over rough terrain, delivering all sorts of agricultural products, finished goods, and news of the world; even today, in many places in Colombia mules still provide reliable, sturdy, and economic transportation. Thus it is not at all unusual to see a mule, donkey, or other *animal de carga* (animal charged with carrying) in the center of rural and even moderately populated communities.

15. Plaza musicians
Source: CGM, 2009
Place: Guaduas, Cundinamarca

A typical scene on a Sunday afternoon: a local band plays in the center of Guaduas, Cundinamarca. This photo shows part of the cultural life of a small town; more than five hundred music schools exist in Colombia, most with some support from the government. The schools train young people to play music, an alternative to less glamorous activities and/or organizations competing for the attention of the youth. These town bands generally perform at town celebrations and during the commemoration of national holidays and religious feasts.

16. Jacqueline Bouvier Kennedy with Carlos Lleras Restrepo
Source: BPP, Anonymous, n.d.
Place: United States

Carlos Lleras Restrepo was elected president of Colombia in 1966, as a Liberal during the National Front. To help industrialize Colombia, he pushed ISI policies—Import Substituting Industrialization—much to the dismay of Washington. He openly rejected the advice of the Washington-based IMF (International Monetary Fund) and World Bank but never sought to separate Colombia from Washington's centrifugal pull. This undated photo of the Colombian president with Jacqueline Kennedy suggests a warm, collaborative relationship between Colombia and the U.S. despite underlying tensions generated by Lleras's independence before the IMF.

Chapter Six

Economic Unity

The contemporary Colombian economy is a modern, diverse, market-driven economy, managed by an entrepreneurial sector of the nation's elite. During the second half of the twentieth century, the economy avoided the disruptive boom-bust cycles of its Latin American neighbors, most notably Venezuela, Argentina, and Brazil. However, in 1999, the economy fell into a great recession that crippled the construction sector, devastated manufacturing, and pushed people out of agriculture. The recession was characterized by an unemployment rate of more than 20 percent, resulting in social disruption, an increase in crime rates, and a general sense, at the end of the twentieth century, that Colombia was on the verge of becoming a "failed state." Economic recovery began at the beginning of the twenty-first century—thanks partially to the infusion of billions of U.S. dollars in mostly military aid via "Plan Colombia," approved in 2000.

Despite the recent recovery, Colombia remains one of the most unequal societies in Latin America and the world. The Gini coefficient, which measures household inequality, grew from 53.8 percent to 58.5 percent during a ten-year period from 1998 to 2008. Costa Rica recorded a Gini coefficient of 48 percent, and France, 32.7 (for 2008).[1] Approximately 46 percent of the Colombian population of forty-five million lives in poverty, with perhaps as many as 16 percent living in extreme poverty, defined as surviving on less than 1.25 USD per day.

Production in contemporary Colombia has not met the needs of the Colombian population, a trend that dates back to colonial times. The twenty-first-century economy depends on exportation of petroleum and other mineral resources such as emeralds, coal, and gold; manufacturing, especially textiles, paper, and books; and agricultural products, including cut flowers, rice, cotton, sugar, and tobacco. Processed cocaine is another important export from

131

Colombia, but it represents the "off-the-books" segment of economic activity, the informal sector. Much economic activity in Colombia is informal, untaxed, and unregulated, and this blending of formal and informal sectors is an intrinsic part of Colombia's economic flow. Starting in the mid-nineteenth century, the Colombian economy came to depend on the export sector to generate wealth for those who controlled land and labor, yet a dynamic domestic economy emerged and alternated—for decades—with the export sector for dominance: the "debate" over which segment of the economy would prevail led, in large part, to civil war—the War of a Thousand Days, from 1899 to 1902. Disagreements over economic policy have had deep, long-lasting, and at times devastating influences on Colombian society.

COLONIAL COLOMBIA COMPARED

During Latin America's colonial period (1500–1800, approximately), the territory known today as Colombia was poor, compared to its wealthy neighbors to the north and south, Mexico and Peru, respectively. Massive silver deposits became the basis of the Spanish overseas economy, and Colombian precious metal deposits, by comparison to those of nearby colonies, were modest. The Colombian mining sector, based mostly on placer (or riverbed) mining of gold, developed in the western area of the territory, in what today is known as the Departments of Antioquia, Chocó, Cauca, and Nariño. A steady stream of gold was discovered and mined, leading to settlement, commerce, and trade in the western part of the country, but Colombia never came close to matching the economic activity generated by Mexican or Peruvian silver deposits. In the case of upper Peru (modern-day Bolivia), there was literally a mountain of silver, known as Potosí, which created enormous wealth during the mid-sixteenth through early seventeenth century. Colombia's economic growth, from colonial times to the present, can be characterized as gradual and moderate, with a mixed, mostly extractive economy. The architectural splendor, the vast fortunes made from mining and ranching, and the opulence and social dynamics resulting from the mining windfall in Mexico and Peru never materialized in Colombia. So the colonial economy of what today is called Colombia was characterized by modesty, leading to risk-averse behavior, conservative investment patterns, and policies that can be seen as prudent rather than exuberant and irrational. One of the great paradoxes of the contemporary Colombian economy is centered on this exact historical irony: despite the alarming figures of economic inequality, which permits approximately half the population to survive at or below the poverty level, Colombia is viewed by classically trained Western economists as a stable, modern, prudently managed economy.

The capital city of Bogotá, high up in the Andes and isolated from a major river-port system, influenced the subsequent trajectory of the colonial Colombian economy. Bogotá was firmly integrated into the local Andean economy, and trade in foodstuffs and other agricultural products from the interior, including warmer-weather products such as tobacco and cotton, shaped the internal Colombian economy more than trans-Atlantic trade. The port cities of Cartagena and Portobello (today located in Panama) were major centers of human trafficking during the colonial period; enslaved Africans were sold at these markets in exchange for American silver and other minerals and agricultural products. In Colombia, the coastal economy—based at Cartagena—operated in concert with the demands of external markets; the interior economy, based in the highland cities of Bogotá, Socorro in the modern Department of Santander, and Popayán to the south, depended on an internal circulation of goods and products that originated in the soils and workshops of Colombia. The Magdalena River, which drains the Colombian Andes and flows northward to the city of Barranquilla and the Caribbean Sea, integrated the two economies. But the difficulty of travel on the Magdalena—the average trip from Cartagena to Bogotá lasted about a month during the colonial period—meant that true economic integration would remain elusive for Colombia, and so a dual economic system, one based on coastal patterns of trade and external markets and another based on long-established networks dating to the Muisca pre-Columbian civilizations, developed and functioned. Technological innovations of the nineteenth century (for example, the steamship and the railroad) would pull these economies together, and twentieth-century aviation would more thoroughly break down the coastal-interior economic divide. Local economies of scale, based on geographic realities, fostered production and trade patterns that remained functional for decades and established a production paradigm characterized by slow, careful, conservative economic development.

MONOPOLY AND POLITICAL PROBLEMS
IN THE EIGHTEENTH CENTURY

During the late colonial period, beginning in the middle of the eighteenth century, the so-called Bourbon Reforms attempted to control economic activity in the colonies more completely via new policies originating in Spain. These policies were designed to collect more taxes, stimulate economic activity, and cut down on corruption. Monopoly control of certain segments of the Colombian economy characterized Bourbon policy during this time. Given the limited amount of income that could be generated through direct extraction of minerals or foodstuffs, Spanish policy in New Granada decreed that Spain would directly control production, marketing, and the sale of certain key products to include tobacco and *aguardiente* (cane liquor). The tobacco monopoly irritated the people of New Granada and was a source of tension pitting Americans against their overseas rulers.

At this time, the Spanish and British both looked for new revenue streams to finance costly wars, and their policies were remarkably similar. They increased revenue by raising taxes on overseas subjects, tried to restrict trade and prevent the flow of contraband by enforcing trade monopolies, and raised the prices on controlled goods that colonists needed. In the case of the British at Boston, the products in question were stamps, paper, and tea; in the Spanish New Granadian case, the tobacco and *aguardiente* tax increase seems to have overstepped the bounds of what was acceptable. Santander, Colombia, with its mild climate at 1,200 meters above sea level, represented an ideal growing environment for tobacco, and well-watered valleys created small land parcels that proved perfect for tobacco cultivation. High-quality tobacco came from this area of Colombia, and in a time period prior to cinema, television, or the surgeon general, tobacco was a critical recreational and social accelerant for people from all socioeconomic strata. One of the most important rebellions in northern South America would occur as a direct result of a tax hike on tobacco, the 1781 Comuneros Rebellion of New Granada.

The Comuneros Rebellion began in Socorro, Santander, and ended in Zipaquirá, the salt-mining town a mere day's journey from the capital at Bogotá. The rebellion showed Spaniards that people were growing weary of paying high taxes for the privilege of living as colonial subjects. Scholars have debated the degree to which the rebellion is an early cry for independence, but it did force a reconsideration of tax and monopoly policies and gave the people of New Granada encouragement that they could, in fact, organize and pressure a distant government concerning matters of production and taxation. The Comuneros revolt is widely considered an early tax rebellion, not an early cry for independence; it has more in common with the earlier Boston "Tea Party" in faraway New England and less in common with the Tupác Amaru Rebellion (1780–1781) in the Peruvian highlands. Tupác Amaru, a far more complicated rebellion, pitted Peruvian *mestizos* against the indigenous people and the Church against royal authorities and ended with a violent suppression of indigenous cultural expression.

The long, difficult, and disruptive Latin American wars of independence (1810–1826) dramatically set back the Latin American economies, especially in Mexico and Peru, where silver mining activities ground to a virtual halt. In Colombia, where most production was local and supported a regional economic structure, the dislocation was less apparent. David

Bushnell estimates that gold mining fell by approximately 40 percent but notes that mining quickly recovered with the conclusion of the wars, since Colombian gold mining (unlike silver mining in Mexico), was river-based, low-tech placer mining.[2]

Political independence did not imply a radical or dramatic restructuring of the Colombian economy; in fact, economically speaking, Colombia changed very little with the onset of political independence from Spain. The new government provisionally abolished the hated *alcabala* (sales tax), long associated with Spanish abuse, and government revenues were raised through the continuance of monopolies on tobacco and salt. Customs receipts made up a significant percentage, perhaps as much as one third, of national revenues during this time, but Colombia's rugged mountainous terrain prevented the development of an internal economic network; in Colombia, there was no symbolic economic unification of the nation, as was the case in the United States with the linking of the transcontinental train line in 1877. Colombians had to creatively adapt to their surroundings and grow, produce, and trade locally; in the highlands, especially, they could not depend on or afford imported luxury goods, and most Colombians lived an extremely austere existence, shaped by the confluence of geography and climate. In the Colombian lowlands, cotton and sugar were produced for export, but the levels were minimal compared to cotton exports from the United States (especially after the Civil War) or Cuba and Brazil (in terms of sugar production). Tobacco was an important product that spanned the colonial and independence period, and Colombian quinine, produced from the bark of the cinchona tree (found in the highlands of Colombia and other South American nations) and used to treat malaria, grew in commercial significance, especially after midcentury. This so-called quinine boom lasted about thirty years.

It would be inaccurate to write that transportation confounded Colombians. The reality is more complex and since, historically, most of the pre-Columbian, precapitalist people of the territory thrived in high-altitude plateaus and mountain valleys, modern production, accumulation, and trade would have to adapt to the rigors of mountainous geography. Colombian economic development should not be compared to that of other countries during the same time period, especially those nations blessed with abundant natural resources, significant navigable river systems integrated with clear growing seasons, or easily navigable plains—much like the United States, Canada, or Argentina. Scholars have used words such as *divided* and *fragmented* to describe a Colombian economic (and social) reality, and those terms certainly apply when comparing Colombia to the United States' economic development of roughly the same historical time period. Colombians learned how to adapt, improvise, and create, and they did so through agricultural practices and production for domestic markets of basic necessities (clothing, footwear, and household goods, among others). They also developed inter- and intra-regional trade patterns that proved durable and functional. The durability of these economic patterns is remarkable: for example, today, cotton, tobacco, rice, sugar, and *panela* (an artisanal molasses-based sweetener used in candies and beverages) are grown and processed in the same regions and—in the case of *panela*—in the same manner as they were hundreds of years ago.

What has changed, of course, is transportation networks, and the advent of modern aviation has significantly diminished the challenges imposed by geography on Colombia's economic development. Before aviation, however, Colombians faced the challenge of taming the mighty Magdalena River, which flows out of the Andes to the Caribbean Sea. Infrastructure developed at midcentury, especially during the regime of General Tomás Cipriano de Mosquera, who is credited with building modern roads and introducing steam navigation on the Magdalena River. Modern steam freighter service on this river provided a much-needed link between the highlands and the Caribbean and allowed Colombians to imagine a dynamic export system, supported by the massive Magdalena, which, like the Mississippi further north in the United States, profoundly shaped trade, commerce, and economic development in the Andean nation.

Mid-nineteenth-century economic activity, then, centered on regional production and trade of mineral products (gold), salt, tobacco, and cotton; the second half of the nineteenth century witnessed the continuation of tobacco and mining and the introduction of quinine as a significant factor for the Colombian economy. But by the fourth quarter of the nineteenth century, one product would come to dominate and define the Colombian economy and help establish the basis of a modern, fully articulated economic system: coffee. Coffee would help link the rural growing sector with the financial and transportation sector in the cities. Banking and international trade would grow as coffee came to overshadow, in terms of revenue, all other segments of the Colombian economy.

COFFEE

Coffee emerged in the late nineteenth century as the leading export from Colombia. It helped transform the nation, even though, like export booms in other regions of Latin America at this time (that is, wheat and fresh meat from Argentina, copper from Chile, and coffee from Guatemala, El Salvador, and Brazil), reliance on one product that was tied to overseas tastes and markets would generate uneven, unsustainable economic growth. In the case of Colombia, it would lead to a bitterly fought civil war, aptly named the War of a Thousand Days (1899–1902). American historian Charles Bergquist was the first scholar to connect coffee and the export-led economic model with political conflict in his 1986 book *Coffee and Conflict in Colombia, 1886–1910*. He notes how the war, which took the lives of between seventy thousand and ninety thousand Colombians and represented an ideological conflict, turned particularly violent due in large part to an inability among elites to reach consensus concerning the future economic direction of the nation. Those who dominated the Conservative political party were more concerned with the local economy, farming, cattle raising, and the traditional *latifundia* (large-scale landholding) model. Political Liberals were pushing for infrastructural development, finance, and banking modifications that would allow them to pursue an export-based economic model based largely on cultivation, distribution, and exportation of coffee. The war was complicated: it pitted Liberals against Conservatives, coastal residents against citizens from the Andean interior, the landed elite against people with little to no land. Taxation, once again, was a primary factor leading to war in Colombia: the imposition of the 1895 government tax on exports came at a time when overproduction of coffee, on a world scale, resulted in declining profits for Colombian coffee growers and a general sour mood in the country. Neither the Conservatives (who controlled virtually all of the official apparatus of the government) nor the insurgent Liberals actually won the war, which all but dissipated by 1902, resulting in a bitter stalemate.

Ironically, what eventually brought the country back together, so to speak, was the so-called separation of Panama, which occurred in 1903. Colombia was so utterly divided by its civil war that an outside power, the United States, was able to foment an independence movement in the Province of Panama during this time. After the bloodless revolt that led to the independence of Panama, the United States quickly recognized the new republic. Colombians did not exactly forget the tensions that led them to a thousand-day civil war, but a much more powerful adversary to the north helped Colombians to refocus their internal animosities toward an external target—an aggressive, undiplomatic United States. A similar, though not exactly analogous, sentiment could be seen in Mexico after the ambiguously named Mexican-American War (1846–1848), which led to Mexico's losing 51 percent of its national territory and demonstrated the urgent need for political collaboration, at home, to avoid further territorial dismemberment.

By the end of the nineteenth century, according to David Bushnell, coffee represented about half of all export earnings for the nation; by the mid-1920s, after the economic and social dislocation occasioned by the First World War, coffee represented 80 percent of all Colombian foreign earnings, and about 90 percent of all coffee exports went to one place: the United States. Colombia's privileged geographic position allowed easy access to the U.S. market. Colombian geography gave it a comparative advantage over other nations in Latin America for growing and exporting coffee. The coffee bush grows best at a temperate, frost-free climate found in Colombian mountain valleys, particularly in the western part of the country, in the so-called coffee zone, comprising the departments of Antioquia, Risaralda, Tolima, Caldas, and Quindio. A patchwork of railroad investment, especially in Antioquia, supported the coffee economy, and small-scale producers came to define the Colombian model, wherein families would work together to grow coffee for export and staples (beans, cassava, and plantains, among other products) for home consumption.

Coffee production, which is extremely labor intensive, returned more revenues to the middlemen and merchants than to the farmers. In 1927, as a way to control the production and marketing of the most vital product of the nation in terms of foreign exchange, the Federación Nacional de Cafeteros (National Federation of Coffee Growers) was organized by the Colombian government to regulate production, harmonize trade, provide credit, and look after the interests of producers and merchants alike. This organization, which still exists, represented a creative, modern attempt to regularize and balance the economy of Colombia and bring unity to a country and economy that defies unification. Naturally, as pointed out by Bushnell, this organization was dominated by the large growers and merchants, but the creation of the federation ushered in a period of economic planning, collaboration, and cooperation that is rarely emphasized when discussing contemporary Colombian economic development.[3]

Thus, during the first two decades of the twentieth century, coffee came to define the Colombian economy. Coffee production had shifted west and remained in the hands of small-scale producers, and profits from the coffee economy remained largely in Colombia. This helped stimulate early industrialization, which took root at Medellín—the capital of the Department of Antioquia—in the center of the nation's coffee region. Another factor that spurred industrial development was the 1922 indemnification payment by the United States, which was used mostly to modernize transportation networks. The result of negotiations that had led to the 1914 Urrutia-Thomson Treaty between the two nations, this payment of twenty-five million dollars was designed to compensate Colombia for the loss of Panama in 1903.

A significant year in Colombia, 1914 represents the time when frozen U.S.-Colombian relations began to thaw; this is partially due to the opening of the Panama Canal during that year, shortly after the outbreak of the First World War. Colombian president Pedro Nel Ospina (1922–1926) was the sitting president who most benefited from the indemnity funds and used the money to promote public works projects. Many of these projects involved transportation, construction of railroad lines, and other infrastructure improvements designed to facilitate the movement of goods and to support overall economic growth. In 1923, reflecting a new spirit of friendship between the United States and Colombia, the Banco de la República (Central Bank) was established upon the recommendation of the Kemmerer Mission, an economic advisory council from the United States that sought to help Colombia regulate and modernize banking, finances, investment, and interest rate schedules during the heady days of soaring coffee profits.

However, historians date the initial rebirth of U.S.-Colombia commercial and diplomatic relations to the presidency of Marco Fidel Suárez (1918–1921); President Suárez was a firm believer in linking the economic fortunes of Colombia to what he called a *respice polum*, or the "Polar Star"—represented (according to his reasoning) by the United States. But a two-tiered internal tension limited the extent to which the U.S.-Colombian commercial relationship would grow: on the one hand, a significant trade imbalance existed, since most manufactured goods arrived at the north coast of Colombia from Europe, while Colombia relied heavily on the U.S. market for its exports (principally coffee); this meant that U.S. influence over the Colombian economy was limited. On the other hand, credit and investment flowed to Colombia mostly from the U.S. during the 1920s when U.S. banks, bursting with post–World War I investment capital, were eager to advance loans and credit in the Americas.

In addition to this economic reality, Suárez's gaze toward the Polar Star was fraught with cultural tension; he was a man deeply influenced by a nineteenth-century Catholic ethos that viewed U.S. Protestant-style capitalist-industrialist development with great skepticism. The Church frequently warned about capitalist excesses and worried that it would lose its flock to secular labor unions, political parties, and industrialists from abroad. Marco Palacios summarizes Suárez's dilemma by presciently noting how "this recipe of Catholic social doctrine and Yankee progress would put its stamp on 'progressive conservatives' for the rest of the century."[4]

THE PERCOLATING TWENTIES

The 1920s "dance of the millions"—the name given to the decade of prosperity ushered in by the dramatic increase in coffee exports and foreign loans taken by Colombia (when Colombians began to think in terms of millions rather than hundreds of thousands of pesos)—was characterized by increased foreign capitalist penetration of the Colombian economy, most notably by the United States. The north coast of Colombia became the primary focus for cultivation of exotic tropical fruits, at this time primarily bananas. The United Fruit Company (UFCO) had developed a virtual enclave economy in and around Santa Marta and managed the growing, harvesting, and transportation of bananas out of Colombia to the North American markets. UFCO also operated plantations in Caribbean and Central American nations.

In 1928, Colombian banana workers staged a strike, which is seen as a watershed moment in the nation's economic history. UFCO employees executed a work stoppage that brought UFCO operations to a halt in late 1928. As many as twenty-five thousand workers struck for better working conditions and for a greater share of company profits to be returned to them as actual wages rather than worthless (outside the banana zone) company scrip. UFCO management, frightened by the prospect of ripening and rotting fruit in the Caribbean sun, called on the Colombian government to take action, which resulted in a massacre at the main plaza in Ciénaga. Workers had gathered at this town, organizing to march to the departmental capital, Santa Marta, but the workers were mowed down in an extraordinary show of brutality that officially left forty-seven dead. However, most estimates put the number of actual dead that day at between one thousand and two thousand. The massacre was immortalized in Gabriel García Márquez's *One Hundred Years of Solitude*, an account of magic and madness at Macondo—the town he invented to parallel the town where he grew up, Aracataca—in the middle of the banana zone, and about fifty miles south of Santa Marta. García Márquez used the number three thousand to refer to the dead in his account, and that number has come to define the magnitude of the December 6, 1928, tragedy—though most agree that his is an outsized statistic. García Márquez, reflecting on the centrality of fiction to help explain history in Colombia, commented on the strongman he created in one of his earliest novels: "In *The Autumn of the Patriarch*, the dictator says that it doesn't matter if it's not true now, because sometime in the future it will be true. Sooner or later people believe writers rather than the government."[5]

The 1928 massacre at Ciénaga presented a contradiction that was not lost on the Colombian political elite or ordinary Colombian citizens: while the wealthy were dancing and thinking in millions, an important segment of Colombia's new export economy had, in essence, fallen into the hands of foreign subsidiaries, and the nation's poor were being massacred. Colombians energetically organized after this massacre to take back control of their economy and reconsider their economic and political future. This nationalist impulse helped launch the career of a new political star, the young Bogotano lawyer Jorge Eliécer Gaitán, who advocated on behalf of the massacre victims in a series of noisy, sensationalistic public speeches that also forcefully criticized the economic practices and policies of UFCO, its U.S. backers, and its Colombian allies. In 1930, the Conservative Party, which had held power since about 1886, was swept from power in national elections that brought the Liberal Party to power; people in Colombia had grown disenchanted with economic policies and conditions that favored outside corporations' profits over the lives of Colombian citizens, and the 1928 Ciénaga massacre is seen as the beginning of the end of a forty-five-year Conservative political hegemony.

OIL AND INDUSTRIALIZATION

Oil during the 1920s became an increasingly important export from Colombia and is currently its leading export. Since 1948, a state-run oil company, Ecopetrol, has managed the development, drilling, production, and distribution of oil in the country, and contracts are granted by the company to outside oil companies. The excesses of the banana plantation economy, completely monopolized by one company and one nation, led to nationalization, control, and protection of precious, profitable national resources—such as oil—though Ecopetrol, S.A., was partially privatized in 2003 through the sale of shares on the Colombian stock exchange. Colombia is petroleum self-sufficient and exports oil to nations in the region, but its reserves are minimal compared to those of neighboring Venezuela—a nation where roughly 33 percent of the entire nation's GDP is tied to the production and exportation of oil through a state-run oil monopoly, Petróleos de Venezuela, S.A., or PDVSA.

During the fifteen-year period marked by the Great Depression and the Second World War, the Colombian economy continued to export coffee, and by the late 1940s, coffee represented about 72 percent of all exports. Careful, prudent management under the umbrella organization of the Coffee Growers Federation created the conditions for Colombian coffee exports to continue during the difficult depression years. In 1931, Colombians organized the Caja de Crédito Agrario (Agrarian Credit Bank) to offer loans to small producers and keep them afloat during the capital-scarce 1930s. Colombians took advantage of their diverse, regionally based economy to weather the storm, and like other neighboring Latin American nations, they began to rethink their economy and restructure it toward the domestic sector. Economic and political havoc in the United States and Europe (the Great Depression and Second World War) mitigated against a robust international trade at this time, so Colombian industry shifted toward producing for the internal market. Textile manufacturing, based at the industrial center of Medellín, took the lead in the Colombian industrialization plan. The nation also excelled at producing paper, books, clothing, shoes, and household items—particularly furniture—and all of these manufactured goods contributed to the nascent industrialization process, which would grow under the protection of favorable tariff rates and, of course, limited competition from foreign producers.

The conclusion of the Second World War brought, to Latin America in general and Colombia specifically, higher prices for commodities that had been under price-control regulations during the war: thus, sugar, cotton, coffee, and minerals fetched excellent prices on the world market, and the price of coffee in the postwar period reached an all-time high. Colombia's GDP grew by 5 percent per year from 1945 to 1955 despite the onset of uncontrollable rural violence, and demonstrating the degree to which the Colombian economy has managed to push forward, despite major obstacles found along the path. During this period, the economy was managed by moderate bureaucrats wedded to free-market principles with conservative management styles. An example is President Mariano Ospina Pérez, an avuncular, bland businessman who ruled from 1946 to 1950 and was followed by proto-fascist Laureano Gómez, who ruled until his ouster by the military in 1953.

General Rojas Pinilla's regime (1953–1957) was characterized by state intervention in labor matters. The military dictator committed to some high-profile projects to develop the country's infrastructure. He helped build the modern El Dorado Airport at Bogotá, the headquarters of the Ministry of Defense, and the new military hospital in the capital, and he largely stuck to the free-market system favored by the elites and their allies. His regime was marred by a declining price in coffee, and his enthusiasm for labor organization frightened more conservative segments of society. Rojas Pinilla was ousted in 1957 through a national civic strike, and a military junta ruled until the 1958 elections. Thus, in the twentieth century, it is accurate to note that the military interceded only once, in 1953, when General Gustavo Rojas Pinilla removed Laureano Gómez from the presidency. Colombians, unlike Argentines, Chileans, or Brazilians, have shown an aversion to military rule, and part of Rojas's problem with governability was the widely held perception that something was not quite right about his unelected government. Colombians have preferred civilian chief executives, and while tolerating a lot of backroom, behind-the-scenes negotiating (such as that which led to Rojas's coup against Gómez), they have regularly gone to the polls to elect civilians to higher office.

THE NATIONAL FRONT

From 1958 to 1974, Colombia's political elites came together and shared political power. Pointing to the economic significance of this period, historian Marco Palacios describes the National Front as "the golden age of gentlemen's agreements between the leadership of the state and the quasi-corporative trade associations."[6] The cohesiveness of Colombian trade associations, which defended the interests of coffee growers, cattle ranchers, merchants, industrialists, bankers, and others, demonstrates the value placed on sociopolitical stability as a means of realizing profits for Colombian business managers. Economic modernization was a central concern during this period, and openness to the free market, together with prudent management by technocrats and elites (many of whom were trained in the United States) and periodic currency devaluations, made Colombia an appealing economic partner to the United States during the escalating Cold War, a crisis that grew more intense after the 1959 Cuban Revolution. The Colombian economy became fully integrated into the capitalist economic orbit led by the free market priorities of the United States. President John F. Kennedy made Colombia a priority in his plan for hemispheric unity called the Alliance for Progress; Colombia was viewed as an economically stable, democratically inclined nation, and President and Mrs. Kennedy's visit to Bogotá in 1961 represented a critical turning point for Colombia in its self-image as an important player on the world stage.

The National Front political arrangement included a sixteen- to twenty-year economic plan for Colombia based on industrialization. The Colombian business elite did not want to be assigned their historical role of mere producers of primary commodities (coffee and oil, emeralds and bananas); Colombian industry during this time widened to include areas of Bogotá, the north coast, Cali, and Medellín. For example, from the late 1960s to the present, Colombia has assembled automobiles for the domestic market under an agreement with Renault of France.

However, French automobiles rolling off Colombian assembly lines hid a larger, growing, historic problem in the Colombian countryside. From the late 1920s, the agricultural model in Colombia was designed to privilege a growing agro-industrial sector, which led to the abandonment of the traditional *campesino*, that is, small-scale agricultural producer. This created a major migratory process from the countryside to the cities—not only in Colombia but in other Latin American nations as well. The postwar economy stimulated this process, as did Colombian rural conflict in the 1950s–1960s. While some small landholders tried to retain their lands by organizing into what are today the insurgency forces (such as the FARC), other *campesinos* not disposed to joining the rebellion fled to the major cities. Unable to find steady employment, they moved into what are today shantytowns. A solution to this complex socioeconomic reality was proposed by President Carlos Lleras Restrepo (1966–1970): an agrarian reform program. This reform was opposed by wealthy landowners and others who feared that such reform would undermine their economic interests. It therefore never materialized. Thus, from the late 1960s onward, the agrarian economic model in Colombia has favored large-scale industrial agriculture to the detriment of poor country folk. This reality has helped establish the conditions that have favored the social dislocation and tensions that remain part of contemporary Colombian society.

MODERN TIMES

Despite the push for industrialization, the Colombian economy remains dependent on the exportation of primary products. More recently, fresh cut flowers, coal, coffee, and oil have dominated the official Colombian export sector. The flower industry has benefited from lowering air-freight rates since the 1980s, ideal climatic and soil conditions, and an abundant labor force willing to work for low wages. Coal mining at El Cerrejón, the open-pit coal mining operation in the far northeast corner of the nation—the Guajira—has become an important part of the Colombian export sector. Cerrejón, a mining consortium owned by three international mineral corporations, is a multibillion-dollar enterprise that, in 2009, returned 280 million dollars in royalties to the public and private sector in Colombia. That same year, the company exported more than thirty million tons of coal, mostly to Europe; 17 percent of exports went to North America. Five thousand people are directly employed by the company while another five thousand are employed through subcontractors.

The exportation of illegal narcotics, beginning with a marijuana boom on the north coast of Colombia based in and around Santa Marta and continuing later with cocaine processing and export, has distorted the Colombian economy, particularly during the past thirty years. "Narco-statistics" are unreliable by their very nature, but the influx and laundering of dirty capital is seen in the main cities—particularly in the booming construction sector during the 1990s (before the 1999 economic crash), the abundance of luxurious malls, and the construction of high-priced housing in the major Colombian cities. Most Colombians prefer to discuss the legitimate basis of their economy, but tens of billions of dollars have flowed in and out of Colombia in recent years due to the illegal drug trade. However, most of the wealth generated from illegal narcotics remains at the point of sale, that is, in the United States, Europe, or other places where consumers are willing to pay a premium for this particular Colombian export. Colombia is not the only Latin American nation to export cocaine (and, increasingly, heroin) to the north. Peruvian production of cocaine has increased dramatically during the past five years, and Peru is presently the world's second-leading producer of coca leaf.[7]

The Colombian economy has avoided the dizzying "boom and bust" cycles of neighboring Argentina, Brazil, or Ecuador due to careful management by elites who hold degrees from Colombian, European, or U.S. universities. But the political and economic fortunes of the country took a tragic turn in the wake of a wave of political violence that ended the lives of four presidential candidates during the 1990 campaign.

A young Universidad de los Andes–trained economist, César Gaviria was elected president in 1990—a sort of "accidental" president. Gaviria had been campaign manager for the heir apparent to the Colombian presidency, Luis Carlos Galán, who was brutally murdered in August 1989 on orders of drug baron Pablo Escobar. Gaviria's tenure in office represented a clear alignment with the so-called Washington Consensus, which stressed privatization of key sectors of the Colombian economy, including the notoriously inefficient Telecom, the national telephone company, and important segments of the mining sector. The country's civil aviation industry was deregulated in 1991, and the airport at Cali was privatized. This push for privatization and market deregulation (often referred to as "neoliberalism") was rewarded by favorable treatment by the IMF and international investment bankers. Gaviria's presidency was followed, in 1994, by the liberal Ernesto Samper's tenure, marred from the very beginning by accusations of a six-million-dollar infusion of illegal funds into his campaign as the election approached. The United States revoked Samper's visa to travel there, as diplomatic and financial relations chilled substantially. The result of market deregulation, growing unemployment, and the general hostile economic and political climate between Washington and Bogotá fueled a severe recession, which began in earnest in 1999 and lasted about five years. The Colombian economy actually shrank by 4.5 percent during this time period, and unemployment reached 22 percent. Construction came to a virtual standstill in major cities, and the period looked especially grim, given that the guerrilla forces during this time made significant gains in recruitment, their kidnapping operations continued unabated, and they seemed to hold the Colombian military on the defensive.

The economy gradually recovered after a massive infusion of outside aid known as "Plan Colombia"; more than 1.3 billion U.S. dollars (mostly in military aid) helped restore confidence in the Colombian economy during the Andrés Pastrana administration (1998–2002). The neoliberal policies continued during this time and into the Álvaro Uribe Vélez administration (2002–2010). Uribe represented a hard line against the guerrilla forces; he planned to eradicate the FARC and ELN during his presidency, and he pushed for approval of an FTA, or free trade agreement, with the United States. That agreement, passed by the Colombian Senate, stalled in the U.S. Congress for five years but was finally authorized by the U.S. legislature and signed by President Obama in 2011.

The Colombian economy can be viewed as a resilient, market-based, mixed economy where manufacturing, mineral extraction, agriculture, and services combine to create a healthy, growth-oriented system. However, Colombia, as of this writing, is one of the most unequal countries in Latin America and the world. The minimum wage in 2012 is 566,700 Colombian pesos, or three hundred U.S. dollars per month. Poverty in some quarters of Colombia is almost surreal, as one observer recently noted while working in Tumaco, a small Pacific coast town, in 2010. "I've never seen misery like I saw in Tumaco. The children all have a white skin fungus due to the poor water quality; most are from displaced families that have built pathetic stilt homes in the impossible mangrove swamps. Few attend school, and those that do trudge through mud and human and animal feces barefoot."[8] The rich—people engaged in honest business and mining ventures—acquire vast fortunes, while the poor languish with underresourced government programs or rely on private charity organizations to fill in the economic gaps.

Though its benefits are distributed unevenly, the Colombian economy endures. The challenge for future leaders will be to shrink the gap between the wealthiest Colombians and the poorest, thereby helping the poor realize that they, too, are stakeholders in the country's prosperity. Reducing economic inequality would help solve social problems, dampening down the impetus for armed insurgency while helping to unify the nation.

NOTES

1. Zero represents absolute equality and one hundred represents absolute inequality in this formula named for the Italian statistician Corrado Gini.

2. See David Bushnell, *The Making of Modern Colombia: A Nation in Spite of Itself* (Berkeley: University of California Press, 1993), 48–49.

3. Ibid., 173.

4. Marco Palacios, *Between Legitimacy and Violence: A History of Colombia, 1875–2002* (Durham: Duke University Press, 2006), 69.

5. From Ilan Stavans, *Gabriel García Márquez: The Early Years* (New York: Palgrave, 2010), 26.

6. Palacios, *Between Legitimacy and Violence*, 171.

7. *CIA World Factbook*, last modified May 4, 2011, http://www.cia.gov/library /publications/the-world-factbok/geos.pe/html.

8. Paul J. Angelo, private e-mail correspondence to Michael J. LaRosa, October 4, 2010.

Chapter Seven

A Common Space

Building a community that could identify itself as Colombian once the complex process of independence ended was by no means an easy task. Several factors worked for and against such a community, including the social dynamics that were unleashed through partisan politics, the search for a system of commonly held beliefs through Catholicism, attempts at creating common memories, and the creation of institutions such as the armed forces or the National Bank of the Republic. To some degree, the regions were woven together through overarching instruments of governance and public administration. The obstacles presented by geography, however, were formidable, and geography, as discussed earlier, has imprinted a unique identity on Colombia. It was not enough to be known as Liberal or Conservative, to be Catholic and speak the same language, or even to engage in commerce using the same legal tender. In order to form a Colombian community after independence, the state had to establish its capacity to govern immediately and everywhere. People had to be able to move according to the rhythms of business and personal aspirations. Goods needed to find viable and open markets, and trade could not be stopped simply because of the high costs of transportation. Public opinion needed to be informed by what was happening in all corners of the country and the world. In short, people, goods, ideas, and institutions needed to flow easily throughout the country's territory—both the territory that was actually occupied and that which was slowly being incorporated through the forces of demographic change and colonization.

The nation as we know it today is a political community. A previous chapter explained how Colombia is a country of nations. From the period of the early republic, it was difficult to accept that cultural diversity and ideological pluralisms could coexist within one political community. The idea that the nation needed to be culturally homogeneous held sway. Thus, a concerted effort was made to implant throughout the country a unified idea about civilization. This idea, created by urban elites, was a hybrid that brought together democratic-liberal institutions and principles, the ideals of capitalist bourgeois thinkers, and the norms and practices of Catholicism. The notion of inhabiting one common national space was thereby founded in the certainty that elites had about their view of civilization. From 1830 until the profound social crises that lasted from about 1960 to 1980, the fundamental objective of governance was to force all populations to meet these elite ideals of civilization. Thus, at the end of the twentieth century, a paradox became evident. The geography had been largely reined in through agile and efficient modes of communication, but the cultural homogeneity that elites imprinted since the end of the nineteenth century was clearly not viable. Instead, the late twentieth century witnessed acceptance of cultural diversity and plurality as essential components of the Colombian social order. In other words, today it is clear that the national community can only be political, and for this reason, the territory it occupies is political as well.

In Colombia, the distance that separated people was not measured in miles but in traditions. Cultural niches had been constituted over the course of centuries, fostered by a geography that separated Colombians by high mountain ranges, deep valleys, and dense jungles. These obstacles impeded the consolidation of a national community—that is, a group of human beings who shared a common identity, lived under a common set of rules, and were conscious of inhabiting a common space. Therefore, in order to achieve this national ideal, a tremendous economic, technological, and administrative effort was put forth not only by the state but also by the private sector. Such a task required immense capital so as to build more efficient systems of communication. The private sector was indispensable in this respect, but the state needed to accumulate administrative experience in order to contract out the public works that would be developed. These efforts gave shape to the institutions and mechanisms of control that guaranteed the execution of planned projects. Today, two hundred years later, the accomplishments are obvious; nevertheless, the aforementioned paradox remains. Unity has been created over the territory, reaffirming Colombia as a political community in terms of participation and interests, but the nation is still only loosely homogeneous in a cultural sense.

The purpose of this chapter, then, is to explain the creation of a space that became national as a result of the reduction of distances through the construction of multiple systems of transportation, however disarticulated. Also involved in this process was the implementation of efficient communication technologies and the interregional diffusion of ideas and news to create a more well-informed public with a shared public opinion. These elements gave shape to a common space. After two centuries, these were the primary circumstances that made Colombia a singular political community within the world order of nation-states.

FROM HORSE PATH TO HIGHWAY

The republic inherited from the colonial period a preference of settlement that privileged the interior Andean areas of the country at one thousand meters above sea level or higher. These were the regions that had been inhabited for centuries by indigenous peoples who had actively sought out fertile lands at healthier altitudes, away from sea-level pests and swamps that were common to the so-called hot lands. The Spanish conquistadors also preferred these higher-elevation lands, and they took advantage of the already-existing labor force in these regions. Only two cities developed on the Colombian Caribbean coast during the colonial period: Cartagena and Santa Marta. The other exceptions to the interior high-elevation model are the few dozen or so mining towns that sprang up in territories that were uninhabitable but attractive for the riches they held. Another territory that lay outside the settlement pattern should also be mentioned: the few villages of mixed-race peoples on the banks of large rivers that functioned as ports for the transit of goods and people to the mountain towns. However, excluding Cartagena and Santa Marta, the principal cities and villas remained in the mountain ranges, far from the sea and the large rivers, and were themselves isolated from one another by high altitudes and deep chasms that led to nearly insurmountable transportation difficulties.

In many places during the colonial period, the people constructed roads over pre-Columbian routes and made them passable not only for humans but also for mules, horses, and oxen. Some of these acquired the rank of Camino Real—a "royal road." The Camino Real was paved with cobblestones and met special characteristics of water management and the control of elevation over the surface of the road. All these roads, royal or otherwise, provided for human foot traffic but never more than this basic function. None served as a path over which wheeled vehicles could pass. The wheel was used only in the interior of population centers, perhaps on some haciendas, and in mining areas. The broad lane that inaugurated an entrance to Santafé from the west was a significant novelty in the eighteenth century, and so was the road that connected Bogotá with Zipaquirá via the Puente del Común at the turn of the nineteenth century. But the only way to get from Bogotá to Popayán in the southwest, to Cartagena on the coast, or to Medellín was via foot or on the backs of horses or mules. Spaniards at that time traveled in sedan chairs, literally on the backs of indigenous carriers.

These difficulties did not mean, however, that communication was stifled among regions. Quite the contrary; according to modern standards, the rhythm of transportation was slow during the colonial period and costly due to its precarious nature, but people and goods as well as mail, and with it news and edicts of government, reached all populated areas. These voyages were infrequent. Most people did not engage in long-distance travel; most were born, lived, loved, and died in the place of their birth. When individuals did have to travel to faraway places, the travelers prepared themselves for a prolonged absence, which could last months or years. The nineteenth century did not represent any palpable change in terms of speed of travel, but it did witness a significant expansion of roadways and transportation networks. The daunting task of building roads that could sustain wheeled traffic began to take shape given that vehicles could not always follow the footpaths or walkways carved out along mountainsides. Also, these mapped-out routes for walkers crossed obstacles that were impossible for carts and other wheeled vehicles to traverse, for example, hanging bridges made out of henequen rope.

By June 16, 1845, the government issued a decree that inaugurated the first plan for a road network that would guarantee communication between the capital in Bogotá with the cities and ports located on the borders with other countries and on the Pacific Ocean and Caribbean Sea. The routes included Bogotá to Venezuela via Tunja and Pamplona; Bogotá to Ecuador and the Pacific coast via Neiva, Popayán, and Pasto; Bogotá to Buenaventura via Mariquita and the Valle de Cauca River; Bogotá to a navigable port in the Atrato River or to the Gulf of Urabá via Mariquita; a route to the Caribbean via the Magdalena River; and a route that would cross Panama, thereby connecting the Caribbean with the Pacific. To construct or repair these national roads, the state granted parcels of unincorporated land to private entities, which led to the immigration of technicians. A labor force was "recruited" by forcing prisoners to work on these roads.

None of the successive governments of the nineteenth century took the formidable task of expanding the national road network lightly. They dedicated significant funds toward either improving existing roads or opening new ones for horse traffic or wheeled vehicles. Laws and decrees are not the only signs of these efforts. Evidence can also be found among the national budget allocations of the period, including funds set aside for civil engineering education. The national government created a military school that would train engineers, and later, the National University in Bogotá and the National School of Mines in Medellín further encouraged infrastructural development. The training of civil engineers capable of confronting and defeating the mountains was key. Foreign civil engineers were recruited, and foreign technology and materials were imported. Entrepreneurs took advantage of incentives to invest in new roads via the provision of large swaths of what would become valuable state lands after the roads were built. Fundamental to this entire process were the incentives granted by the state and employers so that settlers could go and populate the lands adjacent to the roads. These people took care of the roads as part of their obligation and, at the same time, brought their products to the markets that sprang up along the new road.

Thus, the country began the twentieth century served by an extensive road network that primarily comprised horse paths and some roads that allowed for wheeled vehicles. The logic and goals were simple: to move products to nearby markets and, if those products, such as coffee and tobacco, were designated for export, to find ways out to the Magdalena River or to the western port of Buenaventura. Similarly, for the state, these roadways needed to ease communications among people and allow freedom of movement throughout the country. Because transportation was so important, by 1905 the Ministry of Public Works was created. This ministry was assigned many of the tasks previously delegated to the Ministry of Development. In this way, the state prepared itself institutionally to confront a challenge that had not been satisfactorily mastered: the integration of the country so that people and goods could quickly flow throughout its territory.

Construction projects during the first three decades of the twentieth century defined the future of the country's transport system: a predilection for the automobile, buses, and trucks. Roadways thereby became central to national planning. The first car to move over the Colombian territory did so in Medellín in 1899. Nevertheless, the road trip that inaugurated an increasing preference for automobiles was taken in 1905 by the president at that time, Rafael Reyes, from Bogotá to Santa Rosa de Viterbo in Boyacá, his place of birth. In order to make this voyage possible, the precarious road that linked the two cities via Tunja had to be prepared to allow for automobile traffic. Ultimately, roadways turned out to be more affordable than trains due to the difficult geological conditions of Colombia. Automobiles were much more efficient for travel among cities and towns and for accessing the myriad market towns located in the foothills and valleys that separated them. Railways proved impractical in Colombia due to the nation's physical geography and the specific technical limitations of rail technology. This will be examined in greater detail, but for now it is important to note that railway lines were never able to efficiently transport goods and people within the Colombian mountainous territory. By the time railways were constructed within a system that never was quite completed, roadways had already come to dominate the nation's transportation needs.

The impetus from the national and departmental governments to improve old dirt roads and to build new roadways occurred during the first decades of the twentieth century. By 1930, a total of 107,615 kilometers of roadways were viable for transportation; yet, of the grand total, only 5,743 kilometers (or about 5 percent of the total network) were viable for motorized vehicles. Nevertheless, in 1930 many Colombians still used mules as their primary form of transportation. By 1946, 17,900 kilometers of roads were made viable for motor vehicles. Of these, 391 kilometers had been paved. Not until 1970 was the entire road from Cali to the western port of Buenaventura paved, a route that is fundamental for the international commerce of the country, as it links the interior with the only major Pacific port.

Note that in the United States, it was not until the Eisenhower administration (the 1950s) that the country organized and built its national interstate highway system. By the end of the twentieth century, the entire Colombian network of roadways had been constructed and paved. The central government was then in charge of 16,776 kilometers of roadway that connected the capital cities of each department with the national borders (except in the Amazon region) and with the main ports on the Pacific and Caribbean coasts. Of this total, only 629 kilometers were two-lane highways. This is one of the major challenges of the national highway system that needs to be addressed in the twenty-first century. The departments and municipalities now control 147,500 kilometers of roads—many of them still unpaved—which are vital for the economy of the country. They are the roads that connect the municipal centers with the major cities of the country.

STEAMSHIPS AND RAILWAYS

Government officials and entrepreneurs had taken a variety of transportation methods into account early in the nineteenth century. But the implementation of steamship navigation and railways was impossible until the costs could be justified by the adequate size of markets, a significant need to move people, and sales of products destined for export. By the 1820s, the administrations of Bolívar and Santander granted Juan Bernardo Elbers, a German entrepreneur who became a naturalized Colombian citizen, the official privilege to engage in steamship navigation along the Magdalena River. In effect, as of 1825, two steamships, the *Bolívar* and the *Santander*, plied the waters of that river, but their coverage was limited to the area near the mouth of the river, and service lasted only a few years. Other similar attempts also failed. Not until 1850 was steamship navigation consolidated along the Magdalena. Over the course of those twenty-five years, economic monopolies had been abolished, commerce had been expanded thanks to products being sent downriver for exportation, and new trade routes were established that looked toward the Magdalena as a source for markets in other areas of the country.

By 1926, eighteen firms operated eighty steamships, and they pulled 155 barges that together towed over six hundred thousand tons of merchandise. This was the epoch of maximum development for steamship navigation along the Magdalena River. By the mid-twentieth century, the importance of the Magdalena as a shipment lane had significantly declined as other forms of transportation supplanted the steamship by eliminating costly transshipment of merchandise from ship to truck or, less frequently, from ship to train. Overland transportation became more common since it could better handle transportation from ports on the river to distant populations in the interior. Other obstacles that further hindered steamship development involved the dramatic, damaging cycles of rain and dry seasons, the cost of fuel, and, in general, the lack of sufficient return on the transported merchandise. By the mid-twentieth century, merchants increasingly preferred aviation as the most secure means of transportation and ultimately the most economic way to travel from the capital to the coast and the exterior. Thus steamship transportation along the Magdalena River is now a mere memory.

The Magdalena River was not the only waterway that served to facilitate steamship navigation. The Atrato River on the west coast was a key transportation route. *The Esmeralda* arrived in Quibdó in 1852 and was used by a joint stock company starting in 1855. Additionally, some segments of the Cauca River were navigable, connecting Cali with La Virginia starting in the late nineteenth century until 1928, the year that railroad service began between these two points. The Zulia River allowed Cúcuta to connect with the Maracaibo Gulf via steamship in the final years of the 1880s. The Meta River in the eastern plains was used beginning in the mid-nineteenth century; it was easily navigated by steamships and, when reaching the Orinoco River, connected the center of the country with the Atlantic Ocean. The Putumayo River, in the southeast Amazon basin, facilitated commerce in quinine and, especially, rubber. This also occurred along the Amazon River once Emperor Pedro II of Brazil declared free trade in 1867. Other rivers allowed for travel via steamships, such as the Bogotá River, which facilitated shipment of coal to the capital in the late nineteenth century. Taken together, these non-Magdalena river routes were marginal to the economic development of the country and ended up being supplanted by roadways and motorized vehicles and, to a lesser degree, by rail.

The rail system with its multiple cars and locomotives and parallel tracks, which profoundly impacted how humans around the world tackled long distances beginning in the early nineteenth century, was a public preference in

Colombia from very early on. But, as with steam navigation, this mode of transportation could be implemented only when freight and passenger demand brought in real profits. The construction of the first railway began in 1850 when the Colombian government authorized North American entrepreneurs to build what would turn out to be one of the first and most profitable railways on the American continent: the Panama Railway. This line, by 1855, crossed the Isthmus of Panama from Colón to Panama City. Some years would pass before each of the federal states in Colombia would propose construction of their own railway lines. The states believed railways would facilitate the transport of local products to regional markets, especially to capital cities, and would facilitate the exportation of goods to the Magdalena River, toward Cartagena and Barranquilla at the Caribbean or Buenaventura at the Pacific. When the country unified in 1886, this drive to build railroads intensified; however, now the central state assumed as its duty the continuation of public works and initiated new railway projects that were key for the country's development. Thus, a coherent system of roadways, railways, and steamship navigation emerged and was designed to optimize the transportation of merchandise and passengers.

Table 7.1 presents the main lines and rail routes constructed in Colombia throughout its history, detailing the years in which each railroad construction began, when each was finalized, and the length of each trajectory. The duration of these projects is noteworthy—these figures suggest the severity of difficulties to be overcome. It is also important to note how the lines connected with one another. For example, the Valle of Cauca line connected with those of Antioquia and the coffee regions of the states of Caldas, Risaralda, and Quindio. The railway of the savannah of Bogotá connected with that of La Dorada, and this route, in turn, met up with Puerto Berrío and Santa Marta. The Bogotá to Girardot railway connected with the line that ran from Flandes to Neiva (Villavieja). Thus an interconnected system, one that streamlined communication, was created. Finally, as is evident from the table, railways were no longer constructed after the mid-twentieth century. The last line built linked La Dorada with Santa Marta in 1961; the crisis of railroads—precipitated by their limited profitability—coincided with the crisis in steamship navigation along the Magdalena.

The crisis of the rail system was not really the result of the devilish geography that posed so many obstacles for its construction and function. Railways were a problem because the state did not have the necessary tools to deal with private interests successfully. Private investors and subcontractors engaged in practices that ultimately brought the entire railway-building enterprise to a halt. They changed the routes of the railways for reasons having more to do with potential personal profit than the good of the nation. Investors manipu-

Table 7.1. Railroad National Network

Line or Trajectory	Years of Construction	Length (km)
Panama	1850–1855	77
Puerto Colombia–Barranquilla	1869–1888	28
Cartagena–Calamar	1890–1894	105
Central de Bolívar (Cartagena–Medellín, but only to Gambote)	ca. 1922–1925	nd
RR de Antioquia (Port of Berrío–Medellín)	1874–1929	193
Medellín–Jericó (Río Cauca)	1911–1930	127
Buenaventura–Cali–Palmira	1878–1915–1917	To Cali 173
Cali–Popayán	1914–1926	158
Cali–Zarzal–La Virginia	1917–1924–1928	nd
La Virginia–La Pintada (Rio Cauca)	1928–1951	nd
Zarzal–Armenia	1927	nd
Cartago–Pereira–Manizales	1915–1921–1927	111
Tumaco–El Diviso	1925–1928	109
La Dorada–Ambalema	1881–1907	111
Ambalema–Buenos Aires	1919–1931	65
Ibagué–Flandes	1899–1921	76
Espinal–Neiva (Villavieja)	1919–1930	185
La Dorada–Port of Berrío–Bosconia–Fundación–Santa Marta	1953–1961	nd
Girardot–Facatativá	1881–1910	131
RR of La Sabana (Bogotá–Facatativá)	1882–1889	39
Facatativá–La Dorada (Palanquero)	1925–nd	197
Bogotá–Soacha–Sibaté (RR of the South)	1896–1903–1906	30
Branch, El Charquito–Tequendama Falls	Construction ends in 1927	10
Branch, Sibaté–San Miguel	1925–1929	41
RR of the North (Bogotá–Zipaquirá–Chiquinquirá–Barbosa)	1893–1898–1928; to Barbosa after 1930	nd
Port of Wilches–Bucaramanga	1881–1941	109
Santa Marta–Fundación	1882–1906	94
RR of the Northeast (Bogotá–Tunja–Sogamoso)	1925–1931	nd
Cúcuta–Villamizar	ca. 1879–1926	60
Branch, Cúcuta–El Diamante	1926–1929	42
Branch, La Frontera	1895–1897	16

Source: Víctor Manuel Patiño, *Historia de la Cultura Material.* Tomo 3 (Bogotá: Instituto Caro y Cuervo, 1990–1993). Corrected by Juan Santiago Correa.

nd = no data available.

lated contracts to the benefit of some businesses either by overcharging or by winning breach-of-contract lawsuits. The contracts, generally unclear and/ or overly generous to the railway companies, resulted in lawsuits that were overwhelmingly won in favor of the companies to the detriment of the state. Another factor was the incompetence of public officials who never seemed to be able to verify the excuses companies made for delays. Companies were unable to complete the lines according to the terms of the contract, and there was little to no governmental oversight. Similarly, construction delays, which dragged on in some cases well into the mid-twentieth century and led to only partial utility of the rail lines, meant that this system could not compete with the emerging road network, which, despite its shortcomings, managed to achieve continuity over long distances.

AERIAL CABLES AND AIRPLANES

The coffee grown in the fertile lands of Caldas was first exported out of Colombia in large quantities beginning in the twentieth century. Coffee reached the Magdalena River at Honda on its way to the Caribbean ports after a long journey on muleback. A train line covering this route was impossible due to the terrain. The train that finally was built went toward the Pacific port of Buenaventura, a wise political and engineering decision, but the line was not completed until the end of the 1920s, after the opening of the Panama Canal, which permitted the Pacific ports of Colombia to connect with the Caribbean and Atlantic Ocean.

Before the completion of the rail line to Buenaventura, Colombian entrepreneurs, out of an urgent need to move coffee to markets, found that an aerial cable—loosely equivalent to a ski lift for coffee—could offer a solution. Construction began in 1913, and the aerial cable was inaugurated in 1922. It connected Manizales with Mariquita. Over the course of seventy-two kilometers of cable length supported by 376 towers, the aerial cable transported up to ten tons of coffee and other merchandise per hour on about eight hundred wagons. The cable continued in use until 1961 and became one of the key factors that made Manizales the most important regional center in all of the coffee-growing areas of the country. As a result of the success of this cable, other projects for aerial cars were initiated in the region. For example, in 1927, a line was built from Manizales to the town of Villamaría. Another line was designated to reach north from Manizales to the town of Aranzazu in 1928. A third, begun in 1929, was designed to go west to the Chocó. None of these trajectories was constructed beyond a few kilometers, and these additions had a negligible impact on commerce.

Based on the successful Manizales–Marquita cable, a new line was built from the populations of Ocaña, up in the Andes, to the town of Gamarra, down at the Magdalena River. This facilitated the transportation of merchandise to and from the populous Department of Norte de Santander. Some 204 towers connected over 47 kilometers; the project was inaugurated in 1929 but functioned for only a few years.

The greatest impact on the country's communications was from air transportation. The first few public demonstrations of aerial flights occurred in the nineteenth century with hot air balloons in the cities of Popayán, Bogotá, Medellín, Barranquilla, and Tunja. Other exhibition flights, this time by airplane, took place in the early twentieth century. Passenger aviation that could also carry merchandise and mail began in September 1919 through the creation, by several businessmen from Medellín, of the Colombian Air Navigation Company (CCNA). The company initially owned four planes, which allowed it to win a contract with the national government to transport mail and passengers. The CCNA began operations in 1920 between Cartagena and Barranquilla. In 1921 it launched its first flight to Medellín. Economic problems led to the company's liquidation in 1923; nevertheless, aviation fever spread quickly on Colombian soil. Soon thereafter the Santanderanian Company of Aviation (COSADA) began service in 1923, and the UMCA, or Urabá-Medellín and Central Airways, opened in 1932.

Notwithstanding these developments, SCADTA (the Colombo-German Society of Air Transport) was created by Colombian and German entrepreneurs on December 5, 1919, in Barranquilla; it allowed air transport to take shape definitively in the nation. SCADTA permanently connected the center of the country with the Caribbean coast. The first flight from Barranquilla to Puerto Berrío occurred in September 1920. On October 19, a weekly flight was inaugurated between Barranquilla and Girardot, and on November 18, 1920, the first SCADTA flight landed in Bogotá. Earlier, in March 1920, the national government passed Decree 599, regulating "Law 126," which mentioned air travel in reference to military aviation. This decree went further by regulating aerial navigation overall within the national territory. It was in this way that a long history of air service began that has become widespread over the country and now connects Colombia with countries in South America, North America, and Europe.

MAIL AND COMMUNICATIONS SYSTEMS

A mail system began functioning early in the sixteenth century in what is today Colombian territory, and the Spanish Crown at that time contracted the service to private parties. Beginning in the eighteenth century, with the reforms of King Charles III, the Crown attempted to rein in control over mail by sending to the Americas appointed employees. The mail system became efficient through the direct control of the viceroy, and, fortunately, it was this system that the republican governments inherited. Some historians estimate that at the end of the eighteenth century, mail reached some one thousand places in what is now the Colombian territory and twelve thousand sites throughout the continent.

Enhancing the efficiency of the postal system was one of the major concerns of the Santander presidential administration (1821–1826). The following years were rich in government regulations related to mail handling—some regulations promoted free and open transportation of national and foreign newspapers. Toward the mid-nineteenth century, what was then the Republic of New Granada counted on 154 postal offices, and postal couriers traveled about eleven thousand kilometers carrying letters, official information, and even merchandise among these offices. One century later, in 1948, 1,218 post offices existed throughout the territory. In order to facilitate the postal system and to control costs associated with it, in 1859, stamps were used for the first time in the national postal system. This year was also the year that the first Organic Law of the National Postal System was issued.

But the onset of aviation, as mentioned above, included the handling of mail. This process began in a limited fashion in 1919 and grew steadily during the following years. Thus, the postal system, which is now privatized in the country after having been nationalized in the early twentieth century, strengthened during a two-hundred-year period. It connected people emotionally and financially and provided a sense that Colombians all formed part of the same territory.

The telegraph was a mechanism that proved more powerful than the mail system due to its speed. Parallel to the development of the railways, the first telegraph line ran along the Panama Railway during the mid-nineteenth century. Within the territory of what is now Colombia, the Radical Liberal Murillo Toro administration used state funds and some private capital to construct the first telegraph line, which allowed for communication between Bogotá and the hamlet of Cuatro Esquinas (now known as Mosquera) in the Bogotá savannah, on November 1, 1865. A few months later, in April 1866, this line had reached Ambalema, allowing the tobacco trade to be largely managed from Bogotá. At the same time, in Antioquia, another line was constructed designed to connect Medellín to Manizales. In this way, Medellín was integrated with the recently colonized regions to the south of the city. Something similar happened among those living along the Cauca River. In 1867 shares were sold to develop the company that would unite, via telegraph, the population of Cartago with the port of Buenaventura. That same year, Congress authorized the government to establish communications with other countries via transoceanic cables. All of these developments and the importance given to the new system led to the creation of the Directorate of Posts and Telegraphs. Soon thereafter, a telegraph school opened, and telegraph operation was monopolized by female workers—much in the same way as in the United States, for example, where early telephone operators were predominantly women.

During the next few years, telegraph lines were constructed from Bogotá to Manizales, Medellín, Tunja, and Bucaramanga. In only two years, the system's capacity doubled; thus, by 1875, 2,045 kilometers of telegraph line were in operation. The system had developed to the point where on April 12, 1876, news arrived—in two days' time—from London. The president of Colombia received a telegram that had taken the route of London–Jamaica–Colón–Panama–Buenaventura–Bogotá. In this way, the underwater cable, connected to its overland network, had finally defeated long distances through technological innovation. These telegraph lines strengthened the sensation of inhabiting a space that had somehow become more close-knit.

In 1886, when the federal system had been eradicated under the new constitution, the rapid speed with which communications traversed the territory began to shape Colombian society. For example, the presidential palace had its own telegraph set beginning in 1876. Two years later, the first phone call was made in the capital, although still under experimental conditions. In 1882 Colombia was connected via the Pacific base in Buenaventura with Peru, Ecuador, Mexico, and the United States. Europe was already a communication partner, as referenced earlier, via Colón and Jamaica. Once these feats were achieved, the twentieth century witnessed technological innovations and communication speeds that not even the most optimistic people of the nineteenth century could have predicted; wireless telegraph first, telephone next, then radio, television at midcentury, and then satellite systems and the World Wide Web in the last decades of the century. These developments have profoundly transformed the ways in which the nations of the world and their peoples communicate with one another, redefining dominions and liberties. Colombia is no exception; on the contrary, the nation has continually pushed to remain up to date with the latest communications innovations. As a part of government policy, Colombia strengthened public control over communications systems, creating a new Ministry of the Post Office and Telegraphs in 1923 and hiring a Belgian Communications Mission in 1924.

During the 1920s, amateur Colombian radio enthusiasts began communicating with one another and with people from other countries. Experimental radio transmissions were realized in 1923, and commercial radio broadcasts began in 1930 via private radio stations in the country's major cities: one was called "The Voice of Colombia" in Bogotá, and in Tunja, "The Voice of

Tunja"; HKJ and HKK in Cali; HKT in Manizales; and the following year, "The Voice of Chapinero" in Bogotá; "Echo of the Mountain" and "Medellín Radio" in Medellín; another station in Cali, HKR; and in 1934 (in Bogotá) "La Voz de la Víctor" began to broadcast political news with distinct partisan leanings in the first radio news show of its kind in Colombian history. The local, or at most, regional, nature of radio stations was characteristic of the way the system operated well into the twentieth century. In 1940, La Radio Nacional was created, and it became the official station of the state. As such, it officially represented the country and served as the vehicle of communication for the government.

Colombia nationalized its communications through Law 6 of 1943. The law authorized the government to create a company that unified all the systems of radiotelegraphy that operated in the country. In August 1943, the National Radio Communications Company was created after the purchase of the Marconi wireless telegraph. Four years later, in 1947, the government—through its creation of the National Company of Telecommunications (TELECOM)—executed a similar operation and joined the National Radio Communications Company the following year. Thus, the state was in control of both the radio spectrum—although it did permit private commercial use—and long-distance telephone service, while also regulating local and regional telephone services.

This tendency to control communications from the public sector continued when it came to television. In 1954, the first Colombian television program was aired, and it relied on the newly created television division of National Radio. The following decades witnessed the rapid development of even faster and more efficient forms of communicating. It is noteworthy how quickly new inventions could be implemented in the Colombian territory: telex, fax, satellite, the Internet, and cellular communications. Today Colombia is a nation within which the state may communicate with all of its inhabitants via different media that form the public system, and it may also use, when necessary, the wider-reaching and sophisticated private system that has been developed in Colombia by national and foreign entrepreneurs.

PRINT MEDIA

Finally, the print media must be considered among all media available to create a national consciousness among Colombians. Note, however, that few newspapers became truly national, while several thrived in particular regions. The capital of each department tended to produce news, and thus, in general, newspapers emerged there and communicated the local news to residents. These newspapers, with time and the onset of airmail, could be read in many parts of the country, allowing local news to be received in almost every region of the nation.

The written press and especially the daily newspaper were possible in Colombia only after several factors converged. First, news from other places needed to be known and consumed instantaneously; second, news needed to be transmitted with equal velocity through the printed papers; and third, the printed papers needed, in turn, to reach their readers. This is why the press was local in nature from the very moment it was created in Colombia during the last years of the eighteenth century to well into the first decades of the twentieth. Correspondents and especially subscribers in other cities existed, but the difficulties created by distance and the cost of transportation prevented national print journalism from developing. Thus, local publications of literary, scientific, and general interests predominated and were accompanied by a plethora of pamphlets and libel-ridden documents. But this did not prevent significant technical improvements from developing in the printing press. From the mid-nineteenth century, lithography was introduced in Bogotá, and much later, in 1881, an illustrated newspaper (by Alberto Urdaneta) included elaborate illustrations and images created through engravings. By 1911, the linotype technique allowed for the emergence of daily newspapers that could be produced quickly with reduced costs.

The telegraph, as mentioned above, first allowed for almost immediate information gathering in other parts of the country and the world. Eventually, a world network developed that included national and international correspondents and was facilitated through the purchasing of news from emerging international news agencies. The content of newspapers soon became newsworthy; however, periodicals did not become national until the system of transportation could guarantee that subscribers would receive their papers in their homes no matter where they resided in the country. The possibility of transforming a periodical from a weekly to a daily publication implied not only technical solutions but also economic investment. This was achieved when distribution reached other cities of the nation, and of course, shipment by air was a key solution. It is important to mention two additional conditions that contributed as much as technology to the circulation of newspapers at the national and regional levels: the progress in national literacy rates, which expanded the number of possible readers, and the need to form public opinion, a process that required information to sway the public concerning a particular situation. These factors allowed for an increasing generalization and sharing of information to shape opinions in towns and cities. Thus, institutions—the state and the church to offer two historical examples, but also schools and other places of social exchange, such as the café and the plaza—brought together more and more people to discuss and exchange important political, social, and intellectual ideas.

The Colombian newspapers that eventually became national due to the extent of their circulation are grounded in political centralism. Based in Bogotá, the national newspapers carry mostly news from the nation's capital and its environs. This circumstance is not limited to the past; it continues today. Communal identities are forged by making national news out of events that happen to only a few individuals living in the capital city. In this way, the business of Bogotá becomes the business of Colombia.

One of the most prominent nationally circulating newspapers today is *El Espectador*, which was founded in 1887 in Medellín but later moved its headquarters to Bogotá, the city where it acquired its Liberal leanings and national circulation network. *El Tiempo* was founded in Bogotá more than one hundred years ago, in 1911. Today, it is the paper with the largest circulation in the country and the most influential voice in public opinion; its orientation is openly Liberal. *El Siglo*, now known as *El Nuevo Siglo*, or "The New Century," is published in Bogotá and is of a Conservative political leaning. It was founded by conservative leader Laureano Gómez in 1936 as a mechanism for counterbalancing the power of the Liberals in the presidential administration beginning in 1930. *The Republic*, another national paper published in Bogotá and of an equally Conservative political bent, was founded by Mariano Ospina Pérez in 1954. Today, this paper is the most influential paper that specializes in economic affairs.

The regional press, given its place of origin and the specific sociocultural dynamics of those places, addresses the readership in the areas where it principally circulates. But, as previously mentioned, people who live in other areas of the country, especially if they move, also read particular regional newspapers. Among them it is important to mention *El Colombiano*, a Conservative newspaper founded in Medellín in 1912; *El Heraldo* of Barranquilla, established in 1933; *El País*, created in Cali in 1950; *Vanguardia Liberal*, of Bucaramanga, founded in 1919; *La Patria*, in print in Manizales beginning in 1921; and, among others, *El Liberal*, published in Popayán, which has been in circulation since 1938.

Colombia's complex geography has presented obstacles to national unification, and one of the greatest challenges for the Colombian people has been to create governmental, economic, and communications systems that allow for some sense of unification. The historical record is mixed, but the construction of a national road network, the widespread use of the airplane in the twentieth century, and the adaptation of the radio, television, and Internet to the social and political realities of the nation have allowed for slow yet sustained economic development despite seemingly insurmountable physical obstacles. The ongoing challenge involves creating mechanisms to distribute more adequately and share the richness of the Colombian nation with all Colombian citizens.

Chapter Eight

Cultural Dynamism

Colombia's cultural production has been incredibly diverse, drawing on regional distinctions and identities with manifest ties to the country's socio-political realities. This chapter focuses on uniquely Colombian contributions to world culture, emphasizing plastic arts (painting and sculpture), literature, theater, architecture, and music. During much of the twentieth century, Colombian achievements in these areas were virtually unknown to those outside the country, due in large measure to political tensions in Colombia and, as one historian has written, the centrifugal force of "the enormous vogue of things Mexican."[1] Mexican art, particularly the postrevolutionary muralist movement, captivated the world and overshadowed production in other regions of Latin America. The literary world at the turn of the twentieth century, when it focused on Latin America, featured a few Latin American modernists—Rubén Darío from Nicaragua, José Martí in Cuba, and José Enrique Rodó in Uruguay—but it was not until the late 1960s that Colombian literature achieved international acclaim with the publication in 1967 of Gabriel García Márquez's sweeping, monumental *One Hundred Years of Solitude*. Colombian theater, influenced by European existentialism, emerged with a national identity but not until the 1950s. The contributions of Colombian architects were, until recently, generally overlooked as critics focused on the construction of Brazil's new capital city in the 1950s, the influence of the Swiss modernist Le Corbusier in the south of Latin America, the construction of a University City in Mexico, and the colonial Baroque splendor found in Lima, Havana, Mexico City, and Quito. Colombia and Colombians have rarely been mentioned as adding original or unique value to world architecture. Colombia's impact on world music is important, but Colombia cannot claim anyone (when considering elite music) of the stature of Alberto Ginestera (the Argentine pianist and composer), Heitor Villa-Lobos (the Brazilian composer), the Cuban Ernesto Lecuona, or the Mexican Carlos Chávez. However, unique Colombian popular music is found in the coastal *cumbia*, the western plains music called *musica llanera*, and the north central plains folk music called *vallenato*.

SCULPTURE AND PAINTING

In the *artes plasticas*, loosely defined as painting and sculpture, Colombia's tradition is deep and diverse. The first-time visitor to Bogotá typically visits the recently reconstructed and redesigned Museo del Oro (Gold Museum) and begins to understand the immense talent of the pre-Columbian artisans of what is today Colombia. The incredibly detailed, filigree gold work on display, which predates the arrival of the Spaniards by centuries, suggests a level of craftsmanship, patience, and attention to detail that is the marker of sophisticated, highly structured civilizations. The arrival of the Europeans meant that gold and other precious metals and stones found in Colombia would be used to venerate the Catholic Church, Church traditions, and saints. Thus, one of the most impressive religious sculptures from the eighteenth century is found in Colombia, at the Museo del Banco de la República. Colloquially known as *la lechuga*, or "the head of lettuce," the sculpture, designed to hold the consecrated host during the Catholic mass, is made of 1,485 emeralds and 4,900 grams of gold inlaid with pearls, diamonds, and other precious stones. This object, more formally known as "La Custodia de la Iglesia de San Ignacio de Bogotá," was created between 1700 and 1707 for the community of Catholic priests known as the Jesuits, but the Jesuits sold the piece to the Colombian nation in 1985; the money from the sale helped initiate the Jesuit Plan de Paz, or "peace initiative," in the 1980s. The sculpture is a clear reminder of the direct link between art and politics in Colombia.

An exemplary and unique visual record of Colombia's tropical flora, fauna, and topographical beauty is seen in the drawings of a Spanish physician, José Celestino Mutis, who arrived in what is today Colombia in 1760 and died there forty-eight years later. His impressive collection of drawings was confiscated in 1816 during the independence wars and sent to Spain. They remained there, undiscovered, for some 150 years.[2] Approximately 5,300 drawings were recorded on folio sheets and represent a foundational, visual mapping of New Granada. Mutis was not the only European captivated by Colombia's geography and natural beauty. The German scientist Alexander von Humboldt took a five-year journey (1799–1804) to Cuba, northern South America, and Mexico. He was interested in scientific questions especially related to climate, ocean currents, rivers, and valleys, and his drawings helped Europeans to imagine, with more clarity, the natural wonders of Latin America. Von Humboldt found especially compelling the Central *cordillera* (mountain range) of Colombia, which connects Bogotá and the Ecuadorian capital city, Quito. Later, the Italian engineer-geographer Agustín Codazzi spent ten years in Colombia, from 1850 to 1859, mapping the territory and studying its physical and human geography. He assembled a team of painters, mapmakers, botanists, and others; many of the stylized, folkloric watercolor drawings from his expeditions can be found today in the Colombian Biblioteca Nacional.

Not all Colombian art of the nineteenth century was based upon European scientific or mapping expeditions; the process of independence in Colombia generated an outpouring of artistic expression. The Colombian artist Pedro José Figueroa's *Simón Bolívar, Liberator and Father of the Nation* is held at the Quinta de Bolívar in Bogotá—the home and headquarters of the Liberator during the time he spent in Bogotá. The Colombian painter José María Espinosa produced many portraits of the Liberator, including a pencil sketch depicting a gaunt, defeated Bolívar completed shortly before his death on December 17, 1830. Bolívar was not the only hero of independence painted in the early nineteenth century: Policarpa Salvarrieta, heroine of the independence movement, who served as an informant for the insurgents and was executed by the Spaniards in 1817, was a popular artistic subject. An anonymous work housed at the National Museum in Bogotá depicts her final walk to martyrdom.[3]

The nineteenth-century art tradition in Colombia, influenced by the political process of independence and the work of the various scientific, mapping, and geographic missions from Europe, broke dramatically with the colonial tradition of art as religious art. Colombia's first art school, the Escuela de Bellas Artes, dates to 1886 during the period of conservative political ascendency known as the Regeneration; Bellas Artes served as a conduit through which the latest artistic trends of Europe, more specifically Madrid and Paris, would be received in the country. Modernism, which emerged at the beginning of the twentieth century, flourished in places with expanding urban centers and an influx of European migrants. Not surprisingly, Buenos Aires, São Paulo, and Mexico City became important centers of Latin American modernism. Colombia, with a capital city some six hundred miles from the Caribbean coast, was not an important destination for nineteenth- and twentieth-century European migrants, and thus the modernist movement would never take a firm hold.

The country's first modernist painter—and director of the School of Fine Arts—was Andrés de Santamaría, a Bogotá-born artist who spent most of his life in Europe and died in Brussels in 1945. The art historian Jacqueline

Barnitz describes him as the nation's first modernist for his "perverse color combinations."[4] Santamaría's work was not well received in his native country during his lifetime, but changing tastes and sensibilities prevailed, and his reputation as a major force in Colombian art was established during the 1960s, twenty-five years after his death.

Two painters from the western city of Medellín (not including Fernando Botero, who is discussed later) made a lasting contribution to Colombian art in the twentieth century. The muralist Pedro Nel Gómez created extraordinarily detailed renditions of Colombian history and culture, but his work was regionally focused on the forces that moved Medellín and the surrounding Department of Antioquia, that is, gold production, work, family life, and violence. His huge murals decorate the municipal building in downtown Medellín, and at the central Parque Berrío Metro station in Medellín the entire history of Antioquia is depicted in a uniquely Colombian homage to the famous Mexican muralist Diego Rivera.

A controversial painter from the outskirts of Medellín, Débora Arango, who died in 2005 at the age of ninety-eight, offended the sensibilities of some conservative Catholic Colombians with her stark depiction of the female body. She also criticized official society with art that was strongly political: in one painting, she depicted the Colombian president Laureano Gómez as a fat toad. She confronted the Roman Catholic Church in her work and did not shy away from depicting the country's violence. Arango painted during most of the twentieth century and came to be viewed, after initial setbacks and criticisms (including the closing of one of her shows in Franco's Spain), as a daring and creative representative of Colombian art.[5]

Colombians who had a major impact on Colombian and Latin American sculpture in the twentieth century include Edgar Negret and Eduardo Ramírez Villamizar. Negret was born in 1920 in Popayán, in the southwest of Colombia, and spent a good deal of time (c. 1948–1963) living abroad, mostly in New York, Paris, and Barcelona, but he returned to Colombia in 1963. He served as a cultural emissary for artists in Europe, Colombia, and the United States, and one of his pieces, *Dinamismo*, "[an] eight-foot-long exterior structure," is found at the corner of 7th Avenue and 72nd Street in Bogotá, outside the entrance to the Banco Ganadero.[6] Similarly, Eduardo Ramírez Villamizar, born in 1922 in Pamplona, Colombia, lived abroad, training and visiting studios in France, Spain, and Italy; he also spent considerable time in New York City, and in 1973 he produced a piece titled "De Colombia a John F. Kennedy" (From Colombia to John F. Kennedy), a modernist tribute to the late president who visited Colombia in 1961. The piece sits on the grounds of the Kennedy Center in Washington, D.C.

Ana María Hoyos, born in Bogotá in 1942, is a renowned Colombian artist whose paintings, drawings, and photographs have captured, more than other

Colombian artists, the essence, colors, and texture of the north Colombian coast and the dignity of the people who live and work there. In addition to Hoyos, the work of four male painters provides a broad perspective of Colombia's twentieth-century artistic production: that of Enrique Grau, Alejandro Obregón, Luis Caballero, and Fernando Botero.

Enrique Grau, raised in Cartagena, was born in 1920 and died in Bogotá in 2004. Self-taught as a painter, he achieved international fame with his paintings influenced by European baroque. Like many acclaimed artists of his day, he traveled to Italy and France and was warmly received in New York, where his work was presented at MOMA (Museum of Modern Art) and at the Guggenheim. Alejandro Obregón (1920–1995) was born in Spain to a Spanish mother and Colombian father. The artist settled in Colombia after 1955, at Cartagena on the north coast; he lived in the south of France during the early years of La Violencia. Obregón tackled the Colombian violence directly in his work. In fact, he dedicated a series of paintings to the violence, as a form of visual journalism, much in the same way as the contemporary Colombian painter Fernando Botero completed and displayed a controversial series of drawings based on the U.S. military's Abu-Ghraib prison abuse scandal in Iraq in 2004. One of the principal pieces of Obregón's series, *Detalle de un genocidio*, is on display at the Museo Banco de la República in Bogotá; the piece depicts, in a somewhat abstract fashion, the dead body of a pregnant woman.

Luis Caballero, unlike Débora Arango, focused on the male nude and died at fifty-two years of age in 1995 in Paris. He left his homeland as a twenty-six-year-old and never returned to live in Colombia. Early in his life, Caballero learned that Colombian sensitivities were not aligned with his work, and he found a more receptive audience in Europe. But when conservative tastes and Catholic Church condemnations fell out of fashion during the late 1960s and 1970s, Caballero was recognized as a master and an important representative of Colombian cultural development. This changing Colombian artistic mood can be attributed, in large part, to the work of the Argentine art critic and *alta-patrona* Marta Traba, who helped introduce abstraction and other European, Latin American Southern Cone, and U.S. artistic trends to Colombia. She spent considerable time in Bogotá and is principally associated with the founding of the MAMBO—Museo de Arte Moderno de Bogotá.

The most famous and internationally acclaimed Colombian painter, Fernando Botero, was born in Medellín in 1932 and now lives in Italy and New York. His work is easily recognizable: his expressive, overweight figures and still-life paintings are popular throughout the Western world, and Botero is one of the most financially successful artists of his generation in Colombia and in the world. His work is political in a subtle and playful way; he depicts military and church officials as "portly," suggesting an exaggerated sense of self-importance of these historic institutions. His work is found in the most important galleries throughout the world; the Museo Nacional (Bogotá) houses a significant collection of the painter's works. However, the most complete collections of Botero's paintings and bronze sculptures are found at the Museo Donación Botero in Bogotá and the Museo de Antioquia in Medellín. In 2000, the artist donated to the museum in Bogotá 123 pieces of his work and eighty-five pieces from his personal collection, including works by Chagall, Picasso, Robert Rauschenberg, and the French impressionists. He donated a similar number of works to the Museo de Antioquia in his hometown of Medellín, transforming overnight the two Colombian cities into important centers of contemporary Western art. Botero's strong sense of regional identity is found in virtually all of his work, and his donation helped reform the urban center of Medellín. The Museo de Antioquia was inaugurated in 2004, in an elegant downtown art deco building that served as the main municipal building for the region. The year 2004 coincided with a second massive donation by Botero and the construction of the Plaza de Las Esculturas (Sculpture Plaza, better known as "Plaza Botero") in front of the museum, which displays dozens of Botero's large bronze sculptures.

LITERATURE

Colombian creative capacity extends to other areas of the arts: the leading literary figure in Colombia and, arguably, in all of Latin America is the Colombian Gabriel García Márquez, a man with a prodigious literary talent who was recognized by the Nobel Committee in 1982. García Márquez is the only Colombian in history to have won the Nobel Prize and one of only six Latin Americans to win the Nobel Prize in Literature. Gabriel García Márquez, born in 1927 in the north coast town of Aracataca, is the product of a long, rich literary tradition in Colombia, and his major work, *One Hundred Years of Solitude* (1967) is a reflection of *realismo mágico*, where the magical and the real are largely indistinguishable. Many Colombians consider García Márquez a national treasure and a living example of the creative impulse of the Colombian people; others view him with indifference, believing that his worldwide fame has overshadowed the accomplishments of the many other extraordinary Colombian writers who have produced excellent work in the twentieth century. This schizophrenic appreciation is evident, for instance, in the third edition of the frequently cited *Manual de Historia de Colombia* (4th edition, 1992), where, in an eighty-nine-page chapter titled "La Literatura Colombiana en el siglo XX" ("Colombian Literature in the Twentieth Century"), by Rafael Gutiérrez Girardot, García Márquez is mentioned once—in a single sentence.

Before García Márquez, modern Colombian literary production can be considered by focusing on five important writers/intellectuals: the poet José Eusebio Caro; the writer Soledad Acosta de Samper, who was an early champion of gender equality in Colombia; and the poet José Asunción Silva. The most important novelist of the nineteenth century, Jorge Isaacs, produced the romantic novel *María*, and José Eustasio Rivera bridged the two centuries (1888–1928) and penned his powerful political novel *La Vorágine* in 1924 (translated to English as *The Vortex*).

José Eusebio Caro lived for thirty-six years during the earliest days of the republic; he was a politician, essayist, journalist, and romantic poet. The Latin American legacy of fusing literary aspirations (in this case, poetry) and politics seems to have been established with Caro, who was one of the founders of the modern Conservative Party in Colombia. His poetry, much of it highly stylized, was early nineteenth-century romantic in tone. He composed love elegies to Blasina Tobar, daughter of a distinguished Conservative family. Caro's poetry seems outdated and anachronistic by today's standards ("No soy feliz; tu amor, que es mi tesoro/Es quien me roba mi quietud también");[7] but the combination of literary sensibility, journalistic expression, and political ambition became a coherent, practical paradigm for Latin American political leaders. In societies with limited access to education, a hierarchical model of leadership, and a general mistrust among the social classes, those who rose to prominence politically through elevated speech and writing began their "political campaigns" by publishing their ideas in essay format in newspapers or pamphlets. In the United States, there have been presidents who have demonstrated great skill as writers, including Abraham Lincoln, Theodore Roosevelt, and Barack Obama, but citizens of the United States do not identify these men first and foremost as "writers." In Colombia and Latin America, literary erudition translated—not always well—to statesmanship and a pathway to political power. This was certainly the case with at least two Colombian presidents, the well-known writers José Manuel Marroquín and Marco Fidel Suárez. Suárez assumed the presidency in 1918, and his opponent that year was the noted modernist poet Guillermo Valencia.

A nineteenth-century writer with keen antecedent political insights was Soledad Acosta de Samper, who has been described as the "most influential female writer in New Granada during the nineteenth century."[8] She was an early Latin American advocate for women's participation in society. Her upbringing was hardly normative for nineteenth-century Latin America; her father was Joaquín Acosta, a hero of the independence period, and her mother was Caroline Kemble Rowe, who was born in Kingston, Jamaica. Acosta traveled widely as a young girl, learned to speak French and English fluently, and married José María Samper, an important politician and intellectual. Acosta de Samper was an essayist, journalist, travel writer, social commentator, and novelist. Her first book, published in 1869, is titled *Novelas y cuadros de la vida suramericana*. She also published novels that were written from the perspective of strong female protagonists, and she generally tasked her female characters to "search for self-knowledge through experience."[9] Acosta de Samper is considered a leading early pioneer in calling for equal treatment for women, and she insisted on the intellectual capacity of women at a time and in a place where such matters were rarely discussed.

Colombia's most renowned novelist of the nineteenth century was Jorge Isaacs (1837–1895), who wrote one of the most important romantic novels of the nineteenth century, *María*. Isaacs fought in the Colombian civil war of 1860–1862 and recorded, in lush detail, life on a plantation in the southwestern area of the country, in what is today the Cauca Valley. He published this "foundational fiction"[10] in 1867, establishing himself as a leading literary figure in the Americas, a sort of Colombian Mark Twain.

Poetry has always animated Colombian intellectual life, and one of the most important Colombian poets of the later part of the nineteenth century was the mercurial, morose José Asunción Silva, who committed suicide at age thirty-one in 1896. He wrote romantic, sentimental poetry, much of which, it seems, was directed toward his sister, Elvira, whose death in 1892 sent Silva into a downward spiral of despair. His poem "Nocturno," part of which is reproduced below (followed by our translation to English), reflects the mood of both the author and his time period:

> Esta noche
> Solo, el alma
> Llena de las infinitas amarguras y agonías de tu muerte
> Separado de ti misma, por la sombra, por el tiempo y la distancia,
> Por el infinito negro,
> Donde nuestra voz no alcanza,
> Solo y mudo
> Por la senda caminaba—

> This night
> Alone, the soul
> Full of infinite bitterness and agonies of your death
> Separated from you, by the shadow, by time and distance,
> By the infinite void,
> Where our voices never reach,
> Alone and mute
> By this road I wandered—

Silva enjoyed a revival, mostly among university students in Bogotá, on the one-hundredth anniversary of his death; poetry readings, celebrations, and competitions marked the occasion in 1996, and to this day, the Casa de Poesía Silva in the historic colonial neighborhood of Bogotá, La Candelaria, operates as an important cultural center and is a monument to the country's literary tradition and tastes, which tend to favor poetry.

In 1924 José Eustasio Rivera published the important sociopolitical novel *La Vóragine* (*The Vortex*). This novel, which indicted the "rubber barons" and their abusive treatment of poor rubber workers in the Amazon, fused elements of the American journalistic novel pioneered by Upton Sinclair with the work of Brazilian naturalist writer and reporter Euclides da Cunha, who opened up (metaphorically speaking) the Brazilian interior to elites who lived along that nation's coast. *La Vóragine* helped merge the disciplines of Colombian journalism and fiction writing; this art form would be perfected, later on, by Gabriel García Márquez. Tragically, Rivera died in 1928, at forty years of age, after suffering a series of seizures in New York City. He went to New York hoping to find an English-language publisher for his work.

One year before the death of Rivera, Gabriel García Márquez was born in a rural area of the Colombian Caribbean coast into a family of colorful characters who would form the foundation for most of his fiction. García Márquez's immense popularity and fame, in Latin America and the world, has diverted critical reflection from other significant twentieth-century Colombian writers, including García Márquez's closest friend, the writer Álvaro Mutis. The remainder of this segment on Colombian literature will focus on six twentieth-century writers: Tomás Carrasquilla, Álvaro Mutis, Manuel Zapata Olivella, Fernando Vallejo, Laura Restrepo, and García Márquez.

Tomás Carrasquilla was born in Santodomingo, Antioquia, in 1858; he died eighty-two years later in Medellín. He lived most of his life in Medellín, though he worked, reluctantly, in the Colombian capital for a number of years. Unlike many contemporary Colombian artists, Carrasquilla remained in Colombia his entire life and was unimpressed with the fashions, literary tastes, or happenings of Paris and New York. One of his biographers, the Canadian literary scholar Kurt Levy, pointed out that the author's "domain was reality, as reflected in Antioquia, its people and its landscape."[11] His novels and stories came from Antioquia, much like the stories of García Márquez reflect the customs, traditions, and history of Colombia's north coast. Carrasquilla's life has been described by Levy as "uneventful," but this author of stories reflecting the quotidian "trivia"[12] of life in Antioquia reminds the reader of the remarkable power of setting in fiction and the power of literature to capture and distill that which is essential to a region's identity.

A Colombian writer with a rich, varied, and complex life (he worked as a public relations executive for Standard Oil and as a sales manager for Twentieth Century Fox and Columbia Pictures in Latin America; he was a prisoner in Mexico for fifteen months—jailed by the Rojas Pinilla administration—and is now known as a writer of short fiction, poetry, and novellas) is Bogotá-born Álvaro Mutis. Mutis, like García Márquez, has spent most of his life in Mexico City. He became internationally renowned later in life, at the age of about sixty-two, when he published the novella *La Nieve del Almirante*, which turned into a seven-part series of novellas, translated and published in English as *The Adventures and Misadventures of Maqroll*. These captivating novellas reflect the author's international perspective—that is, they are not centered in Colombia or Mexico but take the reader on a variety of monumental journeys that force a comparison with Don Quixote, though Mutis sets his novellas in contemporary time.

Manuel Zapata Olivella was born in 1920 in Lorica, Colombia, and died in Bogotá in 2004. He was one of the earliest Afro-Colombian writers to achieve international literary acclaim. He traveled throughout the Americas and Europe, taught literature at the University of Kansas in the 1970s, and lectured widely on Latin American literature, identity, and culture. His friends included the great Peruvian writer Ciro Alegría, who wrote the prologue to the Colombian's novel *Tierra*, and American poet Langston Hughes. Zapata Olivella's travels are recounted in two works, *Pasión vagabunda* (1953) and its sequel, *He visto la noche*. These works are important commentaries on the treatment of outsiders (in this case, a dark-skinned Colombian man); *Pasión* takes the reader from Bogotá through Central America to Mexico, and *He visto la noche* moves from Mexico to the urban United States in the 1950s. They are critically important works that combine ethnological observation, literary skill, and precise social commentary during the 1950s as the United States was wrestling with the contradictions of segregation, while people in both the U.S. North and South pushed for a more forward-thinking, modern social agenda. Zapata Olivella witnessed all of this and wrote about it as a Colombian, as a black man, as an intellectual.

The controversial Colombian writer Fernando Vallejo has spent the majority of his life living outside of Colombia. Born in 1942, he moved to Mexico in 1971; in fact, in 2007, shortly after the re-election of President Álvaro Uribe (and after having secured citizenship from the Mexican government), Vallejo renounced his Colombian citizenship in a noisy, histrionic outburst that infuriated many Colombians. His 1994 novel *La virgen de los sicarios* is a brief, powerfully unsentimental description of the life of teenage hired assassins and their Medellín milieu; the book was released in English translation in 2001 as *Our Lady of the Assassins* and was adapted into a major motion picture directed by the German Barbet Schroeder in 2000. Vallejo's work is a reflection of the side of Medellín that many in polite society would rather forget, and the author represents an important common denominator in Colombian literary currents: writers who have used the objective reality of familiar surroundings to create works of stark simplicity (in this case) or intricate complexity (García Márquez) without becoming excessively academic or intellectually aloof.

Colombian writer Laura Restrepo (born in Bogotá in 1950) has received international recognition in recent years. Restrepo began her career as a journalist and social critic. Her 2004 novel *Delirium* received wide critical acclaim and cast new light on her earlier work, especially the 1993 novel *Leopard in the Sun*. *Leopard* helped readers understand the onset of the Colombian drug export business, focusing on the 1970s marijuana trade out of Santa Marta. In many significant ways, Restrepo's career path follows that of fellow Colombian Gabriel García Márquez: they are both committed to journalism, they are politically active and outspoken on matters pertaining to the conflict in Colombia, and they both have been involved in helping to solve the supposedly intransigent political problems of their native country. For example, García Márquez helped write the new Colombian constitution of 1991, and Restrepo was recruited by President Belisario Betancur in the early 1980s to promote dialogue with leftist insurgents in advance of his Peace Plan, which largely fell apart in the November 1985 Palace of Justice tragedy.

Colombian literary achievement has been overshadowed by the negative headlines and reports from that nation and by the enormous fame of the nation's vaunted literary star, Gabriel García Márquez. Hardly an aloof prima donna, García Márquez has worked to promote young Colombian writers, his brotherly friendship with Álvaro Mutis is enduring, and he has set up a school to support journalism in Cartagena called Fundación Nuevo Periodismo Iberoaméricano—FNPI (Foundation for New Ibero-American Journalism). Colombian literature, as suggested above, has flourished and would flourish without Gabriel García Márquez, but world literature has certainly been enriched by the work of the "roving and nostalgic Colombian" born in Aracataca in 1927.

THEATER

The Colombian theater has undergone a radical transformation over the past sixty years. Prior to the Second World War, Colombian theater was primarily an elite discourse that focused on safe, predictable religious themes that were neither controversial nor innovative, designed to appease elite sensibilities and not to offend the Catholic Church censure apparatus. The Teatro de Cristobal Colón in Bogotá, reinaugurated in 1892 to celebrate the four hundredth anniversary of the discovery of America (hence the name Cristobal Colón, Spanish for Christopher Columbus), situated in the center of Bogotá, became a place to promote political and literary discussions, poetry readings, musical performances, and operas. During the first years of the twentieth century, works of drama, often written by the leading political figures of the day, including Rafael Núñez and José Manuel Marroquín (president during the period when Panama was separated from Colombia), were designed to be read among friends rather than presented onstage before an audience.

Antonio Álvarez Lleras was perhaps the most notable Colombian writing for the theater during the first third of the twentieth century. Much of his work was staged through the theater company he created called Renacimiento, or "Renaissance." Two of his early works, *Víboras sociales* (*Social Snakes*, 1911) and *Como los muertos* (*Just Like the Dead*, 1916)—were later adapted to the cinema; the advent of Colombian cinema reinforced and intersected with the work of playwriting during the first thirty years of the twentieth century.

The actor and theater director Víctor Mallarino, during the middle of the twentieth century, deeply influenced Colombian theater as director of the National School of Dramatic Art. But dramatic events occurred that would forever change Colombian theater: during a ten-year period, from 1945 to 1955, Bertolt Brecht was introduced to Colombia, the "nueve de abril" occurred, and modernist journalism, literature, and theater coalesced in an innovative journal called *Mito*, which was edited by the poet Jorge Gaitán Durán and literary critic Hernando Valencia Goelkel.

Mito would be compared to the journal *Sur* published in Buenos Aires by Jorge Luis Borges and *Orígenes* in Havana, directed by Alejo Carpentier. But unlike Argentina and Cuba, Colombia received a relatively low number of European immigrants during the first fifty years of the twentieth century, so *Mito* was designed to bring Europe to Colombia, that is, to organize and translate the current intellectual trends in Europe and publish those ideas in Bogotá. Leading modernist thinkers, including Brecht, Sartre, and Beckett, were among the European authors published in *Mito*. Brecht became the central influential figure in the emerging and modernizing Colombian theater scene. The young intellectuals who published the journal truly believed that culture, literature, and modernist theater and political thought represented the most efficacious solution for Colombians' political and social development. They were trying to break away from the "old guard," which in their minds was characterized by the "nueve de abril," La Violencia, and decades of political and social intransigence.

Though *Mito* helped to transmit and translate European theater and literary trends to Colombia, a new generation of theater directors produced astonishingly original work, focusing on Colombia's social and political reality, or at least the reality they perceived. Enrique Buenaventura (1923–2003) founded and led the TEC—Teatro Experimental de Cali—and is considered one of the most important twentieth-century playwrights and theater directors in Latin America. Theater in Colombia during this time became a forum through which to engage the Colombian political and social conditions. *Mito* might have introduced European modernism in the mid-1950s, but twenty years later, Buenaventura and others were creating theater productions that were grounded in the country's contemporary crisis. Thus, *Los papeles del infierno* (*Documents from Hell*), a series of one-act plays that explored the human rights crisis in Colombia, moved far away from elite-inspired "salon" theater. According to one scholar, Buenaventura was one of the many directors who "found that the Marxist-inspired 'collective' could create theater directed to large 'popular' audiences rather than the small clique of cultural elites who dominated the national cultural arena."[13]

A wide array of theater companies during this time period, influenced by the political proclivity of Colombian theater, flourished in Colombia, especially in the capital city, including the TPB—Teatro Popular de Bogotá—and the Teatro de La Candelaria. In 1974, the TPB, in collaboration with Candelaria, staged a political work titled *I Took Panama*, which satirically commented on the separation of Panama, sharply critiquing the Colombian ruling Conservative elites of the time period, the U.S. Marines, and, of course, U.S. president Theodore Roosevelt. The work demonstrated the Colombian penchant for combining humor and satire to level serious criticism of political rulers, their predecessors, and policies.

ARCHITECTURE

Architecture is one area that is sometimes overlooked by those considering the creative capacity of the Colombian people. Most first-time visitors to Bogotá see the main plaza, named after Simón Bolívar, and learn that the beautiful neoclassical "Capitolio" that forms the southern segment of the square took more than eighty years to complete. Construction began in 1847 and was not completed until 1928. Plans for this capitol building were developed by the Caribbean-born architect Thomas Reed, who also developed plans for the Panóptico Municipal, which is today the National Museum at 7th Avenue and 32nd Street. That project was begun in 1874. In 1883 the first urban park in Colombia was inaugurated in the capital city, the Parque del Centenario—"Centenary Park." All of these projects were functional, designed to help provide modernization, harmony, and stability to the nation; the capitol building would house the Colombian Congress, the Panóptico served as the jail, and the Centenary Park facilitated outdoor, healthy, public recreation. At this time period, public parks became popular with urban designers throughout the Americas, who saw them as part of the civilizing program of the modern city. Perhaps the most famous urban park, New York's Central Park, initially opened in 1857, and work continued, hewing closely to plans developed by Frederick Law Olmsted and Calvert Vaux, until final completion of the project in 1873.

A couple of important urbanization projects were organized and completed in Bogotá during the twentieth century: the first led to the creation of the Ciudad Universitaria (University City), on the outskirts of downtown Bogotá; the second was a massive housing project, designed to provide safe middle-class housing for the growing urban population in the era of rural violence and prior to family planning.

The National University of Colombia at Bogotá was designed in 1936 as a large park, with space for experimentation with agronomy and agriculture, animal husbandry, and other sciences important to Colombia at that time. The modernist feel of the campus is attributed to a series of innovative architects, among them the German Leopold Rother, who implemented Bauhaus elements in the campus design.[14]

"Ciudad Kennedy"—named for President John F. Kennedy, who visited Bogotá in 1961 and offered funds to help promote social development—was initially planned in the 1960s to house about eighty thousand residents on the western outskirts of Bogotá. Ciudad Kennedy now is home to more than a million residents; the planning phase during the 1960s and 1970s represented an earnest effort on behalf of Colombian architects, social scientists, and urban planners to create safe, pleasant urban housing for the working class. A rapidly growing population, though, overwhelmed the best-laid plans, and today "Kennedy" is a densely populated, chaotic section of the city, distinct from the idyllic, peaceful community envisioned some fifty years ago.

The contemporary architect who defined a unique Colombian architectural style was the French-born Rogelio Salmona (1929–2007), who studied for a decade in Paris under Charles-Edouard Jeanneret-Gris, popularly known as Le Corbusier. Salmona's style is characterized by the use of red bricks manufactured using traditional artisanal methods from the red clay found in abundance near the Colombian capital city. Salmona spent time in Spain and was influenced by the stylized Moorish architecture, and so his work includes the use of decorative arches and intricate fountains. He designed many important buildings in Colombia and is perhaps best known for his residential apartment complex in the center of Bogotá, the Torres del Parque, which circle the "Plaza de Toros"—the Bogotá bullring. He also designed the National Archives Building, the Virgilio Barco Public library—both in Bogotá—and the Cartagena home of the writer Gabriel García Márquez. Salmona's final project, completed after his death, is a cultural center, the

Centro de Cultura Gabriel García Márquez, in the middle of the colonial neighborhood of Bogotá.

MUSIC

Music is an important component of any discussion of Colombian creative capacity. Unique among Latin American countries, Colombian music has emerged into the international mainstream with some contemporary artists including Juanes (né Juan Esteban Aristizábal Vásquez) and Shakira (née Isabel Mebarak Ripoll), who command worldwide audiences. The wide variety of musical traditions in Colombia reflects the regional diversity of the nation. Music from the north coast, for example, is completely distinct from music that is connected to the *llanos*, or eastern plains.

Though Colombia is recognized as a pioneer and leader in popular music, the nation also holds a rich and varied classical music tradition. Concerning European-based classical music, Guillermo Uribe Holguín is regarded as the most influential at the turn of the twentieth century; like his contemporaries in other areas of Latin America, most notably Brazil's Heitor Villa-Lobos, Uribe Holguín's work introduced unique nationalist elements in terms of melody and rhythm, especially his *Trozos en el sentimento popular*—a collection of three hundred piano pieces written between 1927 and 1939.[15]

Colombia's counterpart to Brazilian samba, Argentine tango, and Mexican *ranchera* music is the *cumbia*. British anthropologist Peter Wade's 2000 book, *Music, Race and Nation*, is a critical analysis of the coastal origins of this music, connecting *cumbia* (the term probably originated in the late nineteenth century) to the nation's Afro-Colombian populations. *Cumbia* has become popular throughout the Americas in recent years, though the rhythm and dance is clearly associated with the Colombian coasts, Panama, and the coast of Ecuador. What unifies *cumbia* and its brass-band cousin, "*porro*" music, is an origin in the history and struggles of Afro-Colombian communities. The *cumbia* rhythms and dance, West African in origin, probably began in and around the north coast city of Cartagena, which served as the principal port of entry for enslaved Africans. The Colombian Luis Eduardo (Lucho) Bermúdez (d. 1994) was one of the most beloved composers and artists of Caribbean music; he was known for taking the African rhythms of the *porro* and performing them with a full orchestra. It might seem a bit of a stretch to refer to him as the Elvis Presley of Colombia, but he, like Elvis, made traditional black music "safe" and comfortable for middle-class *mestizos* and whites in the interior cities and throughout the Colombian nation.

The *vallenato*, according to Wade, originated in and around the city of Valledupar near the north coast and generally includes the accordion (an instrument introduced to Colombia in the late 1880s by German immigrants); it is folk poetry from the region put to music. The *vallenato* was popular among the working and lower middle classes in the countryside and cities and became an important form of popular—oftentimes melancholic—expression at parties, celebrations, or other gatherings. Originally performed by men, the *vallenato* gained new and immense popularity in the early 1990s when a young performer, Carlos Vives from Santa Marta, made a recording of traditional *vallenatos* modified with a new, modern, upbeat tempo and performed by musicians trained in the *vallenato* tradition. His 1993 album "Clásicos de la Provincia" became an instant hit in Colombia, Latin America, and some parts of Europe and the United States. Many of the songs performed by Vives had been written earlier by the man considered the most important creator and promoter of the *vallenato*, Rafael Escalona, who was a Colombian singer, songwriter, politician, and diplomat. Escalona died in 2004 in Bogotá.

Bambuco music, considered by some as the national music of Colombia, originated in the Andean region of the nation, in and around the capital. In style, rhythm, and instrumentation, the bambuco imitated the European waltz and polka traditions developed in the mid-nineteenth century. *Bambuco* was hailed as the "national" music of Colombia at a time period when the nation was attempting to define and forge a unique national identity.

A wholly unique music from the eastern plains, *música llanera*, is popular in the Colombian plains and Venezuela. *Música llanera*, also called *joropo* music, is characterized by the use of a small harp, *la arpa llanera*, which generates a unique sound to this regional style of music and dance. Similar to U.S. country music, the *joropo* is distinct to the cattle culture of the plains and is performed at regional events including rodeos, but it is strongly associated with the traditions and culture of the *llanos orientales*, the eastern plains of Colombia.

This chapter has attempted to organize some of the unique characteristics of Colombian art and culture—a national and universal culture, strongly tied to the regions that shape Colombia's history. But the incredible diversity of the painting/sculpture, literary, theatrical, architectural, and musical traditions suggests a young, creative, and dynamic culture that is neither derivative nor imitative of European or U.S. culture. Colombians have been successful at creating literary works of astonishing originality, such as García Márquez's *One Hundred Years of Solitude*; at the same time, they have been able to incorporate, adapt, and innovate as only a *mestizo* nation can. Colombians are comfortable with the hybrid; their culture is not obsessed with pursuits that are purely intellectual, avant-garde, or otherwise divorced from the concerns of daily reality. Colombian culture, shaped by regional realities and restraints and the burdens of history, and conditioned by the serene wisdom of living day to day, is vibrant, often nostalgic, and sometimes uncertain. It is a metaphor for Colombian society.

NOTES

1. See Helen Delpar, *The Enormous Vogue of Things Mexican: Cultural Relations between the United States and Mexico, 1920–1935* (Tuscaloosa: University of Alabama Press, 1995).

2. See Maurico Nieto Olarte, "Ciencia imperial y ciencia criolla en el período de la Ilustración en el Nuevo Reino de Granada," in *Colombia: Preguntas y respuestas sobre su pasado y su presente*, eds. Diana Bonnett, Michael LaRosa, and Mauricio Nieto (Bogotá: Universidad de los Andes, 2010), 193–94.

3. Jacqueline Barnitz, *Twentieth-Century Art of Latin America* (Austin: University of Texas Press, 2001), 3.

4. Ibid., 35–36.

5. Juan Forero, "Débora Arango, 98, Painter of Politically Charged Themes, Dies," *New York Times*, December 13, 2005.

6. Barnitz, *Twentieth-Century Art of Latin America*, 192.

7. Authors' translation from *El serafín y la mujer*: "I am not happy; your love, which is my treasure, is what also takes away my tranquility." From an unpublished paper by Guiomar Dueñas-Vargas titled "José Eusebio Caro y Blasina Tobar: La política, el amor conyugal, y la educación de los hijos."

8. Guiomar Dueñas-Vargas, "El Romanticismo: Las mujeres que escribian." Unpublished paper.

9. Ibid.

10. This phrase belongs to literary scholar Doris Sommer, whose 1991 book is titled *Foundational Fictions: The National Romances of Latin America* (Los Angeles: University of California Press, 1991).

11. Kurt Levy, *Tomás Carrasquilla* (Boston: Twayne, 1980), 124.

12. Ibid., 124, 126.

13. Diana Taylor and Sarah J. Townsend, eds., *Stages of Conflict: A Critical Anthology of Latin American Theater and Performance* (Ann Arbor: University of Michigan Press, 2008), 245.

14. Alberto R. Saldarriago and Lorenzo M. Fonseca, "Un siglo de arquitectura colombiana," in vol. 6 of *Nueva Historia de Colombia* (Bogotá: Planeta Colombiana Editorial, S.A., 1989), 195.

15. Gerard H. Béhague, "Music, c. 1920–c. 1980," in *A Cultural History of Latin America*, ed. Leslie Bethell (Cambridge: Cambridge University Press, 1998), 321.

Chapter Nine

Daily Life

Daily life in Colombia varies dramatically, and what people do for recreation is shaped by social class, region, religious identity, and residency in urban versus rural sectors of the country. Few textbooks published in English deal with Colombian daily life, preferring to focus on violence, drug trafficking, and other lurid topics that frequently find their way into the Colombian evening news. This chapter seeks to explore the cultural forces that move Colombia and Colombians; for example, religious festivals and Catholic feast days are part of the rhythm of the Colombian calendar. The *puente*—the Monday holiday that serves as a "bridge" between the weekend and the workweek—is ubiquitous in the Colombian calendar and symbolizes the enduring strength of the nation's Roman Catholic identity. In any given year, there are nine Monday "puentes" and a total of fourteen holidays that are directly related to the Catholic liturgical calendar. Virtually all of these are official national holidays—days of rest for the Colombian workforce. However, only the most devout Colombians know the name of the Catholic saint being honored on any given *puente*. Another cultural/social phenomenon is the soap opera. *Telenovelas* (soap operas) are watched by all segments of Colombian society, rich and poor alike. Some *telenovelas*—*Betty la fea*, for example—have been exported and translated into other languages and cultures. Colombian soap operas are shown at night, after work, coinciding with the dinner hour, which starts at about 7:30 p.m. in the cities.

This chapter focuses on Colombian popular culture, using examples from the nineteenth to the twenty-first century. We cannot offer a complete analysis of the vast, rich, and fascinating cultural features that help define a unique Colombian cultural identity. While the writings of Gabriel García Márquez are representative of Colombian culture, so too are the *coleos*, or rodeos, found in many small towns but central to the cattle and cowboy culture of the Colombian eastern plains. Fernando Botero's paintings are internationally known. They hang in the most prestigious museums and galleries in the world and reflect his upbringing in and around Medellín, but the Carnival de Barranquilla is a lived experience, celebrated in the streets of the Caribbean city by tens of thousands of Colombians every year before Lent.

POPULAR RELIGIOUS CELEBRATIONS

Roman Catholicism has been the dominant religious identification in Colombia, and up until 1991, with the ratification of a new Colombian constitution, Catholicism was the official religion of the nation. Today a decidedly more secular Colombia still retains the cultural sensation and regularly scheduled religious celebrations of Roman Catholicism. Colombian society, literally, was built around the ideals and priorities of the Catholic Church. Thus, virtually every town in the nation is anchored by a Roman Catholic church at the center. This includes the main cathedral at Bogotá, which forms the eastern side of the main plaza, the Plaza de Bolívar. But the institutional Roman Catholic Church, which is a political, social, and economic power broker in the nation, operates at a level distinct from and sometimes indifferent to popular Catholicism, as expressed in the variety of Carnival celebrations, pilgrimages to holy sites, and devotion to Catholic spiritual leaders (the Virgin Mary, Christ) via their popularized "Colombian" representations (i.e., the Virgin of Chiquinquirá, the Divino Niño Jesús).

The most important popular celebration in Colombia is the Carnival at Barranquilla. The celebration began in the late nineteenth century. Though the traditional Catholic Carnival dates back to medieval Europe, the New World manifestation, whether it is called Mardi Gras in New Orleans or Carnival in Rio de Janeiro, acknowledges the onset of Lent, the forty-day period of fasting and penance before remembrance of the crucifixion of Christ on the cross and the Easter ascension. The celebration before the fast has become more alluring as time has passed, and Barranquilla's carnival is a multicultural, sensuous, raucous street party that paralyzes the city for four days and brings in millions of dollars (and euros) from Colombian and foreign tourists. Carnival celebrations in Colombia follow, historically, the northern trajectory of the Magdalena River. An earlier Carnival was celebrated in the river port city of Mompox, a city eclipsed by the growth of Cartagena and later Barranquilla. The modern carnival has lost any identification with or control by the Catholic Church; though its history is Catholic, the contemporary carnival is secularly spirited. It is a celebration of music, dance, the human body, and the exuberant joy that helps to unify this city, at least during a four-day period before Lent.

The Carnival at the southwestern city of Pasto is unique in that the celebration takes place during the period leading up to los Reyes Magos, or January 6, which Catholics celebrate as the day the three kings arrived to see the newborn Christ at Bethlehem. In Pasto, this celebration is referred to as the Carnival de Negros y Blancos, or the "Carnival of Blacks and Whites," which has been recognized as a Patrimonio Cultural Inmaterial (Cultural Heritage designation) by UNESCO. The celebration probably has its beginnings as a pre-Columbian agrarian celebration infused with African slave traditions—notably the recognition of January 5 as a "day free from work" that was granted through the Crown via official petition. On January 5, the city celebrates; people dress in black and paint their bodies with black face paint in celebratory solidarity with an official day of freedom from servitude. The next day, January 6, is Día de los Blancos ("White Day"), when everyone applies talc to their faces and bodies to imitate whiteness. This is the final day of the celebration, the day of the arrival of the kings. This celebration is fascinating in the way it attempts to reproduce the cultural heritage of the people who historically populated the city of Pasto and the region; indigenous elements, Afro-Colombian culture and traditions, and European history are brought together, all organized around the centralizing force and tradition of the Roman Catholic Church and Catholic liturgical calendar.

Another example of the intricacy of Colombian culture—and also the degree to which Colombians are an adaptive people, comfortable with synthesis—is the Carnival de Riosucio, or La Fiesta del Diablo, the "Devil's Festival," in the Department of Caldas. Riosucio combines Catholic tradition (it is a January celebration, designed to intersect with the arrival of the three kings on January 6) with a holiday inspired originally by indigenous agricultural festivals. The celebration became institutionalized in the mid-nineteenth century and reflects back to the Spanish conquest of the sixteenth century. The Riosucio Diablo is neither a cruel nor anti-Catholic devil. Rather, the devil and masks represent an integration of the three primary cultures in the region—indigenous, European, and African—designed to show the universality of the culture in Riosucio, Caldas. The festival suggests the celebratory nature of the people and the degree to which Colombians can create celebration and joy out of symbols and traditions designed to frighten and terrorize.

Two popular activities for the working classes in Bogotá are intercity pilgrimages of sorts. One is to a sanctuary, which was constructed between 1650 and 1657 at the top of a hill overlooking the savannah of Bogotá. This "Cerro de Monserrate" is at 3,152 meters above sea level, and people walk up a path to visit the statue of the "Señor de Monserrate," which is a depiction of the fallen, tortured Christ heading off to crucifixion. The truly devout make the pilgrimage on their knees, out of respect for Christ's suffering. At the site, inexpensive food is available for purchase, Catholic mass is said regularly, and high-end restaurants are available for the more affluent Colombians and foreign tourists.

The "20 de Julio" is a lower-middle-class neighborhood in the south of Bogotá. There, in the early twentieth century, an Italian Silesian priest, Father John Del Rizzo, started worshipping the Christ child (Divino Niño Jesús, the "Divine Baby Jesus"), and a church was built in honor of the Christ child in the center of this neighborhood. The 20 de Julio is a popular pilgrimage site, and people from all over the city, from all classes of Colombian society, venture there, especially on Sunday, to attend mass, socialize, and seek the help of the baby Jesus to solve a social crisis, cure an illness, or assist with some other special need. The Divino Niño is depicted as a happy, light-skinned, blond-haired child, dressed in a pink tunic with his arms outstretched. He stands on a base inscribed with the Spanish "Yo Reinaré," or, simply, "I will reign." The symbol is important for contemporary Colombians, especially those living in the chaotic city of Bogotá with as many as eight million residents. Colombians visit the church and are comforted by the welcoming, embracing, and loving child who helps them not necessarily to forget about their daily problems but to focus on another dimension: the openness, warmth, and childlike exuberance that await all in the Kingdom of Christ.

Despite the historically strong ties between the Colombian nation and the Roman Catholic Church, there is no "Colombian saint"—that is, the Roman Catholic Church has never canonized a Colombian as a saint, a person who has performed heroically and miraculously in service to the Church and to mankind during his/her lifetime. There are two Peruvian saints (Santa Rosa of Lima, San Martín de Porres) and a Mexican Saint (Juan Diego). San Pedro Claver, the Spanish Jesuit who lived from 1580 to 1654 and spent most of his life ministering to arriving slaves at the port city of Cartagena, is perhaps the closest Colombia has to a saint. Claver embraced the slaves and treated them with kindness upon their arrival to the slave-trading center, though he never fought against the institution of slavery. Still, for his time, he was unusual given the fact that he went out of his way to treat the newcomers as human beings, and the most important Jesuit church on the north coast of Colombia is dedicated to Claver; his mortal remains are entombed there, on the altar in a glass case for all to see.

SPORTS

Colombians of all social classes participate in sports, especially soccer, which became professionalized in 1948 in Colombia after a strike in Argentina forced many talented players in that nation to move to the Bogotá region. Soccer has been a source of immense joy and frustration for the Colombian people. In 1989, for example, the soccer squad from Medellín won the "Copa Libertadores"—the most important club competition in Latin America—but the team "Nacional" struggled under accusations of accepting illicit funds from Colombian drug kingpins. In 1994, Colombia, for the first time ever, qualified for World Cup competition in the United States. But the competition turned disastrous when Colombian midfielder Andrés Escobar committed a "self-goal" and Colombia was eliminated from the tournament in a 2–1 loss to the United States. Almost immediately after returning to his native Medellín, Escobar was murdered outside a bar, presumably on order of those (or someone) who had lost vast sums of money betting that Colombia would advance to the quarter finals of play. Uruguayan writer and intellectual Eduardo Galeano, an astute observer of contemporary Latin American culture, wrote a short book about soccer and, reflecting on the tragic murder of Escobar, shrewdly noted that "La violencia no está en los genes del pueblo colombiano, pueblo celebrador de la vida, loco de alegrias musiqueras y futbolera—violence is not in the genes of the Colombian people, a people who celebrate life, who are crazily happy about their music and soccer."[1]

Before the professionalization of soccer in Colombia—before the arrival of the Spaniards to America—natives in what today constitutes the Bogotá high plateau played a game called *tejo*. People still engage in this competition, usually on Sundays or feast days, and the matches are usually accompanied by an alcoholic beverage (a fermented corn beverage called *chicha*; today the beverage of choice is beer). *Tejo* is a curious game that involves throwing a metal or iron disc from a distance into a box of clay packed with small gunpowder caps, or *mechas*. The player who hits the most *mechas* (which explode when struck) wins; *tejo* is generally played outdoors by men.

Colombians have excelled at a number of international sports. Bogotá-born Juan Pablo Montoya raced, from 2001 to 2006, with two Formula 1 teams and won at the highest level of world competition. The athletic, affable Colombian golfer Camilo Villegas has had success on the PGA tour, and as of this writing in 2011, Colombians are making a name for themselves in international tennis competition. A story by Greg Bishop in the *New York Times* ("Colombians Build a Tennis Future," August 30, 2010) notes the achievements of two young Colombian tennis players, Alejandro Falla and Santiago Giraldo. The story was written in advance of Colombia hosting the Davis Cup, the most prestigious event in international men's tennis, in September 2010.

Colombia diverges from Latin America in its enthusiastic support of cycling. Though success in international competition has been waning over the past decade, Colombian racers regularly turned in competitive finishes at the leading world venues for cycling, including the Tour de France: in 1988, Fabio Parra took third place in the tour, and Colombian Luis "Lucho" Herrera had great success on the international cycling circuit, including a win in 1987 at the Vuelta de España, the Tour of Spain. Colombia's unique geography, with many mountains and valleys connected by winding, steep roads, allows for amateur and semiprofessional cyclists to train in and around the capital city. The Colombian Federation of Coffee Growers sponsored a team, Café de Colombia, featuring a team jersey that depicts the icon of the Colombian coffee federation's advertising campaign, Juan Valdez, and his trusted donkey, Conchita.

Ten Colombians have played in the major leagues of baseball. Three Colombians remain active in the major leagues: Cartagena's Orlando Cabrera, Barranquilla's Edgar Rentería, and Ernesto Frieri from Arjona. Baseball, from the earliest days of the twentieth century, has had a sort of pan-Caribbean appeal, following the path of the United States Marines and military forces in the late nineteenth century and leading into Teddy Roosevelt's "big stick" Caribbean policy of the early twentieth century. Baseball is not a Colombian "national" sport to the degree that soccer and cycling are. But many Colombians follow the U.S. pastime, paying particularly close attention to the teams that employ the *costeños*—the young men from the Colombian coast who represent Colombia in the U.S. major leagues.

A sport and cultural event that is practiced with great passion in the eastern plains of Colombia, particularly in and around the city of Villavicencio, is called *coleo*—a sort of Colombian-Venezuelan rodeo. *Coleo* is a gathering, a celebration of the culture and tradition of the eastern plains, and a demonstration of the work, art, and struggle of the *llaneros*, the people who live on the plains. *Coleo* comes from the Spanish verb *colear*, which in the infinitive translates as "to wag one's tail." The eastern plains of Colombia is a region strongly characterized by cowboy culture, and cattle raising predominates socially and economically there. The *coleo* is a competition in which two cowboys on horseback are tasked with taking down a young bull by getting behind the beast and pulling on its tail until it loses its balance and falls over. The fall is important: the more dramatic and sensational, the more points earned. The Colombian rodeo differs from the Texas rodeo in that the South American bull is approached from behind; rodeos in the United States and Canada focus on riding and roping the horns. Unlike the Spanish bullfight, neither the Colombian *coleo* nor the U.S. rodeo engage in a matador-bull duel to the death, though many animals are injured in *coleos* and sent off to the slaughterhouse. Recorded or live *joropo* music is played during the *coleo*, and beer is relatively inexpensive and plentiful at the celebration. Since 1997,

Villavicencio has hosted the annual Coleo World Cup; a recent competition, the XIV Encuentro Mundial de Coleo, was held in October 2010 and was won by Ángel Rigoberto Zambrano Brito from the city of Arauca, which borders Venezuela. Panamanians, Brazilians, Argentines, and Venezuelans are Latin American neighbors who practice *coleo*, which can be classified as sport, social activity, or cultural unifier of the people of the Latin American plains.

Women have not received widespread recognition in the Colombian sporting scene; in Cuba, women have excelled in individual and team competitions, and the Peruvian and Brazilian women's volleyball teams and the United States women's soccer and basketball teams have excelled in international competitions. But Colombian sports heroes have mostly been men, and that is unlikely to change given the centrality of soccer (men's soccer) in the Colombian imagination, celebrated and reinforced by the Colombian media conglomerates and society at large.

BEAUTY PAGEANTS

One arena of society where women do, in fact, have power—a strange, sometimes surreal type of power—is through the "Reinado de Belleza," the Colombian beauty competitions. Each November in Cartagena, the national beauty pageant takes place. As in the United States, the Colombian pageant is the final competition in a yearlong nomination process, in which a representative from each Colombian department (state) participates. The competition attracts a wide national television audience, and beauty pageant winners at the state and certainly national level are public figures in Colombia; they are expected to participate in charity and social events and uphold admirable standards to be imitated by younger Colombian girls. Colombian intellectuals—including the writers Laura Restrepo and Gabriel García Márquez—have ridiculed the event for its one-dimensional focus on Colombian physical feminine beauty. But like any media event, in Colombia or elsewhere, corporate sponsorship allows for a lavish show and a weeklong lead-in to the actual event. Critics have contended that the show is elitist and unrepresentative of Colombia at large and that the display of expensive gowns, jewelry, and luxury accessible to an infinitesimally small percentage of Colombians is irresponsible. Others offer a more nuanced view of the competition, stressing the theatrical dimension of the competition and the entertainment provided by the pageant. The current director of the national pageant, Raimundo Angulo, comments that the Miss Colombia pageant could, one day, turn a poor, steamy coastal city into "the Monte Carlo of the Caribbean," though that remains to be seen.[2]

American journalist Simon Romero's fascinating depiction of the "dual" beauty pageants in Cartagena shows the importance of the beauty pageant to the nation's history and consciousness. While the "official" pageant proceeds with the international jet set in attendance, a concurrent celebration of the city's independence from Spain (in 1811) takes place "during a tumultuous street festival" in the poorer neighborhoods of Cartagena.[3] This parallel competition and celebration more accurately reflects the socioeconomic reality of an extremely poor city that is more black than white and where the vast majority of women have never slipped into a haute couture evening gown. Cartagena is a city accustomed to struggle: during the independence war with Spain, Cartagena suffered a terrible siege in 1815 that lasted months and resulted in the deaths of about 6,500 residents, or about one-third of the total population of the city.

The Miss Colombia beauty pageant made it into U.S. news in May 2001, when late-night comedian and television host David Letterman made a crude joke on his show, which indirectly compared Miss Colombia to a *mula*, or a person who is hired (or coerced) to ingest and transport across national boundaries pellet-shaped latex capsules filled with illegal narcotics. Letterman apologized, but only after Andrea Noceti, Miss Colombia of that year, threatened to sue him. Both parties quickly entered into a truce, formalized when Noceti agreed to appear in New York City on *Late Show with David Letterman*. Mr. Letterman's band greeted Miss Colombia's onstage entrance with a rousing rendition of the Colombian national anthem.

RETAKING THE COLOMBIAN URBAN CENTERS

During the late 1970s and 1980s, the industrial city of Medellín became known as one of the most violent, terrifying places on the planet, for non-Colombians and Colombians alike. The city had physically sprawled outside of the geographically imposed boundaries (it sits at about 1,800 meters in a central mountain valley), and poor people moved up the sides of the mountains, settling there while fighting for basic infrastructure including sewerage, clean water, electricity, and elementary schools for their children. The elite pushed back to El Poblado, an enclave neighborhood in the south, as the poor took most of the north and the surrounding east-west hills.

The drug cartel violence of the 1970s through the 1990s created great social tensions in Medellín, and at roughly the same time as the violence escalated in 1979, city leaders began planning for a metro system. In 1995, the Metro of Medellín opened and helped unify a fractured city and society. The metro immediately became a source of civic and national pride, as Colombians were able to demonstrate to the rest of the world that they could plan, engineer, and execute large-scale infrastructure projects that could help solve modern urban problems while bringing a city and a people together. The metro became the envy of the nation, but plans to extend the metro into the vast *comunas* (poor neighborhoods) via a "cable car" system seemed impossible technologically and highly improbable, given the vast social tensions present in those areas. However, in 2004, "Metro Cable Linéa K" opened, bringing people up into the Santo Domingo neighborhood, a vast, sprawling slum with hundreds of thousands of residents. "Linéa J" opened in 2008 to serve people living on the eastern slope of the mountain, and the metro system has helped solve some of the city's problems of transit while bringing a modicum of unification to the city of three million. With greater physical access to the poor neighborhoods of Medellín, city leaders and urban planners have been building parks, schools, libraries, and other civic projects in these once neglected, marginalized, and feared neighborhoods. Perhaps the most impressive project to date is the Parque/Biblioteca España, a monumental library and park built high up in the Santo Domingo neighborhood. The project was financed by the Spanish government.

Bogotá, by the mid-1970s, emerged as one of the largest population centers in Latin America and perhaps the fifth-largest in the region, behind Mexico City, São Paulo, Buenos Aires, and Lima. The city's problems grew increasingly complex with growing insecurity, a lack of adequate housing, and low investment in public transportation. The chilly, rainy, dark, and perpetual late-fall feel of Bogotá contrasted sharply with Medellín's "eternal spring" optimism, pleasant climate, and civic pride—particularly after the inauguration of the metro. With a population of roughly eight million, Bogotá's fortunes changed in positive terms as a result of the dynamic, creative leadership of mathematician, philosopher, and former rector of the National University Antanas Mockus Sivickas, who ascended to the second-most-important elected post in the nation: mayor of Bogotá. Mockus used theatrical tactics to help residents of Bogotá save water (he starred in a television commercial, filmed while he showered), obey traffic laws (mimes were hired to publicly embarrass jaywalkers), and pay taxes. Next, the technocratic, U.S.-educated mayor, Enrique Peñalosa, and the more socially oriented mayor, Luis Eduardo "Lucho" Garzón, continued modernizing Bogotá via investment in parks and public libraries. They also prioritized the goal of meeting basic infrastructural coverage (electricity and water) for all homes; homicide rates fell, and plans were developed for construction of an urban transportation system that would operate on the same principles as a metro, without prohibitively expensive and disruptive tunneling. Strong leadership, a commitment to big infrastructure projects, and prudent fiscal management resulted in the inauguration in December 2000 of the TransMilenio transportation system—modeled after a similar system in Curitiba, Brazil. Despite some setbacks, including major engineering miscalculations in construction of the dedicated bus lane, new lines are currently being added to bring coverage to the north-south-west corridors of Bogotá, and it is estimated that 1.5 million people use the system daily.

In Bogotá, three new public libraries opened during the first decade of the twenty-first century: the Virgilio Barco near the Parque Simón Bolívar, el Parque Biblioteca Tunal in the south of the city, and El Tintal in the remote west. These libraries, designed to provide access to computers, books, and study space for all residents of the city, are intended to help shrink the achievement gap between the wealthy, who have in-home libraries and access to excellent private libraries and study spaces at the city's many private schools and universities, and the majority of the citizens of Bogotá, who cannot afford private education. The mainstay of the public library system, the Biblioteca Luis Ángel Arango (BLAA), in the middle of the colonial section of the city, remains a dynamic cultural center. The BLAA is visited by scholars, high school and university students, and children from the surrounding neighborhood and serves as the anchor of a public system that includes more than one hundred libraries.

Unifying elements in Colombia's capital city also include many urban parks, including the Parque Central Simón Bolívar and the Parque Metropolitano Tercer Milenio, or the "Third Millennium Metropolitan Park," which opened in 2002. Simón Bolívar Park can be compared to New York's Central Park, though the Bogotá park is larger. It is a place people from all social classes enjoy; there are miles of walking and jogging paths, a man-made lake adorns the center, and the park is carefully monitored by uniformed security guards. The Third Millennium Park was planned in the late 1990s, and the first section of the park opened in 2002; this park was built in a dismal central-city neighborhood, "El Cartucho,"[4] known for criminal activity, to which Bogotanos from the north sector of the city (the more affluent, in general) would never venture. But after taking down more than six hundred structures, the city built a forty-one-acre urban park designed to revitalize downtown Bogotá, reduce crime in the city, and provide a safe space of transit and recreation for all city residents. Unfortunately, there are few advocates for the homeless in Bogotá, and it is difficult to calculate where the people who lived in this neighborhood went, but most agree that they were pushed farther into the west and south of the city, where the majority of the population lives in poverty that ranges in condition from poor but dignified to unbearably destitute.

Another key activity that brings together all classes harmoniously in Colombia is the weekly *ciclovía*, or literally "bike lane," that runs Sundays from 7 a.m. to 2 p.m. in Bogotá and has recently been introduced in other Colombian cities. The *ciclovía*, started in 1976, is a highly organized Sunday (and Monday holiday) takeover of the principal roads by bicyclists, joggers, walkers, and skateboarders. It is estimated that two million people participate weekly in Bogotá. The *ciclovía* turns the city into a sort of open park; along the route people set up stalls, selling soft drinks, juices, and snacks. Entrepreneurial Colombians bring their tools to the street and set up "repair stands" for citizens who run into minor mechanical mishaps. In the early days, *ciclovía* extended only along the principal north-south thoroughfare known as the "Séptima" (7th Avenue), but now the routes extend along most of the major city thoroughfares. People of all ages, social classes, and professions participate in the weekly *ciclovía*, which has become a model program for Colombia and Latin America.

RADIO, TV, AND SOAP OPERAS

Technological change helped break down the walls of isolation perceived by many Colombians, isolation imposed by the accidents of geography. The intense regional identifications—a hallmark of Colombian society—began a national dialogue of sorts with the advent of three important technological developments: the airplane, the radio, and finally, in 1954, television, which was introduced to Colombia by General Rojas Pinilla. In 1919, in the Caribbean port city of Barranquilla, SCADTA (Sociedad Colombo-Alemán de Transportes Aeréos), generally credited as the first commercial airline in the Americas, was founded by German immigrants living in and around Barranquilla and was later organized as Avianca Airlines, which still exists today as Colombia's national airline. Avianca is no longer a "Colombian" company, as a majority share of the airline was purchased in 2004 by the Brazilian airline tycoon Germán Efromovich. Air transportation began an important process of modernization in Colombia and helped Colombians feel more connected to other regions of their own nation and the world, though in the earliest days of aviation only the wealthiest Colombians could afford to travel by airplane.

Ten years after the advent of air transportation, the radio arrived in Colombia, also in the city of Barranquilla. Radio networks in Colombia—including the two powerful networks RCN and Caracol—have helped to bring unity to a nation divided by mountains and valleys. The growth of radio occurred with the ascent of the Liberal Party in 1930. Liberal leaders allowed for a mixed public-private financing arrangement that brought outside funding to this new technology, and radio investment grew, particularly after 1931. Colombian citizens learned the details of the nation's short war with Peru in 1932 thanks to radio broadcasts, and advertisers soon learned the power of this new medium to sell products to Colombian citizens. Colombian radio was unique in the Americas thanks to the creation of Radio Sutatenza in 1947; it was an educational radio network founded by Father José Joaquín Salcedo in the rural community of Sutatenza, Boyacá, north of the Colombian capital. Father Salcedo hoped to bring literacy and education to peasants living in rural Colombia, in places where teachers were absent, school houses had never been constructed, and the future for the people was, at best, static. Eventually the station moved to Bogotá, and it became a powerful tool of popular education, receiving funding from outside benefactors including the World Bank, General Electric, and the Inter-American Development Bank. The station's broadcast center was visited and blessed by the pope in 1968. Controversy erupted in the 1960s when a young, political, rebellious priest, Father Camilo Torres Restrepo, accused the station, its founders, and backers of harming the people it purported to help via the radio's excessive anti-Communist teachings. Father Torres viewed the radio station as a tool of the most reactionary elements of society, in concert with their outside funders. Despite his concerns and those of others on the political left, the radio station continued to broadcast until the early 1990s, when it was absorbed by the Caracol radio network.

Television came to Bogotá with great fanfare in June 1954. Television— like the introduction of radio some twenty-five years earlier—changed the social dynamic of the Colombian household. According to Colombian journalist and social critic Oscar Collazos, "Colombian families placed the television first in the living room, then the bedroom—it offered the possibility of family unity without conversation, families could eat together without sitting at the table and become 'informed' without reading newspapers."[5] The new technology forced social change within the household but also introduced images of other places to those Colombians who had never traveled outside of their city or region. Advertisers could use the new technology to sell products and expand markets, politicians seemed more tangible, and politics became more immediate and important. The changes initiated by television in Colombia were dramatic, though initially, it is estimated that only 1,500 televisions were available to see the first transmission on June 13, 1954, broadcast from the basement of the National Library.[6] By 1960, approximately 80 percent of the Colombian territory was receiving television transmissions,[7] and while this new technology did not solve social problems or reduce poverty, it did help forge and unify the modern Colombian nation, a unification project that seemed impossible at the beginning of the twentieth century. By 2008, it was estimated that about 85 percent of Colombian households had televisions. Thus, prominent Colombian historian and journalist Eduardo Lemaitre, who died in 1994, was not exaggerating when he wrote that "three things have given this country of countries a nation with common principles and have given it a compact to exist as a singular unit: the Constitution of 1886, the Magdalena River, and the television."[8]

Television in Colombia has been derided for its supposed superficiality, with excessive focus on feminine beauty, style rather than substance, and a proclivity for showing gory violence on the evening news. But the Colombian *telenovela* developed a following in Colombia and Latin America that is now legendary. Soap operas from Mexico, Colombia, Brazil, and Venezuela are seen throughout Latin America and in U.S. markets with significant Latin American populations—Miami, New York, Los Angeles, Chicago, and south Texas, for example. The Colombian soap opera is known for outstanding production quality and excellent acting and writing, and two recent soap operas are worthy of mention. When *Café con aroma de mujer* (*Coffee with the Scent of a Woman*) was produced in 1994, it mesmerized the Colombian nation. The soap opera appeared at a time when Colombians were searching for an escape from the daily routine—a routine that had turned deadly and dreary. *Café* distracted people from the recent past and helped them to focus on something else. The story line seemed, at first glance, to dwell on cliché: beautiful female plantation worker falls in love with wealthy businessman. The series, however, dealt with important social issues pertinent to Colombia and Latin America at that time. Those issues included human trafficking, prostitution, and women's ability to ascend in a male-dominated universe, together with the enduring power of love. The series was filmed on location in the Colombian "coffee zone" and helped foster a boom in tourism to the lush, mountainous coffee cities, principally Pereira, Manizales, and Armenia.

A few years later, in 1999, *Yo soy Betty la fea* captivated the nation. The story of "Ugly Betty"—the brainy secretary who works behind the scene to help save the fashion company that employs her and becomes romantically involved with the boss—was so popular in Colombia that it was recast into a successful television series in the United States, playing in prime time for four seasons starting in 2006 as *Ugly Betty*. Colombians were impressed that a creative product designed for the Colombian nation could compete on the world stage, particularly in the powerful and extremely competitive U.S. prime-time network television market.

GASTRONOMY, COLOMBIAN STYLE

Colombian cuisine is rarely mentioned as one of the great cuisines of the world in the way that French, Chinese, Italian, or Mexican cuisines are regarded by food experts and critics. Colombian cuisine varies from region to region and between socioeconomic class. The traditional Colombian diet is meat based, and no meal is considered "proper" unless it contains some type of meat (beef, pork, chicken, or fish) as the main dish. Potato, rice, and corn are staples in Colombia, together with yucca, plantain, and every type of tropical fruit imaginable. The Colombian diet is high in carbohydrates: a typical working-class lunch might consist of a piece of beef accompanied by white rice, potatoes, and pasta.

While Colombia does not have a "national" dish, the *ajiaco* probably comes close. It is a potato stew made from three distinct varieties of locally grown potatoes, seasoning, rice, and pulled pieces of tender chicken. It is served with capers, sour cream, and avocado. *Ajiaco* is the main meal on Saturday afternoon, when families are gathered together for lunch; carbohydrate and calorie rich, it is designed to feed large numbers of people. In Medellín, the focus is on pork and beans: the *bandeja paisa* is the regional dish from Antioquia and, like *ajiaco*, it is meant to feed everyone in the extensive Medellín household. The *bandeja* (or "tray") consists of ground beef, sausages, rice, fried plantains, a flat corn cake called *arepa*, beans, avocado, and a fried egg on top. The plate is lightly seasoned with salt. Colombians, in general, are averse to heavy spices and, unlike their neighbors to the south (Peruvians) or to the north (Mexicans), tend to prefer bland food. The coastal regions of Colombia have their own cuisine based on the availability of fresh fish. Fish is served with white rice, fried plantains, or—a delicacy of the coastal region—*arroz con coco* (rice made with fresh coconut).

UNIVERSITY LIFE IN COLOMBIA

The official education numbers for Colombia appear promising but can be deceptive. For example, from 2005 to 2007, the percentage of children from five to sixteen years of age who were enrolled in school jumped from 88 to 90 percent. *Attendance* is a relatively ambiguous term and does not account for vast differences in quality of education services available. Extremely rigorous, internally accredited private schools can be found in all of the major cities in Colombia; these are the schools supported by the wealthy elite. Poorer schools, in rural areas, are only marginally staffed, and basic infrastructure is limited. The overall literacy rate for Colombia is about 90 percent, and more Colombians are attending university today than ever before. From 2002 to 2007, according to reliable statistics from DANE (the National Administrative Statistics Department of Colombia), the percentage of students enrolled in either public or private universities grew by 7.4 percent, to 31.8 percent.

Public universities, including the nation's flagship Universidad Nacional de Colombia at Bogotá, offer a university education modeled after European and U.S. programs. Many of Colombia's leading intellectuals, attorneys, social scientists, artists, scientists, and engineers graduated from this university, informally referred to as the "Nacho." Admission is granted based on the results of a comprehensive, selective admissions exam. Tuition—once free— is now paid on a sliding scale according to the family's income and ability to pay. Strikes, protests, and political demonstrations are legendary at the National University, but the university continues to train professionals, many of whom become leaders in their respective fields. Similarly, the University of Antioquia in Medellín has trained the technical elite who have worked to secure the city's reputation as the nation's leading manufacturing center.

Private universities have been growing in number and prestige during the past two decades, with many Colombians having earned advanced master's and PhD degrees in the United States and Europe; these professionals, re-turning to work in Colombia, have organized important master's and PhD programs at universities such as Los Andes in Bogotá, the Pontificia Univer-sidad Javeriana, the National University, and the Universidad del Norte in Barranquilla, among others. In Bogotá there has been a proliferation of high-quality master's programs in history, literature, economics, cultural studies, and geography, to name but a few. The University of Los Andes recently opened a medical school, and the Jesuit-run Universidad Javeriana's tradition of training lawyers and theologians dates back to colonial times. Of course, private schools charge tuition that only the salaried class can afford to pay, but students at excellent private universities in Colombia represent a wide range of the socioeconomic strata; sons and daughters of attorneys, business-men, professors, and physicians—most of whom earn at levels significantly below their peers in the United States—generally attend private universities. However, sons and daughters of mine workers, taxi drivers, or police officers rarely attend such elite institutions; many in this socioeconomic class find a place in the public universities, though the *cupo* (slots) are limited and de-mand for space always exceeds capacity.

While this chapter could never be fully representative of daily life in Colombia, we have tried to demonstrate the complexity of contemporary Colombian society and the many opportunities that Colombians have to express common cultural traits. A nation divided by geography, Colombia has had difficulty unifying around a national cultural ethos. The Roman Catholic Church provided unity by introducing and reinforcing the Catholic calendar's holy days of obligations and feasts. Modern technology arrived and brought some unifying elements of daily life, mainly in the form of ra-dio and television, and the related transmission of national sporting events and beauty pageants. A nation as divided as Colombia, by geography, race, social and economic class, political power, education, and *apellido* (family name) can never come together completely and earnestly, but innovative and intelligent Colombians have worked hard to create infrastructure, parks, programs, transportation systems, and university curricula that help Colombians focus on what unites them as a people and a nation rather than what has historically divided society.

NOTES

1. Eduardo Galeano, *El fútbol a sol y sombra* (Bogotá: Tercer Mundo Editores, 1995), 230–31.

2. See Simon Romero, "Dueling Beauty Pageants Put Income Gap on View," *New York Times,* November 30, 2010.

3. Ibid.

4. "El Cartucho" was the informal name given to this sector of downtown Bogotá, abandoned by the middle class in the 1950s and taken over by the homeless, many of whom made their living from a variety of illegal activities; they did provide an informal but efficient recycling program for the city and earned money by selling scrap metal, paper, and other recyclables—hence the name *cartucho*, which roughly translates to "used, scrap cardboard boxing material."

5. Oscar Collazos, "Aparece la Televisión," www.colombialikn.com. Accessed February 8, 2011.

6. Raymond Leslie Williams and Kevin G. Guerrieri, *Culture and Customs of Colombia* (Westport: Greenwood Press, 1999), 45.

7. Ibid., 46.

8. "Asi arrancó la odisea," *Semana*, June 6, 2004.

Chapter Ten

Colombia and the World

During the nineteenth and twentieth centuries, Colombia's relationship with its Latin American neighbors, Europe, and the United States evolved in a substantial and systematic manner. This chapter studies two centuries of Colombian external relations, focusing on the Andean nation's relationship with its territorial neighbors, the complexity of its European alliances, and the growing interest of the United States, particularly after the 1823 Monroe Doctrine. The chapter concludes with recent collaborations and tensions between the United States and Colombia—collaboration in the form of funding through "Plan Colombia," which has directed about eight billion dollars in mostly military aid to Colombia since 2000. Also, we study the recent relations with two Andean neighbors, Ecuador and Venezuela. The legacy of Peruvian-Colombian relations is explored, with a focus on the relative peace and collaboration between those two nations after an unfortunate war in 1932. Brazil and Colombia share a large Amazonian border, and transshipment of illegal narcotics has been a recent source of stress between the two nations. Those stressors have been magnified by Brazil's emergence as a regional and world power with a concurrent determination to defend its borders against illegal smuggling.

Of course, Colombia's modern external relations must begin with a focus on the colonizing European power, Spain. But the story of independence has been carefully outlined in earlier chapters of this book, and once the break from Spain was complete by 1819 at the Battle of Boyacá, the task of organizing the Colombian nation ran parallel to reorganizing its European alliances and relations. The new Colombian nation looked—generally—to Great Britain for economic advice, to France for cultural and philosophical principles, and to the United States, begrudgingly, for technical support.

Latin America's relationship with the young neighbor to the north, the United States, began as a series of misunderstandings perpetuated by prejudicial, jaundiced commentaries. As early as 1811, Thomas Jefferson worried about the Latin American independence movement, suggesting Latin Americans were neither ready for nor capable of true independence. "I fear," wrote the statesman regarding the Latin American independence movements, "the degrading ignorance into which their priests and kings have sunk them, has disqualified them from the maintenance or even knowledge of their rights and that much blood may be shed for little improvement in their condition."[1] The great Liberator of the northwest segment of South America, Simón Bolívar, had an equally myopic but certainly more nuanced view of the neighbor to the north. David Bushnell, in a brief but fascinating study published in 1986, reported on Bolívar's "ambivalence" toward the United States, best illustrated by the Liberator's declaration, written in a letter in 1829, one year before his death. He asserted, "I think it would be better for South America to adopt the Koran rather than the United States' form of government, although the latter is the best on earth."[2] Bolívar is best known, perhaps, for his unambiguous, provocative, and somewhat prophetic comment in another letter dated 1829. He warned, "The United States . . . seems destined by Providence to plague America with torments in the name of freedom."[3] Bushnell suggests that the monarchist-leaning Liberator was lamenting the United States' push for republican governments in Latin America against the more monarchist aims of Great Britain, a society that would have a much greater influence in Latin America, including Colombia, during most of the nineteenth century.

THE EARLY DAYS

In 1823, the United States expressed its interest in influencing Latin American politics and trade in the famous Monroe Doctrine, which was widely misinterpreted as a doctrine of intervention. President James Monroe's doctrine was a warning against future European attempts at recolonization in Latin America, as the wars for independence entered the final phase. Great Britain was the dominant Western power in 1823, and the British presence in Latin America, including Colombia, was deep. For example, Simón Bolívar benefited from British soldiers of fortune at the decisive Battle of Boyacá, and the British supplied, "on credit, substantial amounts of military equipment to the patriot forces."[4] Colombian independence allowed an opening up of critical Caribbean ports, and British imports flooded Cartagena and Santa Marta. With the British directing New Granada's foreign trade in the earliest days of the republic, Colombia's debt mounted, and by the middle of the 1820s, immediately after independence, the new nation found that it could not afford the interest payment on exorbitant loans issued by British banks.

New Granada was directly involved in an intense rivalry in the Caribbean for markets and influence waged between the United States and Great Britain. France, Britain, and the United States were all interested in a transisthmian (across what is today Panama) route as a way of extending their trade networks. The British made inroads on the Caribbean coast of Central America (the "Mosquito Coast" of Nicaragua and British Honduras, later the Republic of Honduras), and French colonialism in the Caribbean endured for much of the century. French interest in the Caribbean grew particularly after the 1848 revolution in France that witnessed the election of Louis Napoleon Bonaparte—who three years after the election annulled the results and ushered in the Second French Empire. This empire was characterized by an aggressive foreign policy with repercussions for Latin America, especially in Mexico and the Caribbean. The Second French Empire lasted until 1871.

Also in 1848, the United States ratified the Bidlack-Mallarino Treaty, which combined commercial interests (United States products in New Granada were treated, with regard to tariff, equally) and the isthmus question. The United States agreed to support the "perfect neutrality" of the Isthmus of Panama provided that U.S. citizens could freely pass through the isthmus as they pleased.

By 1855, the privately owned and operated (U.S.) Panama Railroad opened, linking the Caribbean port city of Colón to the capital city of the Province of Panama, Panama City on the Pacific. The discovery of gold in California in 1849 provoked a rush of U.S. east coast–based speculators to the far west, and the safest, most comfortable route, particularly with the opening of the railroad, was via the Isthmus of Panama. Stephen J. Randall has reported on the profitability of the railroad and noted how it "was the single most significant revenue source for the Colombian treasury from the turbulent 1850s until the contract was revised in 1867."[5]

The presence of a U.S. railroad company in Panama created a trio of tensions between Panamanians, North Americans, and Bogotanos; the parties argued over control of tax revenues, land rights/access, and freight rates, among other concerns. Tensions boiled over on several occasions, but the most often reported incident is known as the "watermelon riot" of April 15, 1856. This violent episode, which began ostensibly over lack of payment by a U.S. citizen for a slice of watermelon, left about two dozen dead. Unfortunately, as demonstrated by the riot, tension and mistrust defined the relationship between Bogotá and Washington, though United States investment in Colombia grew, especially with the conclusion of the U.S. Civil War in 1865. The U.S. investment pattern favored transportation—including steam transportation and railroad projects in the Colombian interior—but most U.S. investment during this time was focused on Panama. Fourteen million dollars is the estimated U.S. investment in Colombia by 1881, and, according to Randall "the bulk [of this investment] was represented by the Panamá Railroad."[6]

THE CANAL PROJECT

Discussion of a trans-isthmian canal became a priority in the 1860s, especially with the successful construction of Suez in Egypt, a project initially developed by French engineer and entrepreneur Ferdinand de Lesseps. The Suez opened in 1869 after approximately ten years' work. In Colombia, however, the United States failed to take action on an 1870 treaty which would have allowed for construction of a canal through Panama. During this time, the United States considered a possible route through Nicaragua and a Mexican route through Tehuantepec that involved, essentially, hoisting ships out of the Caribbean Sea onto a platform that would be pulled over land on parallel trains running from the Caribbean to the Pacific. This project was never undertaken.

After extensive vacillation on the part of the United States, the French attempted to build a canal in Panama. Ferdinand de Lesseps, whose success with Suez made him somewhat of an international celebrity, organized and financed a canal project, and construction began in 1881. But the Lesseps Panama project was never supported by the United States, which opposed an expansion of the French presence in the Caribbean. The engineering company went bankrupt by 1889, and it is estimated that forty thousand workers, mostly from Jamaica and other Caribbean locales, died of yellow fever and malaria while working in the Caribbean heat for a French company that was mismanaged and crippled by massive fraud, graft, and corruption. Though approximately 40 percent of the canal route had been dug during a seven-year period, the Lesseps project was a monumental failure and, in theory, a cautionary tale for European economic expansion abroad.

With the French collapse in the Caribbean, the United States' determination to build and occupy a canal grew dramatically, and the competition between the European powers and young American upstart to succeed in a trans-isthmian canal project can be compared to the space race of the 1950s and 1960s between the Soviet Union and the United States. Several factors influenced the United States' push for a canal, not least of which was the ascension to the presidency in September 1901 of Theodore Roosevelt. Having served as secretary of the navy, he advocated for a "two ocean" navy and believed that U.S. military and economic power was a direct function of a strong naval force. The United States' short war in 1898 with Spain in the Caribbean placed Cuba and Puerto Rico under de facto command of the United States. Guam and the Philippines in the Pacific fell under United States influence, but only after a lengthy, bloody campaign in that theater. By the turn of the twentieth century, the canal question was revisited with urgency by the United States, which increasingly viewed its economic and military health as contingent upon a direct sea route connecting the Caribbean and Pacific.

Colombia, during this same time period, underwent major systemic change, highlighted by the promulgation of a new constitution during the 1880s and the onset of a major civil war in 1899. The Colombian political "regeneration" of 1886 ushered in a sustained period of Conservative rule during the presidency of Rafael Núñez and Miguel Antonio Caro, who as vice president presided in Núñez's frequent absences and would take over for the ailing president in 1892. As noted previously, the new Conservative regime of 1886 represented a return to centralist rule and emphasized Colombia's Hispanic and Catholic traditions and culture. A year after the promulgation of the new constitution, Colombia signed a concordat that initiated a special relationship between the Holy See and Colombia and, in practical terms, meant that Colombia would officially observe the rules of the Roman Catholic Church.

But not even an agreement with the Holy See could prevent the chaos that would ensue toward the end of the nineteenth century; as the United States was concluding its war with Spain in Cuba, Colombia began a protracted civil war aptly called the "War of a Thousand Days," which lasted from late 1899 until early 1902. The war pitted Liberals against Conservatives; political intransigence combined with economic exigencies created the perfect storm, and the devastating war complicated new negotiations for the construction of a canal through Panama.

After intense lobbying in Washington, Congress reached the decision to pursue a canal through Panama rather than Nicaragua; both routes had their supporters and detractors, but the Panama route, though technologically complex, was already 40 percent completed thanks to the prior efforts of de Lesseps. The Hay-Herrán Treaty was ratified in early 1903 by the United States Senate but was rejected by the Colombian Senate. Colombians worried about the loss of sovereignty over Panama, as their nation was slowly beginning the recovery from the devastating War of a Thousand Days. Colombians understood their weakened position in negotiating a major treaty with the youthful, feisty, and determined Roosevelt administration.

President Roosevelt was none too pleased with Colombia's decision to reject Hay-Herrán, and he famously referred to Colombians as "contemptible little creatures."[7] Undeterred, the U.S. president moved to support an independence movement in the Province of Panama, conspicuously positioning the U.S. destroyer *Nashville* in the waters off Colón. When Colombian troops attempted to cross the isthmus to rescue their officers stationed at Panama City, U.S. troops prevented the Colombians from boarding the Panama Railway, which was partially owned by U.S. investors. A few days after declaring its independence from Bogotá, the United States recognized Panama as an independent nation, and a new canal treaty was written and signed by both parties. Philippe Buneau-Varilla, the French promoter of the Panama Canal project, was credentialed as the official minister in Panama, and the Panama-U.S. Canal Treaty was ratified in early 1904. Work on the project ensued immediately thereafter, and the canal was opened to traffic in 1914.

Teddy Roosevelt's intervention, his open disdain for Colombians, and his disregard for diplomatic procedure led to a freeze in United States-Colombian relations for more than a decade. Ironically, during the period after Colombia's "loss of Panama" up through the worldwide economic crash of 1929, Colombia remained remarkably stable, politically and economically. Colombian sensibilities had been so thoroughly offended by Teddy Roosevelt's assertiveness that the mere mention of normalizing diplomatic relations with the United States was enough to force not one but two Colombian presidents out of office. Rafael Reyes, who ruled from 1904 to 1909, began the process of normalizing relations with the United States, but he was driven from power since any negotiation with the "colossus of the north" was viewed, by his detractors, as "a betrayal of national interests and honor."[8] A few years later, President Marco Fidel Suárez, from humble origins in Antioquia, was less opaque in his dealings with the north: he concluded that Colombia must, at all cost, attach itself economically, socially, and culturally to the United States. He also pushed for passage of the treaty that would normalize relations between the two nations, the Urrutia-Thomson Treaty, which was ratified in 1922. Suárez had to step aside as president in 1921 due to allegations of corruption, but in reality his attempts to facilitate negotiations with the United States earned him the enmity of his detractors. Pedro Nel Ospina, the Conservative technocrat from Medellín, was the acting president when normalization was achieved and, of course, his administration benefited from the twenty-five-million-dollar indemnity paid by the United States. This capital, together with easy credit during the 1920s, helped finance infrastructure development in Colombia, especially railroad projects, roads, and investment in oil fields.

1928

While investment opportunities would facilitate diplomatic relations between Colombia and the United States during the 1920s, a major conflagration ensued involving a U.S.-owned company, United Fruit Company (UFCO), and its Colombian subsidiary, Magdalena Fruit Company. Magdalena Fruit Company purchased bananas from local landholders, while UFCO owned most of the transportation network (the railroad) and controlled the price, export structure, and marketing of bananas in the region. Local Colombian producers and workers were at the mercy of UFCO. By the late 1920s, Colombia had emerged as the third leading exporter of bananas in the world, but with growing labor organization in the region, the strike that ensued at the coastal town of Ciénaga in 1928 seemed inevitable. Colombian soldiers moved in to put down the strike, and on December 6, 1928, the army fired live ammunition into the crowd of strikers.

The Colombian government's brutal response to the strike at Ciénaga, combined with the economic hardships imposed by the worldwide economic crash that began ten months later in October 1929 and divisions within the ruling Colombian conservative elite, resulted in a change in Colombian leadership by 1930. The presidential election that year was won by the Liberal candidate Enrique Olaya Herrera. It was the first time the Liberal Party had held the presidency in Colombia since the late nineteenth century. Despite this dramatic political shift, one enduring feature of Colombian society during this time is the relative strength of its ties to the United States—a relationship that would grow stronger during the course of the twentieth century and into the twenty-first. The events of November 1903 suggested an alternative path for U.S.-Colombian relations, but after President Suárez's "north star" policy, the final negotiation of the Urrutia-Thomson Treaty and payment of the twenty-five-million-dollar indemnity, overall diplomatic relations improved progressively and systematically. This relationship can be seen as functional and practical given that the United States has been the main market for Colombian primary exports and the Colombian external migration trend has favored the United States as a destination since, roughly, the 1960s. Compared with the United States' historical relationships with other Latin American nations during the twentieth century, the U.S.-Colombian relationship is actually a model of pragmatism and stability. For example, U.S.-Mexican relations have been fraught with tension, military intervention, and intrigue. The U.S. relationship with the Dominican Republic has likewise been complicated by multiple military interventions, the latest occurring in 1965 during the presidency of Lyndon B. Johnson. That intervention signaled the end of President Kennedy's goodwill gesture toward Latin America, the Alliance for Progress. United States-Cuban relations, as of this writing, are frozen in a state reminiscent of the pre-1960 Cold War. U.S. direct and indirect military intervention in Nicaragua persisted during much of the twentieth century, and the current state of diplomatic relations between the United States and Venezuela, Bolivia, and Ecuador is, at best, strained.

President Olaya went out of his way to appease U.S. business interests, especially during the early years of the Great Depression. However, his administration was not as friendly to its southern neighbors, especially Peru. The so-called Leticia Affair in 1932, which lasted for about eight months, was actually a war between Peru and Colombia over territory in the Amazon near the Colombian city of Leticia. As discussed in chapter 5, Peruvian civilians seized land that bordered on Leticia, in open defiance of the 1922 Salomón-Lozano Treaty that ceded Leticia to Colombia. Colombia faced a daunting challenge in moving troops to Leticia. The navy had to sail from Cartagena into the Atlantic and then up the Amazon River (through Brazilian territory) to reach Leticia, and airplanes were used to land Colombian troops in the region. The conflict was really more an "affair" than a war, and by May 1933, a cease-fire was declared and mediated by the League of Nations, and a peace treaty was signed the following year. Colombians organized energetically to defend the territory, a sparsely populated land in the jungle seen by only a handful of citizens, and spent the equivalent of about ten million U.S. dollars in recovering the territory. Munitions were sold to Colombia by the United States, committing the Colombian government to massive (by 1930s standards) military spending, which, according to one historian, represented "a costly diversion of scarce resources and energy and drove the government toward a moratorium on its foreign debt payments."[9]

WORLD WAR II AND JORGE ELIÉCER GAITÁN

Colombia's involvement in World War II was significant and supportive of the Allies, despite the strongly pro-fascist sentiments of its emerging Conservative leader, Laureano Gómez. Colombia's Francophile ruling elite was frightened by the prospects of worldwide Axis domination, and by late 1943 the nation declared a state of belligerence against Germany in retaliation for the sinking of a Colombian naval vessel. Colombia never sent troops into battle, like Brazil, nor did Colombians fly missions abroad, as did Mexican pilots in the South Pacific. Colombia nonetheless cooperated fully with the Allies, as directed by Washington. U.S. military missions were formally organized with Colombia, and Colombian military personnel received training in the United States. Colombia was encouraged to freeze German assets, purge German pilots from its airline (which would be renamed "Avianca" during this time), and cooperate economically with Allied powers. The United States sought to control the Colombian market for export products deemed critical to the war effort, including oil, balsa wood, quartz, and platinum, and as a result of the Colombian collaboration, the government received direct U.S. economic assistance through the Export-Import Bank.

During this time period, the most significant political leader of Colombia's twentieth century emerged. Jorge Eliécer Gaitán was born in the center of Bogotá, in a grimy neighborhood named Las Cruces. He earned a law degree from the National University at twenty-one years of age and went on to complete a specialization in criminology in Rome. His fame grew in Colombia when in 1929 he dared to litigate against the U.S.-owned United Fruit Company, claiming that the company provoked the 1928 Ciénaga tragedy that led to scores of Colombians being killed. Gaitán's anti-imperialist discourse won him support among the urban poor and connected him to the coastal residents who saw, firsthand, the devastating effects of the UFCO enclave economic structure that kept Colombian workers entrenched in poverty while American management lived nearby in other-dimensional luxury.

In Bogotá, Gaitán became a fiery champion of the urban poor and was appointed mayor of the city in 1936; he ran for president of the republic ten years later but never received the recognition or support of the official Liberal Party. The ruling elite thought of him as a dangerous upstart and referred to him derisively as "el negro Gaitán"—which translates (politely) in English as "that dark-skinned Gaitán"—a reference to his mixed-blood, *mestizo* features. On the day he was killed by an assassin's bullet, Gaitán was working in his downtown office, preparing to compete in the 1950 presidential elections. His death touched off a wave of urban rioting throughout the country and led to growing intransigence between the two political parties. The urban poor's hope for a significant say in the running of the Colombian state seemed to evaporate when Gaitán died; many poor people assumed that the killing of the Liberal leader was orchestrated by Conservative elements within the country. Conservatives, of course, blamed the Communists. Coincidentally, on the day of his death, the Ninth International Conference of American States was meeting in Bogotá, tasked with drawing up a charter for the Organization of American States. The significant fact that Colombia was selected as the site to organize the OAS—the organization designed to provide post–World War II hemispheric solidarity and collaboration—is generally lost on the more dramatic events that unfolded on April 9, 1948. Complicating the historical record further is Fidel Castro.

The Cuban leader (who assumed power in Havana eleven years later) was also in Bogotá on April 9, 1948, so conspiracy theorists have long held that "international communism" was responsible for the rioting that followed Gaitán's assassination. Castro's presence in the Colombian capital had nothing to do with pushing the communist revolution forward; he was participating in a student meeting that had been organized to coincide—as a form of protest—with the official OAS delegation meeting. Gabriel García Márquez, in his memoire *Living to Tell the Tale*, reports—ironically—that Gaitán's appointment book for April 9, 1948 was marked "Fidel Castro, 2 pm"; Gaitán was killed at 1 p.m. Fidel Castro was motivated and politicized by the events in Bogotá following Gaitán's death, but he was a young Cuban student activist, and his 1959 revolution in Cuba was clearly influenced by what he saw on a dreary April day in Bogotá. It is not at all surprising that Castro was in Bogotá, protesting the OAS organizational meeting: politicized students in Colombia and throughout Latin America were suspicious of any international organization that would be led by the United States, the undisputed Western power in the postwar world.

Gaitán's death is often blamed for ushering in the undeclared ten-year civil war in Colombia known simply as La Violencia—"the violence." But rural violence had begun much earlier, in the 1930s, when poor people were forced to compete for increasingly scarce land. An agrarian reform measure of 1936 seemed to exacerbate rather than alleviate tensions. Political intransigence at the national level, a worldwide economic downturn, and a growing social gap between those with power and wealth and those without are some factors that explain the violence. Gaitán's murder was an urban phenomenon, but people who identified with the populist leader—a man who always spoke of *el pueblo* (the people)—were fed up with government policies that ignored the struggles of the rural poor. And the growing violence, urban and rural, demonstrated both the fecklessness of the national government and the degree to which the government did not, in fact, govern over or control the entire Colombian nation.

The reality of two hundred thousand violent deaths in an undeclared civil war is certainly something no society would wish to dwell on, but that is exactly what has happened. Colombian and foreign scholars who focus on Colombia have turned research on "the violence" into a sort of cottage industry: dozens of scholars from Colombia and abroad have published dozens of works on the phenomenon of the violence in Colombia, leading some to believe that violence is the only issue that defines the nation.

A Colombian Roman Catholic priest, Father Camilo Torres Restrepo, entered the academic debate concerning Colombian "violence." In 1963, he published his own essay titled "La violencia y los cambios socioculturales en las áreas rurales de Colombia." Father Torres was an internationalist who completed a master's degree in sociology at the Catholic University of Leuven (Louvain) in Belgium in the 1950s, where he was deeply influenced by the French worker priests movement, initiated in Marseilles by Father Jacques Loew. This was an effervescent period for worldwide Catholicism, and young European priests were trying to systematically understand the horrors of World War II and the role of Church officials in a world of growing complexity, marked by violence and poverty. Father Torres was a gifted student, orator, and thinker, and he returned to Colombia prepared to take on entrenched socioeconomic and political structures. For example, Torres, in his essay, suggests that the violence had produced positive changes for the rural folk (the *campesinos*) of Colombia and had a modernizing effect since it pushed people into cities and helped them "mature" in terms of socialization and social mobility. Shortly after publishing his essay on the violence, Father Torres would become directly engaged in the violence as a guerrilla fighter with the ELN. He joined the group in October 1965 and died in combat four months later.[10]

How the outside world would come to view the Colombian violence is summarized in a 1986 review article by British historian Eric J. Hobsbawm. The writer tries to make sense of the violence in Colombia, publishing in the *New York Review of Books*. Hobsbawm, like many scholars who have studied the violence, opens the article by categorizing Colombia as a place "long . . . known for an altogether exceptional proclivity to homicide."[11] However, what only a handful of authors have focused on is the remarkable set of policies developed by Colombians to stem the violence. Colombians created a political power-sharing arrangement known as the Frente Nacional, or "National Front," whereby political liberals and conservatives would alternate in and out of the presidency for two terms each. This would, in theory, give everyone a stake in Colombian society and would correct for some of the historic abuses of power that defined both nineteenth- and twentieth-century Colombian political development.

KOREA AND THE ALLIANCE FOR PROGRESS

The Violence alone does not define Colombia during the 1950s. Colombian armed forces, for example, participated in the United Nations–sponsored military conflict in Korea (1950–1953). Colombia was the only nation from Latin America to participate in this Cold War conflict; its participation is a direct function of the virulently anti-Communist rule of President Laureano Gómez, an ultra-Conservative politician known to his detractors as "El Monstruo"—"the Monster." Gómez, who would be removed from power in 1953 by military coup—a rarity for Colombia during the twentieth century[12]—hoped to receive military assistance from the United States as repayment for service in Korea. Colombia received millions of dollars in military aid and training for its military officers and troops and was firmly aligned with the United States.

Colombia's links to the United States grew during the 1960s. The Cuban Revolution of early 1959 pushed the United States to pay closer attention to Latin American society as a whole, rather than only the economic, political, and military elites. John F. Kennedy's election to the White House in 1961 represented a new era of youthful, creative leadership, and he was admired in Latin America for his charisma, vitality, and Roman Catholicism. Kennedy quickly identified Colombia as a vital link to his new program for Latin America, the "Alliance for Progress," which was formally launched on August 17, 1961, in Uruguay, via the Punta del Este Charter. The alliance was designed to show that "progressive capitalism rather than communism was the most effective means of improving Latin America's material conditions of life."[13] Latin America was to receive about twenty billion U.S. dollars in mostly development aid during the 1960s, and Colombia became a sort of showcase for the alliance. The new administration in Washington was impressed by Colombia's commitment to democratic rule, the intelligence and preparation of its managing economic elite, and the overall collaborative relationship that had developed between Washington and Bogotá since the 1920s. President Kennedy and his wife, Jacqueline, visited Bogotá in mid-December 1961 and used this occasion to promote the alliance and the social development that was its main feature. Alliance funds helped build schools, hospitals, housing, and center-west segments of the Colombian capital city were planned and developed with the help of the Kennedy initiative. An area that now houses more than one million people was inaugurated "Ciudad Techo," later to be renamed "Ciudad Kennedy."

Funding to Colombia was impressive during the early days of the alliance: about twenty-five million U.S. dollars in development grants flowed to Colombia during 1961 and 1962, and another twenty-two million dollars the following year. From 1962 to1963, the "Food for Peace" program, developed by the United States Department of Agriculture, donated about thirty-five million dollars in surplus agricultural products to Colombia, and a thirty-million-dollar "program loan" was sent to Bogotá in early 1962. Interestingly, and certainly distinct from today's reality, U.S. military spending in Colombia was far less significant than social and development spending. Only six million dollars was sent to Colombia in military assistance in 1962; that number grew to 8.4 million dollars in 1963.[14]

Colombia was also the first Latin American nation to receive U.S. Peace Corps volunteers; sixty-one volunteers arrived in September 1961. By the late 1960s, some seven hundred Peace Corps volunteers were stationed there. The Peace Corps volunteers were charged with supporting Colombian "development," but the program was hastily organized, and the young Americans received little practical training and were unable to transform Colombia as hoped. Many of the early Peace Corps volunteers went through a personal and in some cases permanent transformative process while in Colombia, and some of the leading scholars on Colombia in the United States (Bruce Bagley, Chuck Bergquist, and Jim Henderson, to name a few) first encountered Colombia through Peace Corps service.

POPE PAUL VI AND THE CLOSE OF THE 1960s

Colombia's long-standing ties to the Holy See were reaffirmed when Pope Paul VI made his inaugural visit to the nation—the first visit to Latin America by any pontiff—on August 22, 1968. His visit was timed to coincide with the closing of the 39th International Eucharistic Congress, held in Bogotá, and the opening of the II CELAM (Latin American Episcopal Conference) bishops' meeting, held in Medellín in late August 1968. The Medellín meeting established the structure and guiding philosophy of a new, energetic Latin America–led "theology of liberation." Bishops, priests, and academics from all over Latin America came to Colombia to see the pope and to begin the difficult work of connecting the priorities of the Roman Catholic Church to the socioeconomic realities of Latin America.

While Colombians like to think of the 1960s as a decade of collaboration with the United States, increased development, and modernization of infrastructure and cities, a less alluring reality is found in the growth of armed insurgency groups during this same decade. Two groups still in existence today are the Army of National Liberation, the ELN by its Spanish acronym, which formed in 1962, and the Revolutionary Armed Forces of Colombia, or the FARC, founded in 1964. The ELN was organized by university students and other disaffected Colombians who felt their ideas for a more just and inclusive society had been stifled by the hierarchical, elite-driven political arrangement of the National Front (an arrangement that left Colombian structures completely intact). While the ELN was internationalist, inspired by Fidel Castro and his successful 1959 revolution, the FARC was a more local, agrarian-based movement and developed out of the *campesino* class— country folk who felt the political elites in the big cities never represented their interests or priorities.

The FARC's origins date back to the land struggles of the late 1920s and 1930s, when poor people were pushed off their land by more prosperous landlords with connections to the political and military apparatus of the state. In 1964, in an attempt to demonstrate that the state was in charge, the Colombian army bombed an insurgency stronghold in Marquetalia, and at that point, the conflict was engaged. The mostly urban, educated Colombian

Communist Party sought the support of Moscow and viewed the FARC as their loyal armed representatives in the countryside, but Moscow seemed more interested in supporting leftist movements in Central America, Mexico, Cuba, and, after 1970, in Chile under Marxist president Salvador Allende. The FARC still supports an army—of roughly six thousand to eight thousand guerrilla soldiers as of this writing—but they have suffered a series of significant setbacks over the past few years.

Lawlessness extended into other aspects of Colombian society, as demonstrated by the growth in the processing and transshipment of illegal narcotics. Drug trafficking came to define Colombian society during the 1970s up through the present. Marijuana from the north coast of Colombia was grown and shipped to the United States. The so-called Santa Marta Gold became the standard of excellence among marijuana aficionados during the 1970s. The United States worked to convince the Colombian government to commit to a crop eradication program, but this barely affected U.S. consumers, who turned to domestic producers in California and other mild-climate regions in the United States. A much more profitable, easily transportable, and addictive substance became the rage among the affluent urbanites in the United States—the so-called Studio 54 set, named for the New York City nightclub where glamour, disco music, and cocaine were all openly displayed and celebrated.

Unfortunately, many non-Colombians still associate Colombia with cocaine and the notorious leader of the Medellín cartel, Pablo Escobar, who rose to prominence during the 1980s. His organization coordinated and controlled shipments of illegal narcotics out of Colombia, taking advantage of Colombia's geostrategic position (facing two oceans at the northwest corner of South America), its weak government, and its underpaid police force that was susceptible to bribes and intimidation.

CONTADORA, CENTRAL AMERICA, AND COLOMBIA'S NEIGHBORS

While engaged in a brutal, complex, free-flowing narcotics war at home, Colombia became actively engaged in promoting peace in Central America during the 1980s through the "Contadora Initiative," named for the island off the Panamanian coast where the initial meetings were held in 1983. At the suggestion of Swedish prime minister Olof Palme, Colombian Nobel laureate Gabriel García Márquez, and others, Contadora was designed as a regional solution to the seemingly interminable civil wars in Guatemala, El Salvador, and Nicaragua. In all three conflicts, U.S. military aid played a decisive role, though one not always helpful from the perspective of human rights. The other Latin American nations involved in the peace initiative were Mexico, Venezuela, and Panama. Contadora never received support or backing from the United States, which viewed all three wars as part of the larger Cold War conflict between the United States (and its allies) and the Soviet Union. However, Contadora is viewed as an important regional first step in creating peace accords that would eventually end the fighting by 1993 in El Salvador and by 1996 in Guatemala. In Nicaragua, the U.S.-backed *contra* war ground to a halt when the leftist Sandinistas were voted out of office in 1990.[15]

Colombia has had a long-standing diplomatic dispute with Nicaragua over San Andrés, an island off the coast of Nicaragua. San Andrés y Providencia is an official Colombian department, and the dispute over whether Nicaragua or Colombia should exert sovereignty over the territory extends back to the nineteenth century. In the late 1920s, a formal treaty between Nicaragua and Colombia settled the matter with Colombia's claim upheld, but the treaty was abrogated by the Nicaraguan revolutionary government that took power in Managua in 1979. Currently, the conflict has degenerated to little more than a territorial maritime dispute, and Colombians take daily flights to San Andrés from the principal mainland cities to enjoy the tropical beaches and practice their Caribbean English.

Certainly, Colombia's manufacture and shipment of illegal narcotics— mostly processed cocaine and heroin—to the European and North American markets have created tensions with bordering countries. Those tensions continue today and involve a mix of illegal activities at borders between Colombia and Brazil to the southwest, Venezuela to the west, Ecuador and Peru due south, and, to the north, Panama. Illegal narcotics are one leg of a three-legged structure of tension. A second leg is the smuggling of commerce, money, and fuel. The final leg of border tensions involves human migration across borders. These tensions have been most prevalent at the extensive Colombian-Venezuelan border. During the 1970s, when the Venezuela oil boom was in full swing, tens of thousands of Colombians, mostly poor and underskilled, traveled to Venezuela to work low-wage, demeaning jobs. Many returned home as political and social tensions developed in the late 1990s—the tensions that led inexorably to the rise of the mercurial president Hugo Chávez. In Ecuador, the pattern described above is reversed—poor, mostly indigenous Ecuadoran citizens come to Colombia to work, often selling handcrafted items in the urban marketplaces—and they are generally looked down upon by their more affluent, urban Colombian hosts.

Regional relations were severely strained in early March 2008, when the Colombian military briefly entered Ecuadorian territory to kill Raúl Reyes (né Luis Edgar Devia Silva), the number-two commander of the FARC revolutionary group, who had established a camp in Ecuador on the border with Colombia. A total of seventeen people living at the camp were killed in addition to a Colombian soldier. The government of Rafael Correa energetically denounced the raid; Venezuelan president Chávez, in solidarity with his leftist colleague Correa, seemed ready to declare war on Colombia. He called for troops to move toward the Colombian border, but Colombia's president Álvaro Uribe refused to take the bait, and the tensions diminished over time without what many feared might become a three-country war in northern South America.

The 1990s were certainly hectic for Colombia. It was a decade that saw the demise of Pablo Escobar (though not the demise of illegal narcotics shipments out of Colombia), a strengthening leftist insurgency, a growth in paramilitary activity, an internal refugee crisis topped off with a major political crisis, and, last, economic collapse at mid-decade. The Colombian nation survived, but the struggles were intense, complex, and seemingly interminable. The political crisis briefly altered the long-standing collaboration between Colombia and the United States. Presidential candidate Ernesto Samper of the Liberal Party was elected in the spring of 1994, but it was quickly revealed, later that year, that he had accepted an illegal infusion of approximately six million dollars into his campaign; the funds evidently had been bundled by drug traffickers. The accusations, which proved mostly true, led to an immediate cooldown between Washington and Bogotá. The climate grew so chilled that President Samper—the sitting president of the Republic of Colombia—had his visa revoked to travel to the United States. Samper survived the crisis, but the Colombian economy headed into a free fall as society reacted to privatization initiatives of the late 1980s and early 1990s, falling coffee prices during the early 1990s, difficulty in securing investment capital at home and abroad, lower levels of productivity, and limited outside investment due to an ongoing political crisis and social insecurity. When Andrés Pastrana was elected president in 1998, the political crisis with the United States quickly evaporated, and the economy slowly picked up. Pastrana skillfully befriended U.S. president Bill Clinton and convinced the U.S. leader and Congress (but not really the European Union, another legislative body he had courted) of the dire situation in Colombia. Pastrana worried, justifiably so, that a collusion between growers of coca leaf, processors of *pasta básica* and processed cocaine, and the leftist guerrilla groups had become solidified. He described an out-of-control leftist armed insurgency raking in annually about five hundred million dollars through kidnappings, extortion, and "protection" of illegal narcotics operations. He asked for help.

Adding to the mayhem in Colombia at this time, the AUC (the United Self-Defense Forces of Colombia—the paramilitary forces), under the command of Carlos Castaño, was fully operational. The "paras," as they colloquially came to be known, targeted the guerrilla insurgents and anyone they suspected of collaborating with them. Tens of thousands were murdered during this period, and about two million Colombians were displaced from their homes. President Pastrana had to walk a tightrope whereby he assured world leaders that he was in charge while trying at the same time to convince the world that the social situation in Colombia was tantamount to total chaos. Pastrana gave an interview to the CBS show *60 Minutes* in the fall of 1999; speaking calmly, in perfect English, he described Colombia as a historically stable democracy that needed a major infusion of funds to continue functioning as a democratic entity. President Clinton responded by pushing forward the so-called Plan Colombia—a 1.35-billion-dollar (mostly military) aid package designed to "save" Colombia. Clinton mentioned Colombia in his 2000 State of the Union address, and with minimal debate, the U.S. Congress approved the aid package in the summer of 2000.

The terrorist attack on U.S. soil on September 11, 2001, diverted Washington's attention from Colombia and the rest of the Western Hemisphere. President George W. Bush defined three nations as "evil" (North Korea, Iran, and Iraq) and classified a variety of armed groups as "terrorists," including three such groups residing in Colombia: the AUC, ELN, and FARC. At about the same time, from 1999 to early 2002, President Pastrana made a somewhat serious attempt at negotiating peace in Colombia, which was responded to with minimal enthusiasm from the leaders of the FARC and EPL (Army of Popular Liberation). Many Colombians concluded that Pastrana had been outmaneuvered by the FARC leadership, and most citizens expressed anger and humiliation at the insurgents' intransigence. The failed peace together with the growing sense that the country lacked a reliable rudder led to the election of the hard-line governor of Antioquia as president, Álvaro Uribe Vélez, a man who represented neither the Conservative nor Liberal Party structure. He took the oath of office on August 7, 2002.

URIBE AND BUSH: BROTHERS IN ARMS

President Uribe and President George W. Bush became close allies in their respective roles: they shared Texas-sized stories of ranching and rural life, and they were both fond of wearing cowboy boots and hats at press conferences. They developed a genuine friendship, and Colombia quickly became the United States' leading regional ally in the Bush administration's post-9/11 War on Terror. Military aid continued to flow to Colombia; about eight billion U.S. dollars have been directed there since the beginning of Plan Colombia in 2000, though the initial impetus of Plan Colombia, designed to curb the power of the drug smugglers and help Colombians regain control of their nation through judicial, political, and security reforms, morphed after 9/11 into a war against "terrorists"—particularly the FARC. The rebels proved to be more stubborn and elusive than the president imagined, but significant gains were made during Uribe's eight years as president (2002–2010) against the armed resistance. However, the toll in human rights abuses, extrajudicial killings, and military scandals—most notoriously, the "false positive" scandal in which some military commanders were inflating body counts by killing innocent civilians, dressing the dead civilians as subversives, and calling in a weak, stenographic press to help celebrate the "victory"—led to broad condemnation by national human rights groups (such as the Jesuit-run think tank and human rights advocacy group in Bogotá, CINEP) and international groups Human Rights Watch and Amnesty International, among others.

The grim human rights record has had economic and social consequences, most notably in the form of delayed passage of a free trade agreement (FTA) with Colombia. Passage of the Colombian FTA, a priority of the Bush administration, which succeeded in negotiating the agreement in 2006, was delayed for five years. The delay can be attributed, in large measure, to opposition by Democratic Party union leadership in the United States, which looks unfavorably, in general, on FTAs that have pulled high-paying manufacturing jobs away from the United States and union control. Union leaders and their political allies in the United States scrutinized the Colombian FTA on an added human rights platform. It is estimated that as many as three thousand union leaders in Colombia have been murdered since 1986; but with billions of dollars at stake (in 2009, U.S. imports from Colombia were 11.3 billion dollars, and exports represented 9.4 billion dollars), the FTA was signed in October 2011. President Obama, who vocally denounced the Colombia FTA during his 2008 campaign, reversed his position to the glee of big business. Union representatives in the United States and human rights activists throughout the world fought against passage of the Colombia FTA in the United States Congress, but the fate of the agreement became assured when a Canada-Colombia FTA went into effect by mid-2011 and when China began to make—during the past five years—significant economic inroads into the Colombian market.

Human rights abuses and stifled economic opportunity have forced many Colombians to leave the country. It is estimated that more than two million Colombians live outside the nation, in the United States, Western Europe, and Latin America, and Colombians abroad remitted approximately 4.2 billion U.S. dollars in 2009. That figure fell to 3.9 billion dollars in 2010 due, most likely, to the contraction of the U.S. and European economies. Fifty-eight billion dollars in remittance payments were sent to Latin America in 2010, down by about 12 percent from the previous year (2008–2009).

ENTER SANTOS

President Juan Manuel Santos, who assumed the Colombian presidency in August 2010, has begun to redefine Colombia's international relations in important ways: first—and most significantly—he has markedly improved relations with neighboring countries Ecuador and Venezuela and has worked in a more deliberate and prudent fashion (over his predecessor) at creating cordial, collaborative relations with important Latin American nations, such as Argentina, Chile, and Peru. Santos has looked elsewhere, besides the United States, to open trade dialogue, including countries in Europe, and China. His foreign policy has been more balanced and nuanced than that of Uribe, whose foreign policy focused almost exclusively on a sort of obsequious collaboration with the United States.

Santos surprised many by signing, in early June 2011, the Ley de víctimas—"Law of Victims"—which could affect four million people. This new law recognizes all victims of the Colombian conflict, dating back to 1985, and guarantees reparations in the form of cash payments. It also, perhaps more significantly, guarantees that the state will work to return lands taken illegally from rightful owners since 1991. The law was seen as an important first step at controlling and repairing some of the damage done in a long, devastating conflict that always seemed too cumbersome to contain.

From its place in the economic rivalry between the United States and Great Britain in the early nineteenth century, to the separation of Panama in 1903 and, more recently, its conflict with neighboring Venezuela and Ecuador, Colombia's interactions with the outside world have followed a complex but substantive evolution, developing in response to the nation's needs and aspirations. The foreign press has tended to malign Colombia, focusing on a history of regional conflict, violence, guerrilla movements, and drug trafficking. As this chapter has attempted to demonstrate, however, periods of violence and illegal activity are only part of Colombia's story. A spirit of collaboration has long guided Colombia's dealings with the outside world. For example, President Marco Fidel Suárez, in the early twentieth century, initiated diplomatic relations with the United States despite Colombia's lingering resentment over the U.S. intervention at Panama in 1903. He understood the urgent need to collaborate with the growing power to the north. Colombia also collaborated with the Allied powers in World War II, with the United States and the United Nations during the Korean conflict, and with the United States in the establishment of the Alliance for Progress and the Peace Corps. Additionally, Colombia led a peace campaign with its regional neighbors in the 1980s, in what would be known as the Contadora Initiative. In each case, Colombia demonstrated a willingness to engage in and, indeed, initiate international projects to promote its people, its ideals, and its way of life. Of course, Colombia is not perfect, but it is important that constructive contributions of Colombia are not simply overlooked or dismissed. This chapter has shown the depth and complexity of Colombia's international relations and the futility of reducing that history to mere statements about drugs and violence. International cooperation and collaboration will offer Colombia opportunities and challenges in the future, but the viability of Colombia as a nation and society is no longer the subject of international debate.

NOTES

1. Thomas Jefferson to Pierre Samuel Dupont de Nemours, 1811, in *The Writings of Thomas Jefferson* (Memorial ed., Lipscomb and Bergh, eds.) (Washington, D.C.: Thomas Jefferson Memorial Association, 1903–1904, 20 vols), 13:40.

2. David Bushnell, "Simón Bolívar and the United States: A Study in Ambivalence," *Air University Review* 37 (1986): 106–12.

3. Ibid.

4. Frank Safford and Marco Palacios, *Colombia: Fragmented Land, Divided Society* (New York: Oxford University Press, 2002), 98.

5. Stephen J. Randall, *Colombia and the United States: Hegemony and Interdependence* (Athens: University of Georgia Press, 1992), 33.

6. Ibid., 56.

7. Ibid., 83.

8. David Bushnell, *The Making of Modern Colombia: A Nation in Spite of Itself* (Berkeley: University of California Press, 1993), 161.

9. Randall, *Colombia and the United States*, 144.

10. See Michael J. LaRosa, *De la derecha a la izquierda: La Iglesia Católica en la Colombia contemporánea* (Bogotá: Planeta Colombiana Editorial, 2000), chapter 4.

11. E. J. Hobsbawm, "Murderous Colombia," *New York Review of Books*, November 20, 1986.

12. The only other president removed from office in Colombia by military coup during the twentieth century was President Manuel Antonio Sanclemente in 1900.

13. Bushnell, *The Making of Modern Colombia*, 231.

14. These figures are from an excellent 2003 paper presented by Luis Eduardo Fajardo titled "From the Alliance for Progress to the Plan Colombia: A Retrospective Look at U.S. Aid to Colombia," published by the Crisis States Research Center at the London School of Economics and Political Science (UK), 2003.

15. *Contra* is the shortened version of the Spanish word for counterrevolutionary, *contrarevolucionario*. The United States backed the *contras*—described as "freedom fighters" by President Ronald Reagan—against the Marxist-inspired Sandinista government.

Conclusion

Colombia endures as a nation despite difficulties, challenges, and a history that is tragic and dynamic. Colombians do not hide from their past. Indeed, they have learned to confront and incorporate parts of their history that would be more convenient to forget.

Contemporary Colombian currency tells a story about how the nation considers its past. The currency features heroes from politics and literature who have met tragedy: Policarpa Salvarrieta—martyred heroine of the independence struggle who was executed by Crown loyalists in 1817—is remembered on the ten-thousand-peso note. Renowned poet José Asunción Silva, who took his life in 1896, is represented on the five-thousand-peso note, and Jorge Eliécer Gaitán, whose murder on April 9, 1948, touched off urban rioting known simply as the *nueve de abril*, is commemorated on the one-thousand-peso note, along with a couple of his trademark phrases. One of the phrases, "*el pueblo es superior a sus dirigentes*" ("the people are better than their leaders"), shows the politician's ironic skepticism of "politicians."

Geography, more than the Colombian currency, explains the Colombian condition; the land's physical contrasts are dramatic, imposing isolation on peoples who live in the same territory yet identify with their region and neighbors rather than their fellow national citizens. That a nation would be constructed out of this complexity is itself worthy of comment. The only time in the historical period covered in this book when Colombia "deconstructed" was during a hostile outside intervention, in 1903, when the United States organized and executed the separation of the province of Panama from the Colombian mainland. The Province of Panama's separation was a direct function of Colombia's unique global geographic position, that is, the nation straddles two oceans, and in the period prior to aviation, a small strip of coveted Colombian territory linked the two oceans. Today, that territory is known as the Republic of Panama.

Many forces and factors have come together to help unify Colombia. Constitutional processes have shaped Colombia's history during the past two hundred years, as demonstrated in chapter 3; institutions have been forged to unite what appeared permanently fractured. The Church helped unify and, on occasion, divide the nation. Yet a common language, a consolidated, elite-driven historical narrative, and a Western-focused education system all contributed to the forging of the Colombian nation.

The first-time visitor to Colombia—Mutis, Codazzi, and von Humboldt, among the most prominent and productive—is struck by the nation's natural beauty, lush vegetation, and biodiversity. However, until the construction of modern transportation and communication networks, Colombia remained somewhat of an enigma to the outside world. David Bushnell's prescient comment, in the introduction to his 1993 textbook, demonstrates this point: "Colombia today is the least studied and least understood of the major Latin American nations." Bushnell is commenting on the fact that Colombia's history is not easily understood or compartmentalized since it does not follow the historiographical patterns developed by twentieth-century historians, especially those writing from afar. Colombia lacked the long, strong pattern of immigration found in places such as the United States, Argentina, Brazil, Chile, Cuba, Peru, and Uruguay. Colombia also lacked revolutionary tumult and military governance; there was no twentieth-century sociopolitical "revolution" similar to those in Mexico, Cuba, or Nicaragua, and there was no dramatic military intervention, as experienced in Brazil in 1964, Peru in 1968, Chile in 1973, and Argentina in the mid-1970s. Populism in Latin America became an important academic topic in the 1970s and 1980s, but research on populism focused on Brazil under Getúlio Vargas, Peru under Víctor Raúl Haya de la Torre, Mexico under Lázaro Cárdenas, or Argentina under the Peróns; it was seen as improbable to study Colombian populism because the populist leader, Gáitan, died young and tragically, before ever assuming national power.[1]

The outstanding generation of Colombian social historians, forged in the 1960s with the path-breaking work of Professor Jaime Jaramillo Uribe, has shown the world the richness of Colombia's history. These historians have emphasized the importance of understanding Colombia on its own terms. Models and theories drawn up elsewhere—whether they are called "dependency theory," "import-substitution industrialization," or "developmentalism"—never quite resonate or translate entirely in Colombia. Learning about Colombia requires dedication and significant time spent in the country. Unfortunately, a U.S. State Department travel warning that emphasizes the presence of an active guerrilla insurgency and the widely held perception that Colombia is more dangerous than most places in the Western Hemisphere have conspired to keep foreign researchers away from Colombian archives and document collections.

Our book has attempted to show that Colombia, despite its complex historical record, endures, and that the focus on political violence, illegal narcotics, and corruption hides a less dramatic but more important story of constitutional procedure, governments that regularly transfer power after elections, and a concern with social rights of the people, as evidenced by the rethinking and rewriting of the Colombian constitution in 1991. The nation is sustained not only by a constitution and stable, though imperfect, government but by infrastructure (outlined in chapter 7) that has sought to unite the nation. The most conspicuous, remarkable aspect of Colombia, though, is its diverse, complex, and original cultural development. Colombians rally more enthusiastically around their cultural ambassadors than around politicians and business leaders. Colombian cyclists who race in the Tour de France, golfers who compete on the PGA tour, painters whose work features in galleries all over the world, and writers who have won the Nobel Prize are the topic of daily conversations.

Colombian culture is extraordinarily vibrant, but it has been too often overshadowed by the worldwide media headlines that focus—for reasons that are both functional and profitable—on Colombia "the dangerous." Writers, painters, poets, directors of theater, and scholars from diverse disciplines have been animated by "the crisis" (an example of which is represented by the critically acclaimed 1999 gallery show at the Museo de Arte Moderno de Bogotá, "Arte y Violencia en Colombia Desde 1948"),[2] and at the same time, they have worked to challenge the official, accepted historical narrative while pushing back against the forces of hierarchy, elitism, and social stratification.

Which history is the "correct" history of Colombia? We hope that we have shown how that question is both perilous in its implications and impossible to answer. Colombian history is remarkably dynamic, and historians arrive at distinctly different conclusions when writing about the same time period or event. We wanted, in this work, to focus on the forces of unity, the dynamics that we believe have held Colombia together over time. Other works—scholarly and not so scholarly—study Colombia from the perspective of disintegration, failure, catastrophe, or division. Our interpretations and emphases are not necessarily "correct," and future scholars will likely contradict what we have offered here. That is the territory of our profession, which moves and changes as interpretations develop, are debated and promulgated, and are supported or rejected over time. While interpretations will vary, we have little doubt that Colombia the nation will endure and that Colombians will continue to face the challenges ahead of them with a sound spirit of skepticism grounded in hope, fortitude, and the dignity that seems to define them as a people. The quest for a better future is the goal of all civilized peoples, and Colombians have been moving toward that goal—not always evenly, but in a systematic, remarkably creative Colombian fashion.

NOTES

1. Scholars have hardly ignored Gaitán, but the study of Colombian populism would require particular creativity and judiciousness with sources, as demonstrated in Herbert "Tico" Braun's book *The Assassination of Gaitán: Public Life and Urban Violence in Colombia* (1985).

2. This translates as "Art and Violence in Colombia since 1948."

Colombian Chronology, 1810–1991

Year	Politics	Society and Economy	Culture and Science
1810	—Autonomous Provincial Junta —Supreme Junta of Santafé —Act of 20 of July and expulsion of the viceroy —First battle of the National Guard		—Newspapers: *La Constitución Felíz* and *Diario Político de Santafé* —Composition of first patriotic song by José María Salazar —In Cartagena, *Argos Americano* published
1811	—Constitution of Cundinamarca —Federal pact signed —Declaration of Independence of Cartagena —Constitution of Tunja		Antonio Nariño publishes *La Bagatela*
1812	Constitution of Antioquia		

Year	Politics	Society and Economy	Culture and Science
1813	—"Admirable Campaign" of Simón Bolívar —Declaration of Independence of Tunja and Cundinamarca —Nariño's military campaign under way		—Francisco José de Caldas organizes military academy in Medellín —Publication in Mompox of catechism or *Instrucción Popular de Fernández de Sotomayor*
1814		—Sale of communal lands (*ejidos*) authorized —Slaves freed in Antioquia	
1815	Cartagena under siege by Pablo Morillo's army		
1816	—Pablo Morillo takes Santafé —Regime of Terror begins —Viceroyalty re-established		
1819	—Congress of Angostura —Campaign of Freedom —Battle of Boyacá —Fundamental Letter: Republic of Colombia created		
1820	Simón Bolívar declared president by Angostura Congress	—Government declares that schools are to be founded in all villages and towns	

Year	Politics	Society and Economy	Culture and Science
		—First Masonic lodge in Bogotá	
1821	—Cúcuta Congress promulgates new constitution—centralist —Panama declares independence and annexes itself to Colombia	—Free womb law; children of slaves born free —Law—freedom of press —First steamships arrive on Colombian coasts	—Education system of Joseph Lancaster pushed forward in Colombia —French mission hired to push agricultural scientific research
1822	—United States recognizes Colombia —Meeting between Bolívar and San Martín in Guayaquil —Government regulates ministries and organizes properties in the country	In Bogotá, "Industrial Society" created to build an earthenware industry	University of Antioquia founded
1823			National Museum founded
1824	Treaty of Friendship, Commerce, and Navigation between United States and Colombia	English "Colombian Mining Association" re-establishes mining activity in Antioquia	
1825	—Great Britain recognizes Colombia and signs treaty of friendship,	—Census taken: 2,583,799 people —Abolition of colonial taxes	—Newspaper: *La Miscelánea* —Exploration for possible

Year	Politics	Society and Economy	Culture and Science
	commerce and navigation —Abolition of slave trade		interoceanic route through Panama
1826	—Rebellion in Venezuela against Vice President Santander —Anfictiónico Congress in Panama	Protective laws for indigenous persons	—Central University created, Bogotá —General Law of Public Instruction passed
1828	—Ocaña Convention —Dictatorship of Bolívar —War with Peru	Founding of Pácora in new colonization zone, Antioquia	Painter José María Espinosa creates portrait of Simón Bolívar
1829	Military uprising against Bolívar's dictatorship	Shipyard project, to build steamships	Juan García del Río writes *Meditaciones Colombianas*
1830	—Constitutional assembly creates new constitution —Gran Colombia dissolves when Venezuela and Ecuador separate —Simón Bolívar dies	Special privileges offered to those producing bowls, glass, linen, iron, paper, and textiles	
1832	—New constitution creates Republic of New Granada —Francisco de Paula Santander named president	All Indian tribute abolished	Colegio de La Merced created for women

Year	Politics	Society and Economy	Culture and Science
1834		—Census taken: 1,687,129 —Concession granted for steamship navigation on the Magdalena	Three-color flag (yellow, blue, and red) approved as national flag
1835	The Vatican recognizes New Granada	—National system of currency created —First exportation of coffee	Theories of Jeremy Bentham re-emerge in university curricula
1837	—José Ignacio de Márquez elected new president —Penal code drawn up	Economic protection developed	
1839	Civil war "The Supremes" (1839–1842); various provinces rebel against central government, which wins		
1840		Coffee cultivation begins near Bogotá	
1841	Pedro Alcántara Herrán is president of the republic	Judas Tadeo Landínez opens the "Compañía de Giro y Descuento," or first bank, which fails a few years later, causing economic crisis	—Exposition of artistic and industrial products —Newspaper *El Condor* publishes, in every edition, novel of a Colombian author

Year	Politics	Society and Economy	Culture and Science
1843	New constitution approved of, Centralist Court	Census of the republic: 1,931,685	
1845	—Tomás Cipriano de Mosquera elected president of the republic —Major state reforms begin	—Steam navigation on Magdalena River —National road plan to connect capital with Venezuela and Ecuador —Savings bank established in Bogotá	Lino de Pombo publishes his *Recopilación Granadina de Legislación Nacional*
1846	Treaty, Mallarino-Bidlack, between United States and Colombia concerning Panama	Horse-drawn coach: first public transportation system in the capital	—First "normal school" established —Architect Thomas Reed begins construction of Capitolio Nacional—"Congress Building"
1847	Democratic artisan and progressive workers societies formed	—General budget directorate established —Concession signed to build Panama railroad	—Philharmonic Society created at Bogotá —Statue of Bolívar placed in Central Plaza, Bogotá
1848	Two political parties defined: Liberal and Conservative	—Free trade approved —Freedom of agriculture and commercialization of tobacco begins	—Joaquín Acosta publishes *Compendio histórico del descubrimiento y colonización de la Nueva Granada en el siglo XVI*

Year	Politics	Society and Economy	Culture and Science
		—Concession to North Americans for construction of Panama Railway	—Newspapers using "lithograph" published in New Granada
1849	José Hilario López is president	—Death penalty abolished —Manizales is founded	
1850		Liberal reforms	—Chorographic Commission, "Agustín Codazzi" established —Education restrictions ended, university titles abolished
1851	Civil War	—Census: 2,240,054 —Introduction of English livestock "Durham" and "Hereford" —Slavery eliminated —Freedom of press, trial by jury —First roadway built with McAdam's technique	
1853	—José María Obando is president —New moderate constitution		
1854	—José María Melo stages coup —Civil War, Melo falls, and José de Obaldía governs		

Year	Politics	Society and Economy	Culture and Science
1855	—Manuel María Mallarino president —Panama becomes federal state	Panama Railway begins operations	
1856	—Watermelon Riot at Panama; U.S. Marines occupy Colón —Antioquia becomes state after approval of their own constitution	—Colombia third-largest producer of gold in the world —Textile factory (cotton) built at Bogotá	Agustín Codazzi releases his *Geografía física y política de la Nueva Granada*
1857	—Mariano Ospina Rodríguez is president —States created: Santander, Cauca, Boyacá, Bolívar, and Magdalena	Tobacco produced in Ambalema under English control	
1858	—New federal constitution —Republic of New Granada becomes "Confederación Granadina"		—*Manuela* by Eugenio Díaz published in segments in the new literary journal *El Mosaico* —Edition published in France of José María Restrepo's *Historia de la Revolución de la República de Colombia*
1859	Civil War until 1862	—Bank "Botero, Arango e Hijos" created; lasts until 1898	

Year	Politics	Society and Economy	Culture and Science
		—Modern mail system created	
1860	Various states separate	—Steam engines used to clean cotton —Exportation of quinine and indigo	—Ezequiel Uricoechea publishes *Elementos de Mineralogía* —José María Vergara y Vergara publishes *Lira Granadina*
1861	—Dictatorship of Tomás Cipriano de Mosquera —Bogotá set up as federal district —Provisional pact of union gives sovereignty to the states	Disentailment from mortmain decree signed	—National Library moved to disentailed convents —José María Samper publishes his *Ensayo sobre las Revoluciones Políticas*
1863	—New federalist constitution —Confederación Granadina becomes United States of Colombia —Tomás Cipriano de Mosquera elected president	—City of Pereira founded —Tobacco production and exportation grows	
1864	Manuel Murillo Toro elected president	—Banks established —First telegraph message —Infrastructure development: underwater cable and roads	—*Diario Oficial* founded; government publication —Founding of *Gaceta Médica de Colombia* —Medical school founded

Year	Politics	Society and Economy	Culture and Science
1865		Bank of London, Mexico, and South America created	Felipe Pérez publishes his *Geografia General de los Estados Unidos de Colombia*
1866	Tomás Cipriano de Mosquera elected president		
1867	Coup against Mosquera; Manuel María de los Santos Acosta becomes president	Contract written for rail line from Barranquilla to Sabanilla	—Jorge Isaacs publishes *María* —Founding of National University of Colombia in Bogotá
1868	Santos Gutiérrez is president		National Library and National Museum updated
1870	Eustorgio Salgar is president	Banco de Bogotá founded	Education reform, favoring the sciences
1871	Government takes over public education	—Bank of Antioquia created —Colombian Society of Farmers created	University of Antioquia founded
1872	Manuel Murillo Toro is president for the second time		—Decree that the national holiday will be celebrated every July 20 —Rufino Cuervo publishes his *Apuntaciones sobre el lenguaje Bogotano* —Colombian Academy of Language founded

Year	Politics	Society and Economy	Culture and Science
1874	Santiago Pérez is president	—Colombian Insurance Company founded —Bank of Colombia founded —Antioquia Railroad contracted for construction	School of Mines founded in Medellín
1876	—Aquileo Parra is president —National civil war		
1877	Civil war ends, government triumphs	Chaves Chocolate Company founded	Candelario Obeso publishes his *Cantos Populares de mi Tierra*
1878	Julián Trujillo is president	—Digging begins for interoceanic canal at Panama —Contract written for construction of railway from Buenaventura to Cali	Carlos Martínez publishes *Repertorio colombiano*
1880	Rafael Núñez is president	National Bank established with protectionist customs policies	National Institute of Agriculture founded
1881		Work begins on railway lines from La Dorada to Ambalema, Girardot to Facatativá, Puerto Wilches to Bucaramanga, and Cúcuta to Puerto Santander	

Year	Politics	Society and Economy	Culture and Science
1882	José Eusebio Otálora is president	Construction begins on railway line from Bogotá to Facatativá and from Santa Marta to Fundación	—Institute of Bellas Artes established in Bogotá —National anthem composed
1883		—Banco de Crédito Hipotecario established —Banco Unión established in Cartagena	
1884	Núñez is president for second time	Street trolley company established by North Americans in Bogotá	First telephone line in the country, from Bogotá to Chapinero
1885	Civil war; radical Liberals defeated by alliance between Conservatives and moderate Liberals		
1886	—New centralist constitution —Eliseo Payán is president; in 1887 Núñez returns as president —New name for country: Republic of Colombia	Paper money goes into circulation	Rufino José Cuervo publishes his *Diccionario de Construcción y Régimen de la Lengua Castellana*
1888	—Carlos Holguín is president —Strong anti-press laws passed	—Panama Canal Company goes bankrupt	

Year	Politics	Society and Economy	Culture and Science
		—National police founded —Jockey Club founded	
1891	Conservative Party divides between "Históricos" and "Nacionalistas"	—Glass company founded in Bogotá —Bavaria beer company founded in Bogotá	—Society of Medicine and Natural Sciences founded —Julio Garavito begins his astronomical research
1892	Miguel Antonio Caro is president	—Treaty of friendship, commerce, and navigation with Germany and Italy —Law concerning railroads promulgated	—Education reform —Teatro Colón reinaugurated in Bogotá
1894		—Banco Nacional fails —Railway opens, Cartagena to Calamar	José Asunción Silva publishes *Nocturno II*
1895	National civil war: government wins	Colombia becomes coffee export nation	
1898	Manuel Antonio Sanclemente is president		
1899	Thousand Day War begins	—Coffee exports expand	Guillermo Valencia publishes *Anarkos*

Year	Politics	Society and Economy	Culture and Science
		—United Fruit Company established in Colombia —First automobile brought to Medellín	
1900	Coup against Sanclemente; José Manuel Marroquín becomes president		—Electric energy service begins in Bogotá —José María Vargas Vila publishes *Ibis*
1902	In Panama, treaty ending the Thousand Day War signed	—In Medellín, Antioquian Textile Company created —United States buys the shares of the failed French canal company	Colombian Academy of History established
1903	Panama separates from Colombia with U.S. backing	Gold standard established for currency	Carlos Cuervo Márquez publishes *Apuntaciones sobre los orígenes del pueblo Chibcha*
1904	Rafael Reyes is president; closes Congress	—In Medellín, soft drink company Posada y Tobon created, Postobon —Expansion of coffee production in Antioquia —Textile company Fabricato developed in Medellín	—First automobile in Bogotá —Exposition of the painting of Andrés de Santamaría —San José hospital under construction —Geographic Society of Colombia founded

Year	Politics	Society and Economy	Culture and Science
1905	President replaces Congress with National Assembly	—Currency stabilizes —Census: 4,533,777 —"Barco y Mares" granted concession to search for oil	
1907	Military school founded and national army reorganized	—Subsidies in place for exportation of coffee, rubber, tobacco, and cotton —Coltejer established (textiles) in Medellín	First film "shorts" produced
1909	Rafael Reyes resigns presidency; replaced by Ramón González Valencia	—Production of bananas, sugar, and cotton increases —Electric Company of Barranquilla opens	La Academia de Música of Bogotá becomes National Conservatory
1910	—Carlos E. Restrepo is president —Boycott in Bogotá against U.S.-owned streetcar company —Strike, dock workers and railway workers —Reform to 1886 constitution	First Congress of Agriculturalists	—Celebration of one hundred years of independence
1911	—Army reform, with help from Chilean military mission	—Coffee exports grow significantly —First wireless telegraph	*El Tiempo* founded in Bogotá

Year	Politics	Society and Economy	Culture and Science
	—Tensions between Peru and Colombia over Amazon rubber production		
1912	Fighting breaks out with Peruvian soldiers in rubber producing zone, Amazon	—Census: 5,472,604 —Important industrial development at Barranquilla —Radio-telegraphic station at Cartagena	*El Colombiano* founded in Medellín
1914	—José Vícente Concha is president —Urrutia-Thomson Treaty; Colombia will recognize Panama in exchange for twenty-five-million-dollar indemnity	—In Bogotá Electrical Energy and Obregón Textile companies created —Steamship navigation on Sinú and Atrato rivers	Creation of Instituto de Medicina Legal
1916	—Indigenous rebellion under direction of Quintín Lame —Colombia fails to approve Urrutia-Thomson Treaty due to modifications made by U.S. Congress	—Tropical Oil Company of Delaware begins operations —Empresa de Cementos Samper created in Bogotá —Public bus service begins in Barranquilla	Magazine *Cromos* appears

Year	Politics	Society and Economy	Culture and Science
1918	—Marco Fidel Suárez is president —First oil workers' union —Strike, workers at Barranquilla and Cartagena ports	—Súarez makes his *Respice Polum* speech —Census: 5,855,077 —Dock at Buenaventura built	
1919	—Artisans on strike, Bogotá —National air force created	—First Socialist Party Congress —SCADTA created (Sociedad Colombo Alemana de Transportes Aéreos)	
1921	—President Suárez resigns; replaced by Jorge Holguín —U.S. Senate ratifies Urrutia-Thomson and sends twenty-five million dollars in indemnification payment	Coffee exports continue to grow	José Eustacio Rivera publishes *Tierra de Promisión*
1922	Pedro Nel Ospina is president	"Debt prosperity" due to amount of loans sent to Colombia from United States	Miguel Triana publishes *La Civilización Chibcha*
1923	Kemmerer Mission comes to Colombia from United States to help organize national finances	Bank of the Republic established along with superintendence of banks	—Rockefeller Foundation mission helps cure yellow fever outbreak in Bucaramanga

Year	Politics	Society and Economy	Culture and Science
			—First translations of Freud arrive in Colombia
1924	—Oil worker strike in Barrancabermeja —Swiss military mission helps reorganize national army	German Pedagogy Mission arrives	—José Eustacio Rivera publishes *La Vorágine* —Colombian film appears, *Aura o las Violetas*
1926	—Miguel Abadía-Méndez is president —Socialist Party founded	Pedagogic Institute founded in Bogotá	Journal *Universidad* created, directed by Germán Arciniegas
1928	—Strike and massacre of banana workers in Ciénaga —Nicaragua recognizes Colombia's rights to islands of San Andrés and Providencia	Stock market created at Bogotá	Agricultural experimentation station developed in Palmira
1930	—Enrique Olaya-Herrera is president —Communist Party of Colombia founded —First flare-ups of bipartisan violence	Worldwide economic crisis felt in Colombia	—First radio station created in Medellín —The Pontificia Universidad Javeriana re-established in Bogotá

Year	Politics	Society and Economy	Culture and Science
1932	—Jorge Eliécer Gaitán creates UNIR (Unión Nacional Izquierdista Revolucionaria) —War with Peru	—Three-year public works plan with emphasis on highway construction —Banco Central Hipotecario founded	—Porfirio Barba Jacob publishes *Canciones y Elegías* —Eduardo Zalamea publishes *Cuatro años a bordo de mi mismo*
1934	—Alfonso López-Pumarejo is president —Political violence in Boyacá and Santander grows	Eight-hour work day established together with other worker rights	—Luis López de Mesa publishes *De cómo se ha formado la Nación Colombiana* —Colombian Association of Architects created
1935	First Congress of *campesino* workers leads to creation of Workers' Union Confederation of Colombia	Diplomatic relations with Soviet Union	National University unifies at single campus, with institutional autonomy
1936	Reform of constitution of 1886—giving more rights to citizens	—National identity card inaugurated —Agrarian reform (Law 200) —Private property might be limited if social need warrants	—National Symphony Orchestra created —*El Siglo* (newspaper) published —Médical Federación created
1938	Eduardo Santos is president	—Census: 8,701,816 —Law protecting expectant mothers	Inauguration of the new building housing the National Library

Year	Politics	Society and Economy	Culture and Science
1939	—Jorge Eliécer Gaitán named minister of education —Campesinos demonstrate in Viotá (Cundinamarca)	Modernization projects carried out at Port of Buenaventura	—Group of poets known as "Piedra y Cielo" appears —*Revista de Indias* created
1940	Spanish intellectuals fleeing the Spanish Civil War arrive in Colombia	—IFI created— Instituto de Formento Industrial, to push the industrial sector forward —SCADTA's license revoked—WW II —Interamerican agreement regulates exportation of coffee to United States	—National radio network established —First "Salón Nacional de Artistas"
1942	Alfonso López Pumarejo is president for second time	Colombia harmed by WW II–induced economic crisis	
1945	—President resigns; replaced by Alberto Lleras Camargo —Strikes in the Magdalena River Valley severely put down —Constitutional reform	—Grancolombian Mercantile Fleet established to facilitate coffee exports —National Federation of Businessmen established —90% of national exports dependent on coffee	"Circle" of Colombian journalists created at Bogotá

Year	Politics	Society and Economy	Culture and Science
1946	—Mariano Ospina Pérez is president —Union of Colombian Workers UTC) established —Strikes throughout nation —Political violence grows throughout nation	—Colombian Institute of Social Security created —Importation of agricultural machinery	Colombia is site of Fifth Central American and Caribbean Games
1948	—Jorge Eliécer Gaitán killed in Bogotá—riots break out —Ninth Panamerican Conference meets in Bogotá; establishes nonintervention in internal events	—Ecopetrol (state-run oil company) established —Iron works plant established at Paz del Rio, Boyacá	—Universidad Industrial de Santander (Bucaramanga) established —Alejandro Oregón paints *Los muertos del 9 de Abril* —National Museum moves to old Panóptico—jail —Modern Art Exposition
1949	—Ospina closes Congress —Political stability deteriorates; bipartisan conflict grows	—Coffee price rises in international market —National industry consolidates —Visit from Economic Mission of the Banco Internacional de Reconstrucción y Fomento	—University of Los Andes created —Contract drawn up with Le Corbusier to build "Pilot Plan" for Bogotá
1950	—Laureano Gómez is president	—Confederation of Colombian Workers (CTC)	—*El País* founded —La Cumbia spreads internationally

Year	Politics	Society and Economy	Culture and Science
	—Liberal guerrillas of eastern plains form —Colombia participates in Korean War	divides between Liberals and Communists —Political parties divide between moderates and radicals —Measures developed to stabilize currency	—Rockefeller mission helps with agricultural/animal husbandry research in Colombia
1951	—L. Gómez ill; Roberto Urdaneta rules —Liberal Party abstains from political participation	—Census: 11,614,586 —Work code approved —Foreign capital allowed in without restrictions	University La Gran Colombia founded
1952	One hundred thousand dead as result of violence; another five hundred thousand injured	—Oil pipeline operates from Puerto Salgar to Bogotá —Plan to build Hydroelectric plants developed	—Eduardo Caballero Calderón publishes *El Cristo de Espaldas* —Universidad de América founded
1953	Military coup: Lt. Gen. Gustavo Rojas Pinilla takes power	—Banco Cafetero is created —70% increase in military budget	Laureano Gómez publishes his study of Mussolini, Hitler, Gandhi, and Stalin, *El Cuadrilátero*
1954	—Rojas Pinilla "elected" president by National Constitutional Assembly	—Banco Popular created —Economic growth thanks to international price of coffee	—First television broadcast —Eduardo Caballero Calderón publishes *Siervo sin Tierra*

Year	Politics	Society and Economy	Culture and Science
	—Protesting students killed by army in Bogotá	—Bogotá becomes "Distrito Especial"	—Library "Pública Piloto" opens in Medellín
1956	—Rojas creates "Third Force" as alternative to Liberal and Conservative Parties —Pacto de Benidorm (Spain); Alberto Lleras and Laureano Gómez plan to fight dictatorship —Structure of "Frente Nacional" established by Alfonso López Pumarejo	—Minimum wage established —CELAM (Latin American Episcopal Conference) established at Bogotá —Dynamite explosion on center of Cali—many (thousands) killed	Colombians participate in Olympics at Melbourne
1957	—Rojas overthrown via national civic strike; military junta rules nation —Liberals and Conservatives agree to coalition government —Treaty of Sitges (Spain) establishes National Front procedure	SENA ("National Learning Service") established	—Tenth Salón Nacional de Artistas: Fernando Botero wins prize —National school of journalists established —Bogotá establishes Luis Ángel Arango Library, backed by Banco de la República

Year	Politics	Society and Economy	Culture and Science
1958	—Alberto Lleras Camargo is first president of the National Front —Amnesty law for those involved in armed rebellion	International Organization of Coffee created	Gabriel García Márquez publishes, in journal *Mito, El coronel no tiene quién le escriba* (*No One Writes to the Coronel*)
1960	—ANAPO formed by Rojas Pinilla (National Popular Alliance) —MOEC forms (rural student worker movement)	—Colonization of Carare (Santander) pushed by Agrarian Savings Bank —Government pushes metal industry forward	Álvaro Mutis publishes *Diario del Lecumberri*
1961	—Álvaro Gómez (in Congress) denounces existence of "Independent Republics" controlled by guerrilla organizations and asks government to act —Diplomatic relations with Cuba cut —President John F. Kennedy visits Bogotá	—National planning organization develops as government tool —Colombia joins ALAC—Association of Latin American Free Trade —INCORA established, Colombian Institute of Agrarian Reform —Colombia benefits from Alliance for Progress	García Márquez wins prize for his novel *La mala hora* (*An Evil Hour*)
1962	—Guillermo León Valencia is second president of the National Front	Severe devaluation of peso	—Alejandro Obregón wins first prize in the Salón Nacional de Artistas

Year	Politics	Society and Economy	Culture and Science
	—Repressive measures taken against rural social conflict		—*La Violencia en Colombia* published by Germán Guzmán, Orlando Fals Borda, and Eduardo Umaña
1964	—ELN (Army of National Liberation) carries out its first acts —FARC (Revolutionary Armed Forces of Colombia) born in Tolima	—Census: 17,484,508 —CSTC created; Syndicate of Colombian Workers —Crisis in textile industry —French president Charles de Gaulle visits Colombia	Manuel Zapata Olivella publishes *En Chimá nace un Santo*
1966	—Carlos Lleras Restrepo is third president of National Front —Father Camilo Torres, who joined ELN in 1965, dies in combat with Colombian army	—Bogotá Declaration, concerning commercial integration of Andean countries —President Lleras rejects IMF reform suggestions	Theater group "La Candelaria" born
1967	EPL is born (National Popular Army of Liberation) —Student demonstrations, Bogotá	—Control over foreign currency established —PROEXPO established to promote Colombian exports	—García Márquez publishes *Cien años de soledad* (*One Hundred Years of Solitude*) —Álvaro Cepeda Samudio publishes *La Casa Grande*

Year	Politics	Society and Economy	Culture and Science
	—Massacre of sixteen indigenous persons at La Rubiela		—Colombian cyclists have international success —Álvaro Mejía wins San Silvestre Marathon in Rio de Janeiro (Brazil)
1968	—Constitutional reform —Pope Paul VI visits Colombia	Colombian Family Welfare Institute begins operations	Colcultura, Colciencias, and Coldeportes established to support national culture, academic/ scientific research, and sports
1970	—Misael Pastrana is fourth president of National Front —ANAPO accuses government of electoral fraud		
1972	Plan created to fight production, sale, and consumption of illegal narcotics	Agrarian reform ends	First Olympic medal for a Colombian
1973	—New concordat signed with Vatican —M-19 insurgency group forms, separates from ANAPO	Census: 20,666,920	Álvaro Mutis publishes *La Mansión de Araucaima*
1974	Alfonso López Michelsen, president	Economic emergency declared to control inflation	Journal *Alternativa* founded with leftist democratic character

Year	Politics	Society and Economy	Culture and Science
1975	—National civil strike —Diplomatic relations with Cuba re-established	—Eighteen-year-olds declared legal citizens —Economic program calls for greater social spending and support of rural folk —Coffee production grows	—García Márquez publishes *El Otoño del Patriarca* (*The Autumn of the Patriarch*) —Discovery in Sierra Nevada de Santa Marta: the ruins of Buritaca 200 (Ciudad Perdida)
1977	National civil strike		
1978	—Julio César Turbay is president —Estatuto Jurídico imposed for the security of the state, which turns into mechanism of repression for political opposition		Ethnic education for indigenous peoples becomes the policy of the Ministry of Education
1982	—Belisario Betancur is president —Right-wing organizations created —Peace Commission created —Congress approves Amnesty Law	—Colombia decides not to support Argentina in Malvinas War —Colombia joins "non-aligned" nations —President Ronald Reagan visits Colombia —Petroleum economy takes off	—García Márquez wins Nobel Prize in Literature —Caro y Cuervo Institute publishes *Atlas Lingüístico de Colombia* —Arhuacos expel from Sierra Nevada the Capuchin missionaries

Year	Politics	Society and Economy	Culture and Science
		—Cerrejón coal mine exports to Spain —Bogotá-Medellín highway completed	
1984	—National civil strike —Peace Commission and the FARC sign an agreement at La Uribe —Justice Minister Rodrigo Lara Bonilla killed by narco-traffickers —Carlos Toledo Plata of M-19 killed —Peace treaty signed with M-19, EPL, and others	—Capital flight creates crisis —Sales tax implemented —Unión Patriótica (UP) born as result of peace accords with the FARC	—Colombia at Olympic games in Los Angeles —First Bogotá film festival —UNESCO declares Cartagena "Patrimony of Humanity"
1985	—First four drug traffickers extradited to United States —M-19 takes Palace of Justice in Bogotá	—Census: 27,837,932 —Significant increase in oil production —Avalanche of Nevado del Ruíz, burying town of Armero; 20,000 killed —Gold discovered on Brazilian border	First heart transplant in the country

Year	Politics	Society and Economy	Culture and Science
1986	—Virgilio Barco is president —Popular election of mayors approved	—Pope John Paul II visits Colombia —Pacific coast militarized to prevent importation of arms to insurgent forces	—100 years of Constitution celebrated —Casa de Poesia (poetry center) José Asunción Silva opens in Bogotá
1987	—Assassination of presidential candidate Jaime Pardo Leal of the UP —Insurgency forces unite as Simón Bolívar coordinated front in La Uribe —Peace talks between government and Bolívar coordinate	Growth in exports other than coffee	Metropolitan Theater of Medellín opens
1988	—First popular election of mayors —Government recognizes guerrilla as valid political actor —First massacre by paramilitary forces in Magdalena midpoint valley	Inflation reaches 30%	Manuel Mejía Vallejo publishes *La Casa de los Dos Palmas*

Year	Politics	Society and Economy	Culture and Science
1989	—M-19 accepts goverment peace plan —Extradition accepted as government policy —Pablo Escobar takes down Avianca jet —Paramilitary forces declared illegal —Leftist leader José Antequera killed —Bomb destroys DAS headquarters (Administrative Department of Security); another bomb destroys offices of *El Espectador* in Bogotá —Presidential candidate Luis Carlos Galán killed	—United States commits sixty-five million dollars to fight against drugs in Colombia —Inflation at 26% —Silent march in Bogotá, organized by student movement	—National Archive opens —Soccer team "Atlético Nacional" wins Copa Libertadores de América
1990	—César Gaviria is president —Students push for "constitutional assembly" —Leftist presidential candidate	—American Airlines arrives in Colombia —Neoliberal reforms begin in Colombia —Inflation at 30%	—National system of science and technology created —Colombia participates in World Cup, Italy

Year	Politics	Society and Economy	Culture and Science
	Bernardo Jaramillo Ossa killed —Carlos Pizarro, peace broker for M-19, killed —Constitutional assembly approved by election		
1991	—Constitutional assembly writes new constitution; approved July 4 —Peace talks in Caracas between government and guerrilla coordinate	Coffee and oil no longer leading Colombian exports	Fourth Book Fair held at Bogotá

Select Bibliography

Abel, Christopher. "External Philanthropy and Domestic Change in Colombian Healthcare: The Role of the Rockefeller Foundation, ca. 1920–1950." *Hispanic American Historical Review* 75 (1995): 339–76.

Andrade, María Mercedes. *Ambivalent Desires: Representations of Modernity and Private Life in Colombia 1890s–1950s.* Lewisburg: Bucknell University Press, 2011.

Appelbaum, Nancy. *Muddied Waters: Race, Region, and Local History in Colombia, 1846–1948.* Durham: Duke University Press, 2003.

Ardila Galvis, Constanza. *The Heart of War in Colombia.* London: Latin American Bureau, 2000.

Asher, Kiran. *Black and Green: Afro-Colombians, Development, and Nature in the Pacific Lowlands.* Durham: Duke University Press, 2009.

Bergquist, Charles, Ricardo Peñaranda, and Gonzalo Sánchez. *Violence in Colombia, 1990–2000: Waging War and Negotiating Peace.* Wilmington: SR Books, 2001.

Braun, Herbert. *Our Guerrillas, Our Sidewalks: A Journey into the Violence of Colombia.* 2nd ed. Lanham: Rowman & Littlefield, 2003.

———. *The Assassination of Gaitán: Public Life and Urban Violence in Colombia.* Madison: University of Wisconsin Press, 1985.

Bushnell, David. *The Making of Modern Colombia: A Nation in Spite of Itself.* Berkeley: University of California Press, 1993.

Deas, Malcolm, and Alfonso López Michelsen. *Del poder y la gramática: Y otros ensayos sobre historia, política y literatura colombiana.* Bogotá: Taurus, 2006.

Dudley, Steven. *Walking Ghosts: Murder and Guerrilla Politics in Colombia.* New York: Routledge, 2006.

Earle, Rebecca. *The Return of the Native: Indians and Myth-Making in Spanish America, 1810–1930.* Durham: Duke University Press, 2008.

Erlick, June. *A Gringa in Bogotá: Living Colombia's Invisible War.* Austin: University of Texas Press, 2010.

253

Friedmann, Nina de. *African Saga: Cultural Heritage and Contributions to Colombia*. Santa Fe: Gaon Books, 2008.

García Márquez, Gabriel. *News of a Kidnapping*. New York: Random House, 1997.

———. *One Hundred Years of Solitude*. New York: HarperPerennial Modern Classics, 2006.

———. *The Autumn of the Patriarch*. New York: HarperPerennial Modern Classics, 2006.

———. *The General in His Labyrinth*. New York: Random House, 1990.

Guillermoprieto, Alma. *Looking for History: Dispatches from Latin America*. New York: Vintage Books, 2001.

Helg, Aline. *Liberty and Equality in Caribbean Colombia, 1770–1835*. Chapel Hill: University of North Carolina Press, 2004.

Henderson, James. *Modernization in Colombia: The Laureano Gómez Years, 1889–1965*. Gainesville: University Press of Florida, 2001.

Jiménez, Michael. "Traveling Far in Grandfather's Car: The Life Cycle of a Central Colombian Coffee Estate. The Case of Viotá, Cundinamarca (1900–1930)." *Hispanic American Historical Review* 69 (1989): 185–219.

Kline, Harvey. *Showing Teeth to Dragons: State-Building by Colombian President Álvaro Uribe Vélez, 2002–2006*. Tuscaloosa: University of Alabama Press, 2009.

Lasso, Marixa. *Myths of Harmony: Race and Republicanism during the Age of Revolution, Colombia 1795–1831*. Pittsburgh: University of Pittsburgh Press, 2007.

Martin, Gerald. *Gabriel García Márquez: A Life*. New York: Bloomsbury, 2008.

McFarlane, Anthony. *Colombia before Independence: Economy, Society, and Politics under Bourbon Rule*. New York: Cambridge University Press, 1993.

Murray, Pamela. *For Glory and Bolívar: The Remarkable Life of Manuela Sáenz, 1797–1856*. Austin: University of Texas Press, 2008.

Mutis, Álvaro. *The Adventures and Misadventures of Maqroll*. New York: New York Review Books Classics, 2002.

Myhre, David. *Colombia: Civil Conflict, State Weakness, and (In)security*. Princeton: Princeton University Program in Latin American Studies, 2003.

Palacios, Marco. *Between Legitimacy and Violence: A History of Colombia, 1875–2002*. Durham: Duke University Press, 2006.

Paternostro, Silvana. *In the Land of God and Man: A Latin Woman's Journey*. New York: Putnam, 1998.

———. *My Colombian War: A Journey through the Country I Left Behind*. New York: Henry Holt, 2007.

Randall, Stephen. *Colombia and the United States: Hegemony and Interdependence*. Athens: University of Georgia Press, 1992.

Rappaport, Joanne. *The Politics of Memory: Native Historical Interpretation in the Colombian Andes*. Cambridge: Cambridge University Press, 1990.

Rausch, Jane. "Petroleum and the Transformation of the Llanos Frontier in Colombia: 1980 to the Present." *Latin Americanist* 53 (2009): 113–36.

Rodríguez-García, María José. *The City of Translation: Poetry and Ideology in Nineteenth-Century Colombia*. Basingstoke: Palgrave Macmillan, 2010.

Roldán, Mary. *Blood and Fire: La Violencia in Antioquia, Colombia, 1946–1953*. Durham: Duke University Press, 2003.

Safford, Frank, and Marcos Palacios. *Colombia: Fragmented Land, Divided Society*. Oxford: Oxford University Press, 2001.

Sanders, James. *Contentious Republics: Popular Politics, Race, and Class in Nine-teenth-Century Colombia*. Durham: Duke University Press, 2004.

Sweig, Julia. "What Kind of War for Colombia." *Foreign Affairs* 81 (2002): 122–41.

Torres del Río, César. *Colombia siglo XX: Desde la Guerra de los Mil Días hasta la elección de Álvaro Uribe*. Bogotá: Grupo Editorial Norma, 2010.

Vásquez Perdomo, María Eugenia. *My Life as a Colombian Revolutionary: Reflections of a Former Guerrillera*. Philadelphia: Temple University Press, 2005.

Wade, Peter. *Blackness and Race Mixture: The Dynamics of Racial Identity in Colombia*. Baltimore: Johns Hopkins University Press, 1993.

———. *Music, Race, and Nation: Música Tropical in Colombia*. Chicago: University of Chicago Press, 2000.

Williams, Raymond. *The Colombian Novel, 1844–1987*. Austin: University of Texas Press, 1991.

WEB-BASED SOURCES FOR STUDENTS

1. The main library in Bogotá is called the Biblioteca Luis Ángel Arango: http://www.banrepcultural.org/blaavirtual.

2. The National Library in Colombia contains a wide variety of historic sources: Biblioteca Nacional de Colombia: http://www.bibliotecanacional.gov.co.

3. The Center for Research and Popular Education (CINEP) is a Jesuit-run think tank focusing on popular education and human rights. Centro de Investigación y Educación Popular: http://www.cinep.org.co.

4. *El Tiempo* (Bogotá daily newspaper): http://www.eltiempo.com/seccion_archivo.

5. The Pontificia Universidad Javeriana (Jesuit) history department publishes a historical journal called *Memoria y Sociedad*: http://www.memoriaysociedad.javeriana.edu.co.

6. The Universisdad de los Andes history department publishes a historical journal titled *Historia Crítica*: http://www.historiacritica.uniandes.edu.co.

7. The National Archives in Bogotá holds historic documents from the sixteenth century to the present. Archivo General de la Nacion: http://www.archivogeneral.gov.co.

8. General list of NGOs in Colombia: http://www.derechos.org/nizkor/colombia.

9. Human Rights Watch: http://www.hrw.org.

10. A virtual bookstore to purchase books and films from Colombia: http://www.lalibreriadelau.com.

11. Lerner bookstore in Bogotá, an important central-city bookstore: http://www.librerialerner.com.co.

Index

About the Authors

Michael J. LaRosa is associate professor of history at Rhodes College, Memphis.

Germán R. Mejía is professor of history at the Pontificia Universidad Javeriana, Bogotá.